"Ric's book is an excellent introduction to techniques for producing professional sound effects for films, games, etc. It's packed with nuts-and-bolts information that beginning and intermediate level sound designers/editors will find useful."
— Randy Thom, director of sound design, Skywalker Sound

"Ric Viers eats, drinks, and breathes sound effects. If you're a sound designer, editor, or filmmaker, you'll need the Bible!"
— Tasos Frantzolas, founder of *Soundsnap.com*

"*The Sound Effects Bible* is *the* go-to resource for anyone serious about sound creation! Ric Viers generously shares his real-world experience in an absorbing and hard to put down guide to this fascinating corner of the entertainment industry."
— Aaron Marks, composer/sound designer and author of *The Complete Guide to Game Audio*

"Fun, funny, and the most informative source I've seen on the what, why, and how of creating sound effects. This book's a blessing of inspiration, common sense, and trade secrets, a must for everyone planning to get their own microphone for recording our sonic world. Thanks, Ric, for sharing your experience creating those 100,000 humongous, teeny, sloshy, brittle, honking, shimmering, etc. etc. sounds."
— David Sonnenschein, author of *Sound Design*

"Ric Viers manages to not only detail the technical aspects of an underappreciated craft, but explain how a sound effects expert approaches this work from a practical perspective — offering specific examples of how one can capture and later utilize audio that will add depth and character to images."
— David E. Williams, Editor-In-Chief, *Digital Video Magazine*

"If you are interested in learning about the details of sound effects for your own productions — this is the book!"
— Frank Serafine, Award Winning Sound Designer/Composer/ Multimediaist, *Tron*, *Star Trek*, *The Hunt For Red October*, *Brainstorm*

"Ric has really nailed it on this one. There is no other A-to-Z book that a media maker who has limited knowledge of sound effects can use to get a great overview of how sound is matched to visuals conceptually and technically — and then with this knowledge actually make a movie soundtrack."
— Alan Howarth, Composer/Sound Designer for *Star Trek*, *Halloween*, *Poltergeist*, ... :tober, and The Little Mermaid

THE SOUND EFFECTS
BIBLE

RIC VIERS

HOW TO CREATE AND RECORD
HOLLYWOOD STYLE SOUND EFFECTS

MICHAEL WIESE PRODUCTIONS

Published by Michael Wiese Productions
12400 Ventura Blvd. – Suite 1111
Studio City, CA 91604
(818) 379-8799, (818) 986-3408 (FAX).
mw@mwp.com
www.mwp.com

Cover design by Kevin Capizzi
Interior design by William Morosi
Copyedited by Bob Somerville
Photography by Brian Kaurich
Printed by McNaughton & Gunn

Manufactured in the United States of America

Library of Congress Cataloging-in-Publication Data
Viers, Ric.
 The sound effects bible : how to create and record Hollywood style sound effects /
By Ric Viers.
     p. cm.
ISBN 978-1-932907-48-3
1. Motion pictures--Sound effects. I. Title.
TK7881.4.V54 2008
791.4302'4--dc22
                        2008022846

TABLE OF CONTENTS

ACKNOWLEDGMENTS

I would like to thank all of the people that have helped me along the way in my journey. It's been quite a ride so far.

To Bill Kubota and Dave Newman of KDN, for letting me borrow their DAT recorder to record my first sound effect.

To pros like Randy Thom (*The Empire Strikes Back*, *Indiana Jones and the Temple of Doom*, *Forest Gump*, *War of the Worlds*) and Charles Maynes (*Fantastic Four*, *Spiderman*, *Lara Croft: Tomb Raider*, *Twister*, *From Dusk Till Dawn*), for hanging out on forum sites to share their wisdom and insight with other sound designers.

To my mom and dad for all their support.

To Gary Allison, for being a great friend and partner.

To my son, Sean, for being me — only smaller.

To my wife, Tracy, for telling me to go for it.

Thanks!

FOREWORD

Sound Effects — The reason you picked up this book, at least the reason you might be browsing through it right now…. The discipline has an intriguing legacy wrapped up in the art form … from the first talkies to Treg Brown's legendary work at Warner Brothers on their cartoons of the 1930s through the late 1950s … to the digital soundtracks of Middle Earth and *The Matrix*. It has always been a playground of simile and metaphor — and has perpetually challenged its practitioners to higher and higher levels of excellence.

Sound, like image, *must* come from somewhere — and the documentation of that endeavor is what this book is about. Hopefully you can take away from your time with it new understanding and techniques that will allow your work to be something fresh, something different, and most of all something brilliant.

Working with sound presents challenges not dissimilar to photography. In the process of capturing sound, we have many similar concerns and production techniques available. Microphone selection is similar to the selection of lenses and filters a photographer might use, and your recording device and media might also impart sonic qualities to your source material. Other tools in the process will allow great latitude in manipulating the sound in directions impossible in nature.

Ric presents a great set of recording commandments that are invaluable guidelines for your recording, but as they say, you should know the rules before you can stretch, or break them… but there is more to things than just that…. The first rule of recording, no matter what, is: MAKE SURE THE RECORDER IS RECORDING. Even if the levels or mic placement is not quite right, if something crazy happens, at least you will *have some* record of it. So, with that in mind — get to the rest of this book….

Charles Maynes, January 1, 2008

INTRODUCTION

How in the world did I go to film school to learn the craft of directing movies but end up as a sound designer? I ask myself that question all the time. The answer always comes back the same: necessity.

The day I graduated from film school, I quickly pranced off the stage clutching my diploma expecting someone to be waiting for me with my first film deal, which, of course, would lead to my very first Oscar. Needless to say, there was no one waiting for me and I still haven't received an Oscar … yet. Upon graduation, I found myself in the midst of the dawning age of digital filmmaking.

I quickly jumped on the digital bandwagon and began amassing every piece of gear and software I could find to make my own movies. Soon thereafter, I sat down at my new editing workstation and stared at a screen that displayed my first finished video. The picture looked great. The dialogue levels were set just right. The music nearly pushed me to tears. However, there was something missing. It felt dry sonically. I needed sound effects.

I told my wife of my dilemma and a couple of weeks later, I found my very first set of sound effects CDs wrapped with care beneath the Christmas tree in our small apartment. I remember opening the gift. Had I only known the significance of that moment, I probably wouldn't have gone so rough on the wrapping paper. Needless to say, that was almost a decade ago and now I am writing this introduction sitting next to a sound effects library of hundreds of CDs totaling more than 250,000 sound effects. But that's not what's so significant. The truth is that more than 100,000 of those sound effects were created by me for commercial use through the biggest sound publishers in the industry, including Blastwave FX, my own sound effects publishing label. I never saw that coming.

I took my new sound effects CDs and began playing with them on my Digital Audio Workstation (DAW). Wow. They made a huge difference in what I was seeing on the screen. Ambiences helped sell the locations. Hard effects, like door slams, brought rooms to life. Church bells that rang in the distance helped the audience realize that the hero was near the end of his journey. I was hooked. But where could I get more?

A quick search on the newly invented Internet proved disappointing. Professionally produced sound effects libraries were far from cheap. I ordered a free sample disc from one particular publisher only to find that the effects were not produced very well by any standards. There was hiss in some tracks and background noise in others. Why would I pay top dollar for sound material that I would end up having to clean and reprocess before I could even use them in my projects? What to do? After all, I was in Detroit and the nearest professional sound designer was in New York, about 500 miles away. I searched and searched for resources on how to record and design sound effects, but alas, my search proved futile.

At the time, I was freelancing with some big video companies in Detroit, where my story takes place. I had networked with some great guys who were shooting for ESPN, MTV, *Dateline*, and the like. Of course being fresh out of film school, I wasn't allowed anywhere near the camera. So I ended up working a sound mixer and a boom pole. Baptized into the world of television, I found myself associated with some great companies who treated me like family.

After work one day, I spotted a DAT recorder in the equipment room of one of the companies that I worked with. My curiosity was piqued. Maybe this was the answer to gathering more sound effects for my shoestring-budget productions? I asked if I could take the deck out and do some recording with it. Thankfully, they said yes.

The first day was exciting. I made my way to a field in the middle of nowhere and slipped on a pair of headphones. I pointed an expensive microphone (also a loaner) at the trees where some birds were gathered. It was like seeing in color for the first time! I heard everything. I even had to be careful of my own personal movements, because the microphone was picking up the sound of my shoes as I shifted my body weight under stress from holding the boom pole. I thought I was hooked before, but now I realized that I had become addicted.

I raced home with my new recordings and uploaded them into my DAW. I couldn't press play fast enough. Was it as good as I heard in the field? Were my levels set right? Did I accidentally pick up unwanted noise like traffic and planes? Would this work for my own productions?

When I hit the space bar (the default playback key for any editing software), a smile possessed my face. My ears perked up, like a dog hearing the dinner bell. Success. My first sound: FOREST_AMBIENCE.WAV.

What followed were years of gathering every sound I could think of: traffic, door knocks, footsteps, crashes, and more, more, more. With each new sound came a different challenge and a different solution. I enhanced my skills out of necessity and a drive for perfection in every sound I recorded. I found myself learning with no teacher.

One day, I was cleaning out my hard drive and I discovered that I had recorded over a thousand sounds. I was shocked. It was that day that I looked in the mirror and admitted my addiction. I really loved recording sound effects.

I look back now and can't believe how far I've come. What started out as an experiment to fill a need became a lucrative and satisfying obsession. I was fortunate enough to connect with some sound publishers and began working on sound effects libraries professionally. Next came better gear, more experience, and trade shows … oh, the trade shows.

Pandora's box had been opened and there was no turning back. To date, my work spans 150 professional sound libraries totaling more than 150,000 commercially released sound effects. What next? Pass the torch.

This book is my gift to the next generation of sound gatherers. This is a manual. Keep this with your recording gear. Bring it with you in the field. Have it on your sound cart on the recording stage. In it, you will find all of the useful tips that I wish I'd had at my disposal when I started out.

In the following chapters, we will discuss sound fundamentals, recording techniques, Foley tips and tricks, sound design concepts, and more. There is no secret that I am not willing to tell. Well, maybe a few....

About The Detroit Chop Shop and Blastwave FX

The Detroit Chop Shop was founded in a spare bedroom in my apartment in 1997 and has since grown to become the world's largest provider of sound effects, with eight sound designers working full time. Our motto is "Record something new every day." And every day, we live up to that motto. I am surrounded by very talented individuals who record to live and live to record. They are the best and freshest minds in the business and it is an honor to lead them.

The Detroit Chop Shop Crew, 2008

After serving professional sound publishers for nearly a decade, I decided to celebrate my 100th sound effects library by releasing it under my own label, Blastwave FX (*www.blastwavefx.com*). To date, we have released 15 groundbreaking, High-Definition sound effects libraries, including Sonopedia — the world's first professional High-Definition general sound effects library.

The future for The Detroit Chop Shop and Blastwave FX is bright and beautiful. It has been a wonderful journey so far and I can't wait to face the challenges and frontiers that tomorrow brings. But enough about me — let's talk about you!

The Creative Mantra

"Know the tools, so you can break the rules."

As a recordist/sound designer, you will find that creativity always trumps technology. However, it is very important to understand the technology and science behind our craft in order to produce innovative and quality sound effects.

There is a host of monthly publications, magazines, Web sites, and organizations that are specific to the industries of sound and recording. I highly recommend that you research what they can offer you. With today's quickly changing technologies, it is imperative to stay on top of the technology, gear, and scientific breakthroughs in this industry.

However, in order to be innovative it is also important to sometimes forget what we have learned so that we can reach for the horizon in hopes of achieving new sounds and techniques. Sometimes there is a fine line between thinking inside and outside the box. In either case, there is still a box. That box is the standard or constant in the equation. It is the benchmark by which all things are measured. There are reasons why there are rules and there are reasons to break those rules.

So do not be intimidated by new challenges. Instead, be fortified with the knowledge and science of the art. But more importantly, be confident enough to experiment and explore. For it is then that you will cease to be a technician and become an artist.

How to Use This Book

Like most industry books, this book is not intended to be read like a novel. This is a reference book that corresponds to *www.soundeffectsbible.com*. This Web site is full of sound effects samples, videos, tutorials, and additional resources for each chapter in this book.

With that said, let's get started making some noise!

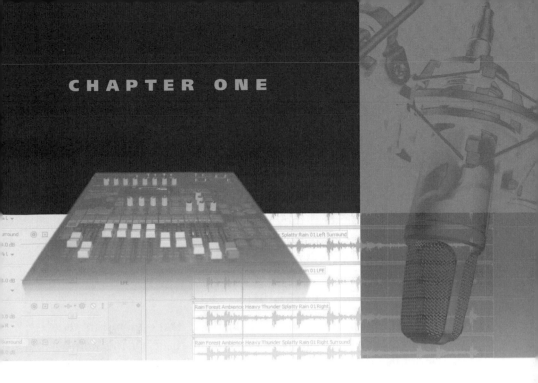

CHAPTER ONE

What Is a Sound Effect?

sound effect

noun

any sound, other than music or speech, artificially reproduced to
create an effect in a dramatic presentation, as the sound of a storm
or a creaking door.

[Origin: 1925–30]

Dictionary.com Unabridged (v 1.1)

Based on the Random House Unabridged Dictionary, © Random
House, Inc. 2006.

Filmmaking is a very complicated process. It is a machine with
dozens of integral parts that have to keep in sync, quite literally,
with one another in order to create the well-balanced and perfectly
aligned product of film. Take away or misalign any of the machine's

moving parts and the product suffers greatly. According to George Lucas (the guy who made a space movie, the name of which I can't seem to remember), "sound is half of the experience." Therefore, sound is half of the machine.

Postproduction is where all of the magic happens for the sound-track of a film. The postproduction sound department has three main stems of audio that they work with: dialogue, music, and sound effects. When mixed properly, the audience will suspend their disbelief long enough to be swept away into the world of the story, believing everything they see and hear. All three of these elements are equally important. There. I said it.

A story can be told using any one of these three elements to convey the emotion. We saw Neo learn of the reality of *The Matrix* in a blindingly white room where all the sounds, save the dialogue, were seemingly sucked away from our ears. We watched Anakin Skywalker make the internal decision of whether or not to betray the Jedi in an almost full minute of nothing but music as he stared across the expansive skyscraper-cluttered landscape of Coruscant in *Star Wars: Revenge of the Sith*. In *Saving Private Ryan* we watch Tom Hanks try to make his way up the beach at Omaha with peri-ods of nothing but sound effects as his hearing toggles back and forth from clarity to deafness.

However, when the dialogue, music, and sound effects are weaved together in a seamless tapestry of aural realism, the story is taken to an entirely different level, such as in the battle scenes in *The Lord of the Rings*. It is in these battle scenes that seemingly every sound — dialogue, music, and sound effects — is heard full on and at full volume. Upon a critical review of the soundtrack, however, one will find that all of the elements are in fact mixed in and out with each other to deliver the maximum impact and chaos of battle. Mixing is truly an art form.

Sound effects are an integral part of story telling. It goes beyond film, television, and radio productions. I have a friend who cannot tell a story without mouthing sound effects to illustrate the events of his tales. My friends and I jab at him and usually reply, "How'd that go again?" Whether or not he's been indoctrinated into the culture of film through avid moviegoing or if it's just because he's passionate about his stories, he feels some need to express certain events of the story through sound effects. They seem to make the story come alive.

The use of sound effects in film helps give weight to a large boulder that may only be made from papier-mâché or even millions of tiny pixels animated through CGI. It can give a sense of impending doom via a ticking clock that tells the audience that time is running out. Sound effects build character to a spaceship the size of Delaware that is, in fact, the size of a skateboard. On a psychological level, a sound effect can invoke fear, such as a chilling whisper or breathing sound coming from the next room of the camp counselor's cabin nestled in the woods of Camp Crystal Lake.

Hollywood has programmed audiences to expect sound from everything they see on the screen. A stormy night contains an endless supply of thunder rolls. Every time a dog appears on the screen, you hear a bark. There is a screeching hawk in every desert scene. Snakes rattle, even if they are not rattlesnakes.

If you pay attention, you can hear the same sound effects being used over and over again in commercials as well. I hear the same gust of wind at least twice a day. If only the sound effects industry paid royalties, that sound designer could have retired by now!

Some sound designers have made clever use of repeating the same sound effect, as a sort of tribute. The "Wilhelm scream" is such a sound effect. You might be scratching your head trying to figure out what I'm talking about. But trust me. You've heard it over and over again.

The Wilhelm scream has been used in every *Star Wars* movie, every *Indiana Jones* movie, *Willow*, *Poltergeist*, *Toy Story*, *King Kong*, and about a hundred other films. The sound is the scream given by a character being eaten by an alligator in the 1950s film *Distant Drums*. The sound was used by Ben Burtt, who named the effect

after Private Wilhelm, a character in another 1950s film, *The Charge at Feather River*, in which the sound effect was reused. As time goes on, more and more films continue to pay tribute to the most recognized scream in cinema.

A sound effect can be defined as any sound recorded or performed live for the purpose of simulating a sound of a story or event. They are used in many industries and applications: film, television, radio, theater, multimedia, video games, cell phones, etc. In this book, we will focus specifically on their uses in film, although with the advent of feature film-style video games and episodic television, those lines are quickly being blurred.

In the film world, there are five main types of sound effects:

- Hard Effects
- Foley Sound Effects
- Background Effects
- Electronic Effects/Production Elements
- Sound Design Effects

Hard Effects

These are the most typical kind of sound effects. They tend to work right off the shelf for images on the screen. Effects found in this category include car horns, gunshots, and punches. With hard effects, there is an absolute sound that is associated with the picture; therefore, performance is not necessarily an issue, whereas with Foley, performance is the key to creating convincing effects.

Foley Sound Effects

Foley, named after the sound pioneer Jack Foley, is the process of performing sounds in sync with picture. The most common Foley sound effects are footsteps; however, there are far more intricate sounds that a performer, called a Foley artist, can make. Foley artists enhance fight scenes with clothes movements and impacts, they use knife-and-fork movements to give a dinner sequence a touch of reality, and they throw paper up in the air for its scattering sound to give the on-screen bank vault explosion life.

Background Effects

Also known as ambiences or atmos, these sounds fill in the empty void on screen and give a sense of location and the surrounding environment. These types of sounds include room tone, traffic, and wind. Background effects (also called BG) do not have a direct correlation to any specific event on screen. For example, if a gust of wind blows through an open window and extinguishes a candle, the sound effect used would be a hard effect. However, if the scene takes place in the Sahara desert and there are gusts of wind blowing, the sound effect used would be an ambience or BG effect.

Electronic Sound Effects/Production Elements

Popular as sources for science fiction effects in the 1960s and 1970s, electronic sound effects are now used mainly as source material for sound design effects or as production elements. Production elements are the electric static, zips, and whooshes heard during radio station IDs and the wipes and title elements used on television shows and commercials. The use of production elements for movie trailers' sound beds and title elements became popular during the 1990s. These elements are metaphorical in nature and purely subjective in their use. Synthesizers and keyboards were the first sources for these kinds of effects; with the advent of DAW plug-ins and their infinite possibilities, they are now also created with organic sound effects that are processed or filtered.

Sound Design Effects

Effects that are impossible to record naturally are designed, typically through a DAW, to produce the desired effect. These effects can range from a simple pin drop that has a faint metallic ring to an army of mythical creatures engaged in fierce battle. Sound designers are audio engineers who have mastered the manipulation of sound waves to create both realistic and synthetic sound effects.

The Science of Sound

Understanding How Sound Works

OUR EARS ARE A VERY sensitive instrument. They help us communicate, both in speaking and in listening. They give us a sense of direction. And the inner drum even helps with our sense of balance.

The principle of sound is simple. Changes in atmospheric pressure cause air molecules to move. Our ears register this movement as sound. Simple enough? But wait! There's more!

Sound Waves

When a rock is dropped into a pond, the water is displaced in waves that radiate from the source of impact. This displacement sends the waves up and down in an outward pattern. The waves decrease over distance due to a loss of energy. Many factors determine the size and shape of the wave: the size of the rock; the force with which the rock was dropped or thrown; the location of the drop — in a pool, pond, or ocean; and so on. This is how sound waves work.

For example, when a hammer strikes a nail, our ears register the event as a loud crack. Scientifically, what happens is that the impact caused a violent change in the air pressure, resulting in the displacement of air molecules sent out in all directions from the event. The sound waves travel to our ears, where thousands of little hairs inside our eardrum sense the vibrations and interpret the event as a sound.

A single sound wave consists of two parts: a compression and a rarefaction. When air pressure is at rest, there is no movement among the equally spaced molecules. However, when there is a disturbance in the air pressure, the molecules float up and down in response to the disturbance like the waves in a pond. The upward movement is called a compression and occurs when the molecules are tightly compacted together. When the air molecules sink below the normal air pressure point, it is called a rarefaction. Therefore, a single wave is made up of one compression and one rarefaction.

The Anatomy Of A Wave

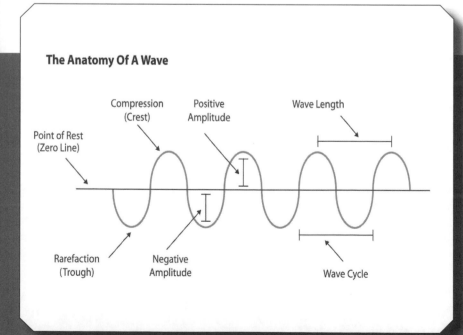

Phase

When sound waves are combined together, the result is more complex waves. When two waves of equal amplitude and frequency are combined, the result is a wave that is double in amplitude. In the event that waves of equal amplitude and frequency are combined but have opposite states of pressure (compression versus rarefaction), the waves can cancel each other out. The result is a thin, weak sound or no sound at all. Phase problems can occur during recording and mixing.

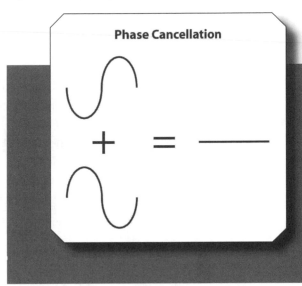

Phase Cancellation

During the recording process, multiple microphones recording the same source can produce sounds that are out of phase when combined together. If these mics were combined onto one channel on the recorder, they would become a single wave. The new sound wave would be the sum of the two waves. This wave might contain little or no audio at all. Once separate sounds are combined onto one track on the recorder, this effect cannot be reversed. However, if each mic is recorded to a separate track on the recorder, the effect can be repaired during editing/mixing by inverting or equalizing one of the tracks.

The Speed of Sound

Sound waves move through normal air pressure at 1,130 feet per second or 770 mph. There are many factors that can affect this speed, such as temperature and being above or below sea level, but this is generally a good gauge. This means that when a sound occurs about a quarter of a mile away it will take one second before that sound reaches your ears. Light travels much faster than sound. The speed of light is 983,571,056 feet per second or 670,616,629 mph. This is why fireworks are seen before they are heard. The explosion that happens hundreds of feet away is seen instantly, because of the speed with which light travels, but the sound takes a half second or so to be heard. It is also interesting to note that sound travels seven times faster in water and 25 times faster through steel.

Frequency

Frequency is the number of complete wave cycles (one compression and one rarefaction) that occur in one second, and it is measured in Hertz (Hz). A sound that consists of 100 cycles per second has a frequency of 100Hz. A sound that consists of 1,000 cycles per second has a frequency of 1KHz (K is for "kilo," or 1,000). The range of hearing for the human ear is 20Hz-20KHz. This is a general statement. The actual hearing response of the average male is 40Hz-18KHz. Women have a slightly better hearing response for higher frequencies than men do.

There are three main ranges of frequencies within the audible frequency range:
Low Range or "Low End": 20Hz-200Hz
Mid Range: 200Hz-5KHz
High Range or "High End": 5KHz-20KHz

Sometimes the mid frequencies are broken down even further:
Low Mid Range: 200Hz-1KHz
High Mid Range: 1KHz-5KHz

The human ear shapes the way that we perceive volume. Higher frequencies are perceived as louder than lower frequencies even when played at the same amplitude. Lower frequencies are often felt before they are heard. This is why subwoofer channels are so prevalent in action films — to put you in the action by enabling you to feel the impact of the explosion instead of just hearing it.

Low frequency sound waves are big, fat, and powerful. It takes a lot of force to produce these waves and they are much harder to control or stop than higher frequency waves. Higher frequencies are thinner and weaker, but can travel much faster and farther than lower frequencies. Low frequency sound waves pass through walls or other surfaces more easily than higher frequencies. That's why it is hard to hear higher frequencies through a wall, such as a human voice talking, but very easy to hear a subwoofer blaring in the next room or even from a car driving down the road.

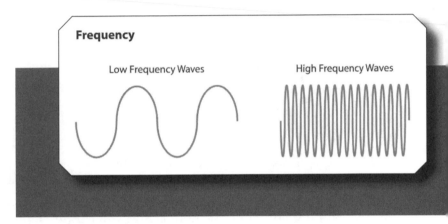

Amplitude

The amount of energy present in a sound wave is known as amplitude. Our ears interpret sound amplitude as volume. The higher the wave is, the louder it is perceived. The smaller the wave is, the softer in volume it is perceived. Amplitude in sound waves is measured in decibels.

Decibels

The word "decibel" is derived from *deci* (from the Latin for "ten") and *bel* (from the name of the inventor of the telephone, Alexander Graham Bell). This is a logarithmic unit for measuring sound. Without diving too far into the mathematics of it all, it is best to understand the basics of decibels. A 3dB increase results in double the power, whereas a 6dB increase results in double the volume. Conversely, a 6dB decrease (or -6dB) will result in 50% of the original volume. So a signal of -24dB that is raised to -12dB will sound four times as loud.

SPL

SPL stands for "sound pressure level" and is measured in decibels. The maximum SPL of a microphone refers to the loudest possible acoustic signal that the mic can handle before distorting the signal. Here are a few references of various SPL in decibels:

Whisper: 35dB

Speech: 65dB

Traffic: 85dB

Rock Concert: 115dB

Jet Takeoff: 135dB

Gunshot: 145dB

Rocket Launch: >165dB

Keep in mind that the distance to source will affect the SPL.

Prolonged exposure to high SPL will result in noise induced hearing loss (NIHL) which accounts for approximately 25% of hearing loss in America. Be careful when recording loud sounds. For example, when recording gunshots or fireworks, use ear protection and monitor your levels via your meters. This is the only time that you should not monitor your recordings with headphones. You only have one pair of ears! If you are pursing a professional career in the sound world, it is important to note that your career is over when you lose your hearing.

The following chart contains the accepted standards for recommended permissible exposure time for continuous time-weighted average noise, according to the NIOSH and CDC. Note that the permissible exposure time is cut in half for every 3 decibels over 85dB in order to prevent damage to the ears.

Decibel Exposure Time Guidelines

Continuous dB	Permissible Exposure Time
85dB	8 hours
88dB	4 hours
91dB	2 hours
94dB	1 hour
97dB	30 minutes
100dB	15 minutes
103dB	7.5 minutes
106dB	3.75 min. (< 4)
109dB	1.875 min. (< 2)
112dB	.9375 min. (~1)
115dB	.46875 min. (~30 sec.)

Note: This chart appears courtesy of http://www.dangerousdecibels. org. Used with permission.

Acoustics

The science of studying sound is known as acoustics. In the sound recording world, the word acoustics is commonly used to describe the sonic characteristics of a room and how it affects sound. Guitars offer a good example of acoustical space. An electric guitar can only be heard at a practical volume if connected to an amplifier; the shape of its body is purely stylistic. But the body and shape of an acoustic guitar allow the sound to resonate and project from the sound hole, naturally amplifying the sound.

Some rooms work the same way. Cathedrals and theaters have shapes and are made of specific materials that are designed to amplify the speaker's voice. Other environments, such as offices, reduce the overall volume with such things as acoustical ceiling tiles or sound-absorbing cubicle panels.

Recording studios and Foley stages are professionally designed and constructed so that the room's acoustics do not artificially color or amplify the sound. They are meant to be acoustically dead, allowing a true reproduction of the sound being recorded or mixed, with no effect from the room.

Some recording stages and vocal booths employ wood or tile to give a certain acoustic signature to the sound being recorded. Generally, in the sound effects world, it is best to record the sounds dry, with no sound of the room or environment. If so desired, reverb and other acoustic imaging can be applied with plug-ins during the edit.

Reverberation

Sound waves that occur in enclosed spaces are subject to a phenomenon known as reverberation. Sound is energy, and sound waves will keep traveling until they lose energy. When these waves encounter a surface, they simply bounce off and head in another direction. When they find another surface, they bounce off again and head off in another direction. These bounces are not limited to wall surfaces. Sound moves outward from its point of origin in all directions. So ceilings and floors are also responsible for this so-called reverberation, or reverb.

Sound-absorbing materials are used to tame the reverberation of a room. Different materials have different absorption characteristics. For example, wood is more absorbent than concrete and foam is more absorbent than wood. In field recording, sound blankets are used to temporarily "treat" a room for reverb and reduce the number of bounced waves.

The Application of the Science

All of the equipment in the world is worthless without the knowledge of how to use it. Therefore, we must dive into the technology and science of recording deep enough to allow us to use our equipment to its full capacity. A good place to start is with the understanding that the recording process is very similar to photography.

The goal is to capture an event to a medium for review at a later time. While great photographers have an arsenal of lenses, filters, tripods, lights, and even stages in which they can capture their subjects, great recordists also have an arsenal of lenses (microphones), filters (equalizers and other processing equipment), tripods (shock mounts and mic stands), lights (amplifiers that help boost the signal to audible levels), and stages (Foley stages, voiceover booths, and recording studios). We must understand the function of each of these tools in order to produce optimal recordings.

The Recording Chain

A recording chain is a system that consists of all the components necessary to record and play back sound. Each recording industry has unique needs that can affect this setup. For field recording, the recording chain can be just a microphone, a field recorder, and headphones. These three components can produce effective recordings with professional results. We'll look at these components a little more closely in the following chapters.

CHAPTER THREE

The Microphone

The Sonic Lens

THE MICROPHONE TURNS ACOUSTIC ENERGY into electric energy through a process called transduction. Microphones include a diaphragm that moves in response to changes in air pressure. The diaphragm then converts this movement into an electric signal that travels through a cable.

Microphone Types

There are two main types of microphones: dynamic and condenser. They both use a different type of diaphragm, resulting in different characteristics in the sounds they reproduce. A third type of microphone is the ribbon, but it is not within the scope of this book.

The dynamic microphone is the more rugged of the two. Its construction makes it perfect for loud, percussive sounds such as snare drums and gunshots. But the diaphragm moves slightly more slowly than the condenser's, which results in a less accurate reproduction of higher frequencies. Dynamic mics don't require external power.

The condenser microphone is the more accurate of the two, but at the cost of being more fragile. Condenser diaphragms usually cannot handle the stress of high-volume sounds for long periods of time. However, in a controlled environment, they can offer a truer reproduction of the original sound. Condenser is the most widely used type of microphone for sound effects recording. Their diaphragms do require powering.

Phantom Power

The condenser's diaphragm uses so-called phantom power to operate, without which it cannot convert an acoustic signal into an electric signal. For phantom power to work, a small amount of voltage must be supplied to the microphone.

This voltage can be sent down a balanced cable from a device such as a mixer or field recorder, both of which typically provide phantom power. Some microphones have an onboard battery compartment that allows them to be phantom powered internally. Typically, phantom power is 48 volts. Some microphones require lower voltages, such as 12 volts. Refer to your microphone's manual before applying phantom power to avoid damaging your microphone.

Proximity Effect

This phenomenon occurs when a voice or instrument is too close to a microphone. The effect is an artificial increase in low frequencies, making the sound boomy or bassy. Moving the sound source a few inches away from the mic usually corrects the problem.

Frequency Response

Each microphone responds to frequencies differently because of the type of material it is constructed from, its shape, and other factors. Frequency response refers to the highest and lowest possible frequency the mic can reproduce. As a rule of thumb, the wider the spectrum of frequencies, the more accurate the microphone's sound reproduction.

Flat Frequency Response

While most microphone frequency responses may appear similar as a specification, the response may increase or decrease in amplitude at specific frequency ranges. Generally, flat frequency responses are preferred in professional microphones. This means that all frequencies are reproduced evenly, with no colorization (added or subtracted frequencies).

However, some microphones are specifically designed to add this colorization, making them preferred choices for certain applications. A good example would be the Tram TR-50 lavaliere microphone. This mic is designed to be hidden underneath the clothing of actors during filming to capture their dialogue. The problem is that when you "bury" a mic, you lose certain frequencies — in this case, higher frequencies — because the sound waves must now travel through the clothes before they hit the diaphragm. To compensate for this, the TR-50 microphone increases its response in the higher frequencies around 8KHz.

There are many other examples of mics that alter their frequency responses as a solution for recording specific sources, such as guitar cabinets, kick drums, and vocals. If you are looking for a

Frequency Response

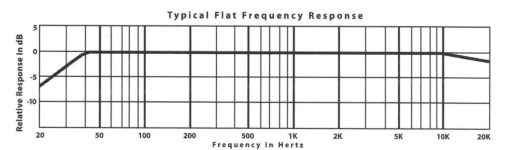

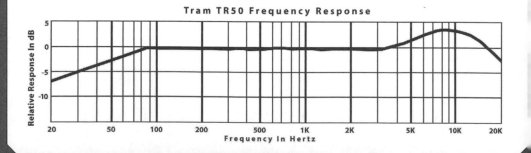

workhorse microphone, it's best to find a mic that has a flat frequency response of 20Hz to 20KHz. This will allow you to record many sources without adding potentially unwanted color to your sound. Remember, you can always equalize the sound after it has been recorded.

High Pass Filter (HPF)

Some microphones and recorders have an HPF switch. Also known as a low-cut filter, an HPF reduces the low-end frequencies at a given point (usually between 80Hz and 110Hz). This is very useful when dealing with sounds or environments that are bass heavy. Sound mixers will often use this switch to reduce air conditioning rumble or other low-frequency sounds when recording dialogue. Generally, the rule of thumb is to record without the HPF and correct the low end during the edit; however, there are some circumstances that will call for its use.

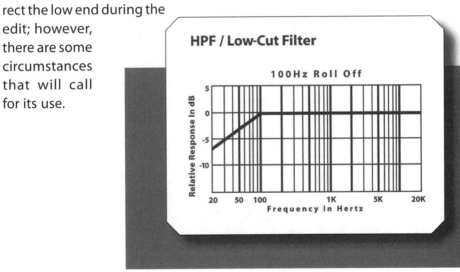

Microphone Patterns

A microphone pattern is sometimes referred to as a pickup pattern. This refers to how the capsule "sees" the sound in terms of direction in front and around the mic. There are five main types of microphone patterns:

Omnidirectional — This pattern picks up sounds coming in a 360° sphere around the capsule.

Cardioid — This is a heart-shaped pattern that gathers sound primarily from the front of the microphone, with some rejection of the sides and all of the rear.

Hypercardioid — This cardioid pattern has a tighter response in front of the mic and some sensitivity in the rear.

Supercardioid — This is a more focused version of the hypercardioid pattern, with higher rejection of the sides and all of the rear of the capsule.

Figure Eight or Bidirectional — This is a dual cardioid pattern that picks up sound from both sides of the microphone.

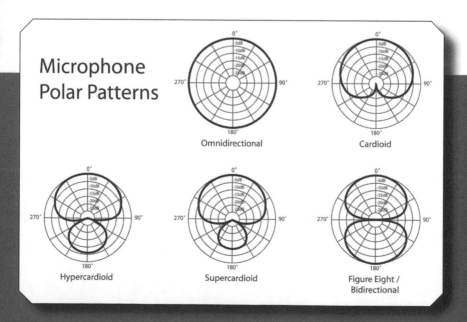

Microphone Polar Patterns

Omnidirectional

Cardioid

Hypercardioid

Supercardioid

Figure Eight / Bidirectional

CHAPTER FOUR

Microphone Models and Applications

Selecting the Right Tool for the Job

MICROPHONE SELECTION IS JUST AS critical as where you place the microphone. There are hundreds of microphones available today, each with its own unique sound and character. Some mics are better for percussive sounds, and others are more suited for ambiences and softer sounds. There are microphones that are better for vocal work and even microphones that are used underwater.

The following is a list of microphone types and examples. This list is not exhaustive by any means. Do some research and find out which microphone is best for your specific needs. Microphones are like guitars: Everyone has a favorite to make magic with.

Stereo Microphones
Stereo microphones utilize one of three main stereo recording techniques: spaced pair, XY and MS.

The spaced pair technique places two microphones apart from each other. The stereo image is derived from the timing and amplitude difference between the two microphones. The drawback to this technique is that it can cause phasing problems.

The XY recording technique places two capsules facing each other at an angle anywhere between 90° (narrow stereo field) and 135° (wide stereo field). This is the most fundamental and widely used stereo recording technique. Some microphones are manufactured as single-point units that house both capsules in the same microphone body. This allows for instant miking capabilities, without the cumbersome task of setup and wiring. This technique provides the best defense against phasing problems during stereo recordings.

The MS stereo recording technique is the more advanced and complicated. This method utilizes a small cardioid capsule facing directly at the sound source to provide the M, or mid, channel. In addition, there is a figure eight pattern capsule placed perpendicular to the mid capsule to provide the S, or side, channel. A matrix decoder is used to produce a stereo image from the two channels (M+S). With this technique, the stereo image can be altered to sound close or distant by adjusting the mid (direct source) and the side (ambient source).

Note: Single-point stereo microphones require a special 5 pin XLR cable to accommodate the signal produced by the additional capsule.

The following are examples of stereo microphones:

Audio Technica AT-825
This is a rugged stereo microphone that uses the XY recording technique with two capsules placed at a fixed 110° angle. This microphone requires a special 5 pin XLR cable.

Specifications
Mic Type: Condenser
Frequency Response: 30Hz-20KHz
Mic Pattern: Cardioid

Mic Capsule: Dual Small Diaphragm
Maximum SPL: 126dB
Phantom Power: 48v

Rode NT-4

This is a high-quality, low-cost, all-purpose stereo microphone that uses the XY recording technique. This mic is perfect for quiet ambiences and general sound effects. The stereo field is slightly narrower than in other stereo microphones. This is due to the dual capsules being placed in a fixed 90° angle. This microphone features two NT-5 capsules and requires a special 5 pin XLR cable.

Specifications
Mic Type: Condenser
Frequency Response: 20Hz-20KHz
Mic Pattern: Cardioid
Mic Capsule: Dual Small Diaphragm
Maximum SPL: 143dB
Phantom Power: 48v

Rode NT-4

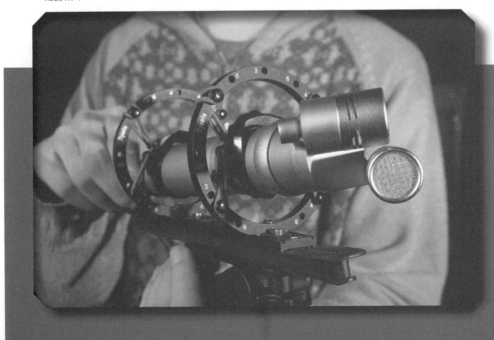

Rode NT-5, Matched Pair

Rode NT-5 (Matched Pair)

Because the NT-5 is a single-capsule microphone, a matched pair can be used for either the spaced pair or XY recording technique. The capsule is the same capsule used on the NT-4 stereo microphone.

Specifications
Mic Type: Condenser
Frequency Response: 20Hz-20KHz
Mic Pattern: Cardioid
Mic Capsule: Small Diaphragm
Maximum SPL: 143dB
Phantom Power: 48v

Shure VP-88

This stereo microphone is a veteran in field recording and uses the MS recording technique. Although a bit heavier than other stereo mics, this is a rugged, tried-and-true mic. This microphone requires a special 5 pin XLR cable.

Specifications
Mic Type: Condenser
Frequency Response: 40Hz-20KHz
Mic Pattern: Cardioid and Figure Eight

Mic Capsule: Dual Small Diaphragm
Maximum SPL: 119dB
Phantom Power: 48v

Shotgun Microphones

Shotgun microphones are designed to focus on sounds in front of the mic and reject sounds to the sides and rear of the mic. The effect is similar to looking through a tube: The only "image" that is seen is directly in front. This is generally true with shotgun microphones. The majority of the dialogue on a film or television set is captured with shotgun microphones (also referred to as boom mics). A shotgun can have the effect of pulling the sound closer, as a zoom lens does.

The following are examples of shotgun microphones:

Rode NTG-1

This is an economical short shotgun microphone. It has a wide frequency response with a bump in the low end around 200Hz.

Specifications
Mic Type: Condenser
Frequency Response: 20Hz-20KHz
Mic Pattern: Supercardioid
Mic Capsule: Small Diaphragm
Maximum SPL: 139dB
Phantom Power: 48v

Sanken CS-3E

This microphone contains three capsules that are arranged to provide a supercardioid directional pattern. This microphone is a favorite with professionals and offers premium quality sound.

Specifications
Mic Type: Condenser
Frequency Response: 50Hz-20KHz
Mic Pattern: Supercardioid
Mic Capsule: Small Diaphragm
Maximum SPL: 120dB
Phantom Power: 48v

Sennheiser MKH-416

The standard in field shotguns for film and television production, this microphone is perfect for recording mono sound effects in the field. Because of its pickup pattern, there is high rejection of super-fluous noise on the sides and rear of the microphone.

Specifications
Mic Type: Condenser
Frequency Response: 40Hz-20KHz
Mic Pattern: Supercardioid
Mic Capsule: Small Diaphragm
Maximum SPL: 130dB
Phantom Power: 48v

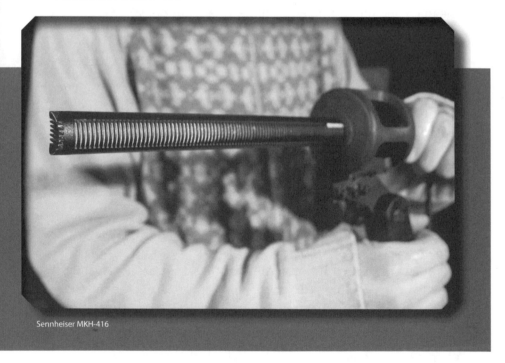
Sennheiser MKH-416

Sennheiser MKH-70

This microphone has an extended 16-inch body that allows for a long throw and high directivity. It features excellent rejection of off axis noise that enables the mic to pick up sounds from farther distances as if they were closer. This mic is commonly used for capturing dialogue on long shots in film and television production. It is the sonic equivalent to a long zoom lens on a camera.

Specifications
Mic Type: Condenser
Frequency Response: 50Hz-20KHz
Mic Pattern: Supercardioid
Mic Capsule: Small Diaphragm
Maximum SPL: 124dB
Phantom Power: 48v

Stereo Shotgun Microphones

Like mono shotgun microphones, stereo shotguns have a considerable amount of directivity, resulting in a focused stereo image. These microphones typically combine a supercardioid capsule with a figure eight capsule to create an MS recording. However, Sanken has developed a stereo shotgun microphone that allows for true stereo imaging. In addition, stereo microphones can generally be used as mono shotguns by using only the supercardioid channel output.

The following are examples of stereo shotgun microphones:

Audio Technica AT815ST

This stereo shotgun microphone has a switch that allows either non-matrixed MS or left and right recordings. This mic can be used to record stereo and mono sound effects in the field. The AT815ST is a 15-inch short shotgun mic with a higher SPL and a longer throw than the 9-inch AT835ST.

Specifications
Mic Type: Condenser
Frequency Response: 30Hz-20KHz
Mic Pattern: Supercardioid and Figure Eight
Mic Capsule: Small Diaphragm
Maximum SPL: 126dB
Phantom Power: 48v

Audio Technica AT835ST

This stereo shotgun microphone has a switch that allows either non-matrixed MS or left and right recordings. This mic can be used for recording stereo and mono sound effects in the field. The AT835ST is a 9-inch short shotgun mic with a lower SPL and a shorter throw than the 15-inch AT815ST.

Specifications
Mic Type: Condenser
Frequency Response: 40Hz-20KHz
Mic Pattern: Supercardioid And Figure Eight
Mic Capsule: Small Diaphragm
Maximum SPL: 102dB
Phantom Power: 48v

Sanken CSS-5

This microphone features five highly directional capsules that are placed in an array. This allows for switching between normal stereo (115° angle), wide stereo (140° angle), and mono recordings.

Specifications
Mic Type: Condenser
Frequency Response: 20Hz-20KHz
Mic Pattern: Cardioid
Mic Capsule: Small Diaphragm
Maximum SPL: 120dB
Phantom Power: 48v

Sennheiser MKH-418S

This microphone is an MS stereo version of the MKH-416 and can be used for recording stereo and mono sound effects in the field.

Specifications
Mic Type: Condenser
Frequency Response: 40Hz-20KHz
Mic Pattern: Supercardioid and Figure Eight
Mic Capsule: Small Diaphragm
Maximum SPL: 130dB
Phantom Power: 48v

General Purpose Microphones

These microphones can be used for a wide variety of situations. They are multipurpose tools on a Foley stage or in the field.

The following are examples of general purpose microphones:

DPA 4012

This is a premier condenser microphone delivering superb-quality recordings. Commonly used for recording instruments such as pianos and violins, this mic has a wider than normal cardioid pattern and features a very high maximum SPL.

Specifications
Mic Type: Condenser
Frequency Response: 40Hz-20KHz
Mic Pattern: Cardioid
Mic Capsule: Small Diaphragm
Maximum SPL: 168dB
Phantom Power: 48v

Rode NT-3

This is a solid Foley microphone that features a focused pickup pattern and great sound reproduction for a low price.

Rode NT-3

Specifications
Mic Type: Condenser
Frequency Response: 20Hz-20KHz
Mic Pattern: Hypercardioid
Mic Capsule: Small Diaphragm
Maximum SPL: 140dB
Phantom Power: 48v

Oktava MC-012
This is a Russian-made microphone that features a low-cost, high-quality sound. This microphone is especially sensitive to low-end rumble and wind noise. Generally, this mic should be used with an HPF when recording movement.

Specifications
Mic Type: Condenser
Frequency Response: 20Hz-20KHz
Mic Pattern: Multiple Capsules — Cardioid, Hypercardioid, and Omni
Mic Capsule: Small Diaphragm
Maximum SPL: 140dB
Phantom Power: 48v

Oktava MC-012

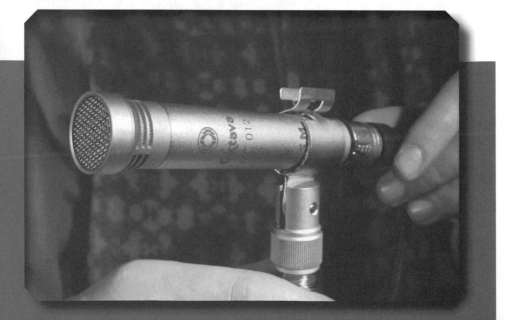

Vocal/Voiceover Microphones

These microphones are designed for miking voices and feature large diaphragms. They provide a smooth and balanced sound for a close-miked voice.

The following are examples of vocal/voiceover microphones:

Rode NT-2000

This is a solid vocal mic that provides excellent sound and carries a lot of useful features such as a variable pickup pattern and a variable HPF.

Specifications
Mic Type: Condenser
Frequency Response: 20Hz-20KHz
Mic Pattern: Variable
Mic Capsule: Large Diaphragm
Maximum SPL: 147dB
Phantom Power: 48v

Neumann TLM-103 Microphone

This is a high-quality microphone used primarily for vocal work. This mic is found in many professional studios.

Specifications
Mic Type: Condenser
Frequency Response: 20Hz-20KHz
Mic Pattern: Cardioid
Mic Capsule: Large Diaphragm
Maximum SPL: 138dB
Phantom Power: 48v

Shure SM58

This is the industry standard for stage/live performance vocal microphones. Although not recommended for sound design work, this mic can be used for vocals that will be filtered to emulate walkie-talkies and CB radios.

Specifications
Mic Type: Dynamic
Frequency Response: 50Hz-15KHz
Mic Pattern: Cardioid
Mic Capsule: Small Diaphragm
Maximum SPL: <180dB*
Phantom Power: None

* Due to the physical characteristics of dynamic microphones, maximum SPL has only been estimated.

Oktava MC319

This is a Russian vocal microphone. The sound it reproduces carries a bright high end. Uses for this mic also include miking pianos and other instruments.

Specifications
Mic Type: Condenser
Frequency Response: 40Hz-18KHz
Mic Pattern: Cardioid
Mic Capsule: Large Diaphragm
Maximum SPL: 140dB
Phantom Power: 48v

Lavaliere Microphones

Lavaliere microphones are typically used in film and television production as an alternative or backup to a boom mic. They can be exposed or hidden and are generally used with a wireless system but can be hardwired into a mixer.

The following are examples of lavaliere microphones:

Sennheiser MKE2-P

This is an extremely small lavaliere microphone that is typically used in film and television production. Its small design allows it to be hidden easier on clothing and costumes. It features an increasing slope in higher frequencies that starts around 2KHz and builds to about 15KHz.

Specifications
Mic Type: Condenser
Frequency Response: 20Hz-20KHz
Mic Pattern: Omnidirectional
Mic Capsule: Lavaliere
Maximum SPL: 130dB
Phantom Power: 12v Internal or 48v

Tram TR-50
This is the industry standard for lavaliere mics in film and television. Its frequency response includes an increase around 8KHz to compensate for miking under clothes and costumes. Its pickup pattern also allows it to be used as a plant mic on sets and inside cars.

Specifications
Mic Type: Condenser
Frequency Response: 40Hz-16KHz
Mic Pattern: Omnidirectional
Mic Capsule: Lavaliere
Maximum SPL: 134dB
Phantom Power: 12v Internal or 48v

TRAM TR-50

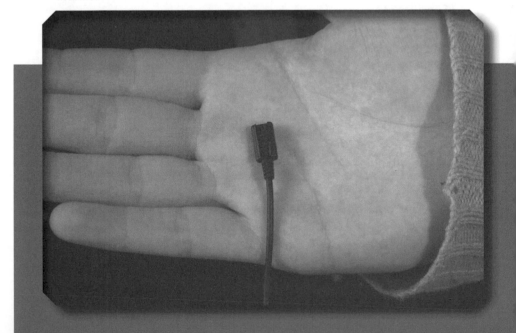

Instrument Microphones

These are microphones that have been designed specifically for miking instruments and can generally handle high volumes without being damaged.

The following are examples of instrument microphones:

Sennheiser E609

This microphone is specifically designed for miking guitar cabinets. It has a high rejection of sounds on the side and rear.

Specifications
Mic Type: Dynamic
Frequency Response: 40Hz-18KHz
Mic Pattern: Supercardioid
Mic Capsule: Large Diaphragm
Maximum SPL: 159dB
Phantom Power: None

Shure SM57

This microphone is the industry standard all-purpose instrument mic. It is very similar to the Shure SM58. The main difference between the two is that the SM57 has a slightly more extended low-end frequency response, and the SM58 has a pop filter.

Specifications
Mic Type: Dynamic
Frequency Response: 40Hz-15KHz
Mic Pattern: Cardioid
Mic Capsule: Small Diaphragm
Maximum SPL: <180dB*
Phantom Power: None
* Due to the physical characteristics of dynamic microphones, maximum SPL has only been estimated.

AKG D112

This microphone is arguably the industry standard for miking kick drums. Its design allows for high SPL (over 160dB) without any noticeable distortion. This microphone is also used for miking bass cabinets, trumpets, trombones, and cellos.

Specifications
Mic Type: Dynamic
Frequency Response: 20Hz-17KHz
Mic Pattern: Cardioid
Mic Capsule: Large Diaphragm
Maximum SPL: 160dB*
Phantom Power: None
* Due to the physical characteristics of dynamic microphones, maximum SPL has only been estimated.

Rode NT-6
This microphone has a distinctive design that allows the capsule to be placed away from the body of the mic via a 10-foot extension cable. This allows the mic to be placed in unique and hard-to-reach areas such as pianos, drums, woodwinds, and brass instruments.

Specifications
Mic Type: Condenser
Frequency Response: 40Hz-20KHz
Mic Pattern: Cardioid
Mic Capsule: Small Diaphragm
Maximum SPL: 138dB
Phantom Power: 48v

Hydrophones (Underwater Microphones)
Hydrophones are microphones designed to capture sounds underwater. These mics are considerably expensive.

The following is an example of a hydrophone:

DPA 8011 Hydrophone
This is one of the most unique microphones in the world. Its design allows it to record sounds when placed underwater or inside other liquids. The microphone body and cable are sealed to prevent liquids from damaging the interior electronics.

Specifications
Mic Type: Condenser
Frequency Response: 100Hz-20KHz
Mic Pattern: Omnidirectional
Mic Capsule: Small Diaphragm
Maximum SPL: 162dB
Phantom Power: 48v

Binaural Microphones

Stereo microphones place the sound in front of the listener. Binaural microphones reproduce how the human head actually hears sound: They are placed inside the ear holes of a dummy head. The recordings produced are more for industrial, musical, and novelty purposes, but with a little innovation, these microphones could be used to produce new and creative sound effects.

The following is an example of a binaural microphone:

Neumann KU 100
Use this microphone when you are looking to faithfully reproduce the way that a human would hear the sound.

Specifications
Mic Type: Condenser
Frequency Response: 20Hz-20KHz
Mic Pattern: Ear Canal
Mic Capsule: Small Diaphragm
Maximum SPL: 135dB
Phantom Power: 48v

Surround Sound Microphones

True 5.1 surround sound microphones have six capsules arranged in a single housing unit. Because there are essentially six microphones, you will need a multitrack field recorder or several two-track field recorders to record the sound.

The following is an example of a surround sound microphone:

Holophone 3-D
Used for sound effects gathering, musical recording, and broad-casting events, this microphone provides a true surround image.

Specifications
Mic Type: Condenser
Frequency Response: 5x20Hz-20KHz and 1x20Hz-100Hz
Mic Pattern: Multidirectional
Mic Capsule: Small Diaphragms
Maximum SPL: 130dB
Phantom Power: 48v

CHAPTER FIVE

Microphone Accessories

Always Use Protection!

THE QUALITY OF RECORDING THAT a microphone produces greatly depends on the equipment that is used to isolate the microphone from its environment. Microphones are vulnerable to wind noise, vibrations, and high sound-pressure levels. Protective gear should be used to reduce these adverse effects. You should always use a microphone with a shock mount. In addition, you should never record outdoors without a zeppelin and a windjammer.

Here is a list of accessories to use with your microphones:

Shock Mounts

Microphones are subject to handling noise. This occurs when vibrations are transmitted to the microphone by direct contact from a hand or through a microphone stand. To reduce this handling noise, place the microphone in a shock mount. A shock mount absorbs the vibration by isolating the microphone from the stand via rubber bands. Handheld shock mounts called pistol grips offer

Rycote Shock Mount

Marshall Shock Mount

General-Purpose Shock Mount

Pistol Grip

the ultimate in portability and are designed to be placed on the end of a boom pole.

Windscreens

Windscreens shield the microphone from excessive air movement, which produces undesirable results known as wind noise. A basic windscreen is a piece of foam that fits over the end of the microphone. Sometimes rubber bands can be used to stop loose windscreens from moving or falling off.

Windscreens

Zeppelin

Zeppelins or Windshields

Zeppelins are long, enclosed hollow tubes designed to have a shock mount inserted inside to keep the microphone shielded from wind noise. These professional windscreens are more commonly used in the field. Zeppelins and shock mounts should be stored in an upright position to avoid excessive strain on the rubber bands inside the mount.

Windjammers or Windsocks

Often referred to as the "fuzzy rat" or "wookie condom," these furry protectors slip over the top of the zeppelin and greatly reduce the amount of wind noise picked up by the microphone.

Windjammer

Hi-Wind Cover

Made exclusively by Rycote, this device is used in place of the windjammer in locations where there is excessive wind.

Hi-Wind Cover

Microphone Stands

Microphone stands come in all shapes, sizes, and prices. There are short stands intended to be placed on a tabletop for voice work or next to a kick drum. There are long boom stands that reach extreme distances for miking an orchestra, for example, or Neil Pert's drum set. For the most part, a cheap mic stand will give satisfactory results. If you are using a stand that has loose knobs or connectors, be sure to secure them with gaffer's tape or rubber bands to stop them from rattling during recording.

Also, make sure to use stands that have rubber feet, which help isolate the mic stand from the ground. In some cases, such as when heavy items are being dropped on the ground to produce effects, it's a good idea to isolate the stand further by placing it on top of a pile of sound blankets to dampen vibrations.

Boom Poles

Sometimes called fish poles, these mobile mic stands extend in length to bring your microphone closer to the action. They are mainly used in film and television production for dialogue recording, but can be very useful for sound effects gathering. There are two types of boom poles: coil-cabled and straight-cabled.

The first has a coiled cable that runs through the center of the pole and is generally not removed. Instead, there is a female XLR jack in the bottom of the pole and a male XLR that comes out of the top. One drawback is that the cable can become tangled inside, making the pole difficult to collapse.

The straight-cabled pole has a standard XLR cable that runs through the center and is designed to be removed to allow external cabling of the pole. The XLR cable appears at the top and bottom of the pole in pre-made holes, making it easy to remove the cable altogether.

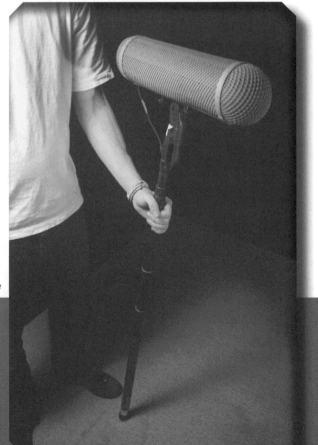

Boom Pole

What's the difference between the two poles? Coiled cables are heavy and bulky. Movements of this boom pole must be graceful to reduce the sound of the cable bouncing around inside the center of the pole. Straight cables are less likely to cause problems, but movements should still be slow and deliberate with these poles as well. It all comes down to application. Coil-cabled poles are perfect for ENG and sound effects gathering, when you do not have the time to deal with your equipment and just need to point a mic at something fast. Straight-cabled poles take a little more time to use and are better suited for filmmaking — when you are sitting at your sound cart with nothing to do for hours at a time.

Pop Filters

Plosive sounds made by the human mouth can cause distortion, or pops, in the audio. These are most commonly made by words that start with "b" or "p." Professional voiceover artists can pull back on these words and create a natural-sounding sentence without drawing attention to the technique. Most of the time, you will need to use a separate windscreen between the microphone and the mouth called a pop filter. This device allows voice talent to speak normally without worrying about controlling their speech on certain words.

Pop Filter

Pads

Pads prevent over-
loading a microphone
preamp when record-
ing sounds with
high SPLs (gunshots,
explosions, human
screams). The pad
attenuates the signal
to a usable level.
Some microphones
have built-in pads.

Pad

You can also purchase pads to plug in between your mic and your
recorder or mixer. Pads come in a variety of attenuations (-10dB,
-15dB, -20dB, -25dB, etc.). An attenuation of -25dB will reduce the
microphone's output signal by -25dB.

Cables

There are two types of cables in the audio world: balanced and
unbalanced.

Unbalanced cables consist of two conductors: hot and ground.
These cables are susceptible to external noise and interference.
They are generally not preferred for long cable runs.

Balanced cables consist of three conductors: hot, cold, and ground.
These cables help shield the audio signal from external noise and
interference. They are generally preferred for long cable runs.

Note: Phantom power can only be used on balanced cables.

Cable shorts are the result of strain and twisting on the cable. Insert
and remove cables by holding the connector firmly. Never yank on a
cable to remove it from a connection. Use strain relief on your cables
when connecting them at hard angles or to gear that can move
around. When wrapping your cables, avoid winding them tightly
around your arms. This can cause the inside wiring to wear down
and become frayed. Loosely roll your cable so that it naturally winds
into a circle. These tips will help protect the life of your cable.

The performance of great gear is often limited by the cables that are being used to connect to the gear. If you can afford to, buy better-grade cables. They will last longer and help shield your audio from external noise.

Cable Testers

When a signal cuts out or crackles intermittently, you need to determine where the problem lies. Between the microphone, the recorder, and your cables, the cables are by far the most likely suspect. Microphones and recorders have internal circuit boards and wiring that are not exposed to the rigors of fieldwork. Cables take the brunt of the abuse.

Cable Tester

You can connect the cable in question to a cable tester to determine if it is indeed the problem. Most testers will display which wire in the cable is having the trouble and other helpful information. A time- and money-saving craft to learn is soldering. Nearly all shorts and signal failure problems can be solved by simply soldering a connection.

External Phantom Power Supplies

Some equipment does not provide phantom power for microphones, or the phantom power supply can go bad. Portable external phantom power supplies can be purchased and stored in your recording bag to power your microphones. The power supplies will require power of their own via AA or 9-volt batteries.

Silica Gel Packets

In general, electronic equipment should be stored away from condensation. Moisture build-up on the diaphragm of a condenser microphone will affect its performance. To prevent this, you can put silica gel packets in your storage cases to absorb moisture. You can find these packets at *www.silicagelpackets.com*.

CHAPTER SIX

Recorders

Tape Is Dead....
Welcome to the Digital Revolution

■ A BRIEF HISTORY OF RECORDING DEVICES

The recorder takes the electrical information transmitted by the microphone and stores it on a medium, such as a hard disk or compact flash card. Through the years, these mediums have changed, but the principles remain the same. Here is a brief history of recording devices.

The Phonograph

The very first sound effect was recorded at 10:30 a.m. on July 16, 1890 in London. In fact, the sound was Big Ben striking 10:30 and was recorded onto a wax cylinder. These wax cylinders were invented by Thomas Edison in 1877 and were the first widely used recording medium for sound. Edison's first attempt involved tin foil as the recording medium, but because of the foil's frailty and short life span of two to three playback passes, the medium was scrubbed for the stronger characteristics of wax. The wax cylinders were used in a device known as the phonograph.

The wax cylinder employed a similar principle to the more familiar vinyl record. At the time of recording, grooves were cut into the wax surface that correlated to the vibrations of the sound event. It was this cutting process during recording that led to the phrase "cutting a record" or "cutting an album." Playback of the cylinders involved a needle that would ride inside the grooves, respond to the vibrations, and transduce them into audible sound. But, alas, the wax cylinders also had their limits. First, their size limited the amount of recording time. Second, they were susceptible to cracks, breaking, and, of course, melting. Third, the wax was known to wear out and break off in pieces after numerous playback passes.

The Gramophone

The gramophone, invented in 1887 by Emile Berliner, replaced the phonograph's wax cylinders with flat discs or records as the recording medium. The platters, as they were called, were far more durable than wax cylinders. This became a standard for recording and mass duplication for nearly a century. To date, records can still be purchased at most local music stores.

The Telegraphone

In 1898, a wire recorder called the telegraphone was invented by Valdemar Poulsen. This device used piano wire as the recording medium and a small electromagnet connected to a microphone to magnetize the wire. The telegraphone was crude, but sturdy enough to be used by the U.S. Army and was later a standard for the corporate world in the form of dictation and answering machines. Wire recorders eventually gave way to the widely accepted magnetic tape in the late 1940s.

The Magnetophone

The magnetophone, a German magnetic tape recorder that used plastic tape developed by Dr. Fritz Pfleumer, was invented in the 1930s. It used the same recording principle as the wire recorder, but it recorded to spools of oxide-coated tape that were easier to store and manage. The magnetophone was the model for modern-day magnetic tape formats.

The Nagra

In 1951, a Swiss inventor named Stefan Kudelski built the first Nagra. Nagras were marketed as portable magnetic tape recorders, and the U.S. military adopted them for documenting battles and other military events. The film industry quickly learned of the Nagra, and it became the standard for location sound and sound effects recording in film until the early 1990s.

Compact Discs

Digital technology began to creep into the recording world in the late 1970s, but it wasn't until 1983 that a true digital recording medium was released to the public. The medium was called the compact disc (CD). Much like a high-tech version of its older brother, the vinyl record, the CD was a futuristic-looking silver disc that carried digital audio in grooves burned beneath its plastic surface with a laser. By the end of the 1980s, CDs were widely accepted as a simple and economical way of distributing music and other recordings to the masses, but it wasn't until the 1990s that CD recording devices became available to the public.

DAT

Sony introduced the first digital audio tape (DAT) recorder in 1987. DAT works like the magnetophone in that it uses magnetic tape to record electromagnetic signals. However, the signals that are recorded on DAT tapes are digital representations of the analog signal. The recorder uses AD/DA converters to encode and decode the digital information stored on the magnetic tape. DAT replaced the Nagra and became the new standard recording medium for the film industry in the mid 1990s.

Hard Disk Recording

Soon after the birth of DAT recording, hard disk recording — the bastard stepchild — was waiting to be born. It uses the same digital technology as DATs but records to far more stable mediums such as removable hard drives and compact flash cards and offer higher sample rates. Hard disk recorders quickly stepped up to the plate as the industry standard for location sound, sound effects gathering, and studio recording. They are a portable solution to computer-based recording, allowing the user to record, edit, and play back digitally recorded sounds.

The evolution of recording devices was at first driven by science, but later gave way to the politics of business and enterprise. Companies raced to be the next deliverer of a storage/recording medium that would yield untold millions in product sales and even more in reprints. As recordists, the benefits we reap from this battle are all sorts of state-of-the-art equipment at very low prices. A recording setup that would have cost hundreds of thousands of dollars can now be purchased at your local Guitar Center for only hundreds of dollars. The revolution has begun!

■ MODERN-DAY RECORDERS

There are a lot of field recorders on the market today. The word "digital" has become synonymous with "professional." This is far from true. Some recorders boast high sample rates and bit depths, but have poor-quality mic preamps and other components. Do some research and make test recordings with different recorders before your purchase. I've returned several recorders after using them because the recordings were just horrible. Be picky. It's your sound.

For the purpose of examining recorders, we will use both the Fostex FR-2 and the FR-2 LE. These units are quickly becoming the new standard for fieldwork. The FR-2 is a professional two-track recorder with an optional time code card. This unit can handle just about anything you throw at it. The FR-2 records in BWFs (broadcast wave file) in resolutions up to 24 bit/192KHz. The FR-2 LE is a more economical solution, at half the price, and records in either MP3 or BWF with resolutions up to 24 bit/96KHz.

Fostex FR-2

Fostex FR-2LE

Gain Staging

Digital field recorders function just like their analog and DAT pre-decessors. The audio signal and gain staging components function the same way. The real difference is the storage medium. Care should be taken when handling the audio signal before the digital conversion step. This is done through gain staging.

How and when an audio signal is amplified is critical to the quality level of the recording. The principle to follow is that the signal should always be amplified the most when it is farthest upstream in the chain. Amplifying a sound downstream will result in system noise and hiss. The idea behind gain staging is that no level should be higher than the previous gain point. For field recording, set your highest level at the trims and not the master.

Two Tracks, Not Just Left and Right

A two-track recorder allows you to record two channels of audio simultaneously. This allows for stereo recording using either a stereo microphone or two mono microphones. When using only one mono microphone, such as a shotgun, you would only record to one channel. Note that on some recorders you have the option of recording a mono microphone to both channels via digital menus. But this does not make your recording stereo. The same information is being sent to both tracks and just wastes hard disk space.

Don't think of two tracks as being just left and right. They are two discrete channels. This will help you in problem-solving complex recording situations and give some room for creativity. For example, if you are recording a loud sound, such as a gunshot, you might want to set up two mics. One mic would be set at a normal signal level and the second mic would be used as a safety backup with a lower signal level to reduce the risk of clipping. Each mic would be sent to its own channel. So, if the first track clips, you can use the second, unaffected track. This would ensure that you end up with at least one usable recording. This is also helpful when you are miking one event from two angles simultaneously.

For example, you can place a mono microphone in front of a door and run it to one channel on the recorder. You can then place a second mono microphone on the opposite side of the door and run it to the other channel on the recorder. You can then perform an event, such as knocking on the door, and record it from two perspectives. In the edit, you can blend these channels together to create a new sound or separate the two channels into their own separate mono files for two different sound effects recorded at once.

A recorder that is capable of recording more than two channels is called a multitrack recorder. There are many options and models of these units available on the market today. The two-track recorder is still the most popular for sound effects gathering.

Clipping

There are two main differences between an analog recorder and a digital recorder. The first difference is the recording medium. An analog recorder stores its information on magnetic tape, while a hard disk recorder stores the information digitally on a micro drive or compact flash card. The second major difference is that analog tape is far more forgiving when the signal is distorted.

Analog signals are imprinted on the tape through the use of magnets. When the signal is too strong, the waveform bleeds off the edges of the tape. A digital signal is stored merely as data: ones and zeros. A digital file has an absolute zero, commonly called digital zero. Any signal that is higher than absolute zero is simply squared off until the next sample that is lower than absolute zero. This is known as clipping. The result is far less desirable than analog distortion and should be avoided at all costs. For this reason, you should always use a limiter when working with a digital recorder.

Note: Clipping and digital waveforms are discussed in greater detail in Chapter Twelve, "Digital Audio."

Limiter

A limiter is an analog circuit that detects when a signal is approaching a predefined level and adjusts the volume accordingly to prevent going over that limit. Limiters are very helpful when working with digital recorders as clipping is very difficult to correct in the edit. All professional recorders have a limiter.

Mic/Line Level

Mic/line switches tell the recorder what type of signal to expect at the inputs of the device. Some recorders also have this switch to determine what type of signal is being sent to the outputs of the device.

Professional line level is +4dBu
Professional mic level is -60dBu
Consumer equipment line level is -10dBV

Line level is a stronger signal than mic level. It is necessary to amplify a microphone's signal through a separate amplifier known as a mic preamp to bring the signal up to a usable level. The gain or trim knobs on a recorder control the mic preamps. The most important feature on a field recorder is the quality of the mic preamps. A top-of-the-line recorder with poor mic preamps quickly loses value.

All microphones send a mic level signal. Some professional electronic equipment will let you select the input and output levels. For example, an audio mixer, such as the Mackie 1604VLZ, has XLR inputs and 1/4" inputs on the same channel. The XLR inputs are used for mic level devices and the 1/4" inputs are used for line level devices. When connecting directly to a microphone you will always set your recorder's inputs to mic level.

Power Supply

Field recorders are different from studio recorders in that they are built to be portable. This means they come with the ability to be powered internally via a battery compartment. Disposable batteries can be costly and adversely affect the environment. Rechargeable batteries such as AAs and 9 volts are useful, but need to be replaced several times throughout the day. Professional battery systems such as the Eco Charge and NP-1 batteries can connect directly to the power jack on the unit. These batteries can offer more than a full day's worth of recording without any additional charging.

Sample Rates/Quantization

Hard disk recorders offer various sample rates and bit depths to choose from. Higher rates use more space on your recording medium. Currently, high-definition audio is considered to be anything above 24 bit/48KHz. This is the standard audio sample rate for DVD audio. The standard for CD audio is 16 bit/44.1KHz.

Here is a chart of approximate file sizes based on bit depth, sample rate, and number of channels (mono or stereo):

MP3 128Kbps 16 bit/44.1KHz

Channels	1 Minute	1 Hour	2 Hours
Stereo	.9Mb	54Mb	108Mb

16 bit/44.1KHz

Channels	1 Minute	1 Hour	2 Hours
Mono	5.2Mb	312Mb	624Mb
Stereo	10.4Mb	624Mb	1.25Gb

16 bit/48KHz

Channels	1 Minute	1 Hour	2 Hours
Mono	5.6Mb	336Mb	672Mb
Stereo	11.2Mb	67 Mb	1.34Gb

24 bit/48KHz

Channels	1 Minute	1 Hour	2 Hours
Mono	8.5Mb	510Mb	1.02Gb
Stereo	17Mb	1.02Gb	2.04Gb

24 bit/96KHz

Channels	1 Minute	1 Hour	2 Hours
Mono	16.5Mb	990Mb	1.98Gb
Stereo	33Mb	1.98Gb	3.96Gb

Note: Sample rates and digital audio are discussed in greater detail in Chapter Twelve, "Digital Audio."

Daily Setup

You should take time to properly set up your unit before you go out into the field each day. It is a good idea to create a checklist that you follow. Here is an example of the checklists that we use at the Chop Shop:

Fostex FR-2 Setup

1. Insert Card and Format
2. Set PHANTOM POWER to ON
3. Set MIC/LINE Switch to MIC
4. Set TRIM(s) to TWO O'CLOCK Position
5. Set HPF (100Hz) Switch to OFF
6. Select TRACK MODE — MONO or STEREO
7. Set QUANTIZATION to 24BIT
8. Set FS(KHz) to 96
9. Set LIMITER to ON
10. Set MASTER FADER to "8"

Fostex FR-2 LE Setup

1. Insert Card and Format
   MENU > Disk > Format > FS/BIT Mode=BWF96/24 > Execute
2. Set HPF (100Hz) to ON
   MENU > Setup > HPF: Off
3. Set SAMPLING/BIT RATE to 96/24
   MENU > Setup > Def.FS/BIT: BWF96/24
4. Set PHANTOM POWER to ON
   MENU > Setup > Phantom: On
5. Set MONITOR MODE to L/R (Stereo) or MONO
   MENU > Setup > Monitor Mode: L/R or Mono
6. Set TRIMs to TWO O'CLOCK Position
   Set MASTER FADER to TWO O'CLOCK Position

Note: Some knobs and faders use numbers as a position reference. For example, on the Fostex units the master knob being set to "8" does not refer to an actual unit of measurement; it is only a relative position on the recorder. This is the same case with the trim knobs being set to the two o'clock position.

Also, presetting the levels does not mean that you will not change the levels in the field. These are just good starting points that will yield a reasonable recording level. When in the field, make adjustments as necessary.

Daily Wrap Up

You should also create a wrap up checklist to follow when you are finished recording for the day. Here is the checklist that we use at the Chop Shop:

Fostex FR-2 & FR-2 LE Wrap Up
1. Remove Card from FR-2(LE) via MENU
2. Dust Equipment with Air Can
3. Wipe Down Cables
4. Store Gear in Case
5. Place Batteries on Charger
6. Transfer Card to a Workstation
7. Back Up Recording to DVD
8. Store Card in Case

DVD Back-Ups

In the days of analog and DAT tape, the reels and cassettes were archived and stored after recording. In the digital age, the audio data on the micro drives and compact flash cards are transferred to a computer. The card or drive is then formatted, erasing all of the data. If the computer crashes, then all of the audio data could be lost. Therefore, DVDs should be used to back up each day's recordings in addition to transferring them to your workstation. Once burned to a DVD, the data should be verified.

In my time, I have seen dozens of hard drives with hundreds of gigs of data burn out, taking all of their data with them. Backing up data is extremely important and necessary. If you haven't lost a hard drive, don't worry: You will one day. Be prepared and have a back-up of everything you record.

Headphones

Headphones are used to monitor the recording and playback of the sounds. They are often referred to as "cans." Closed-ear headphone designs for models like the industry standard Sony MDR-7506 will reduce sound spill from your ears back to the microphone and will help isolate your ears from your environment.

Take care of the coiled cable that is attached to your headphones. You should never head wrap your headphones. This will cause the cable to lose its tension and shorten the life span of the headphones because of shorts in the cable. Always pick the headphones up from the head strap and not the cable or ear muffs. Disconnect the headphones from the recorder by pulling on the quarter-inch plug and not the cable.

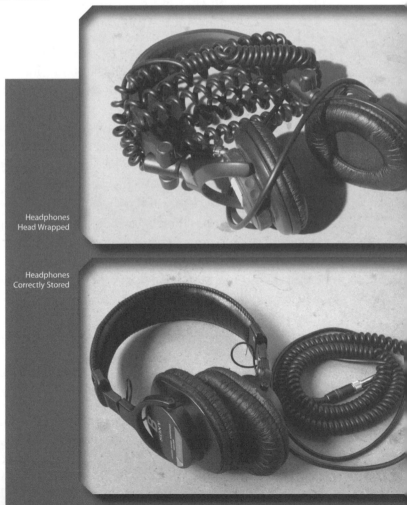

Headphones
Head Wrapped

Headphones
Correctly Stored

The volume level of your headphones will directly correlate to how many years you will be able to work. The bottom line: Monitor at low listening levels. Ear damage is permanent. Always turn the headphone volume completely down before putting on your headphones. This will stop microphone feedback as well as eliminate the chances of exposing your ears to high-level sounds.

Headphone Amplifiers

What you hear through a recorder's headphone amplifier is not always what you are recording. Some recorders are known for having noisy headphone amps. This noise appears as hiss when the headphone volume is increased. However, this amplifier does not affect the sound level or quality of the recording. Each recorder is different and time should be spent experimenting with the recorder to get familiar with the sound of the headphone amp.

Some headphone amplifiers give you the choice of what channel(s) to listen to, such as left only, right only, left and right mono (both channels sent to each ear), left and right stereo, and MS monitoring. If your field recorder does not have this option, third-party vendors make devices that plug directly in between your headphones and the recorder's headphone jack, which can be a powerful troubleshooting tool.

Confidence Monitoring

Confidence monitoring is the ability to listen to what you recorded while you are still recording. This was made possible on tape-based recorders, including DAT, with an additional playback head after the record head. The tape would pass by the record head and the signal was recorded onto the tape. As the tape continued to move, it then passed the additional playback head and would then replay what was just recorded. The space between the record head and the playback head would give the recorded sound about a half-second delay from the original sound. This would let the recordist know that what was just recorded had "stuck" to the tape.

In the digital world, some new hard drive and compact flash recorders are offering this same function through virtual playback heads. It can be a bit confusing to listen to everything with a delay, but the benefit is the confidence in knowing that you have a solid recording. At this time, confidence monitoring is not available on most hard disk recorders.

Connectors

Connectors come in male and female "genders." The male connector has a pin or pins that feed the signal from a device. The female connector has a socket or sockets that receive the signal for a device.

Barrels

A third type of gender is called a barrel or gender bender. These are used to change the sex of a connector. For example, if you need to extend a cable but both cables have male connectors, you would use a female barrel to connect the two male connectors. Barrels are available for all types of connectors.

Audio cables use three types of connectors: phone jack, RCA, and XLR.

Phone Jacks

Phone jacks get their name from the old patch bays that were used by telephone companies. They come in two sizes: 1/8" and 1/4". They come in either balanced or unbalanced connections.

TS (tip/sleeve) is an unbalanced phone jack connector. The tip of the jack carries the hot signal. The sleeve of the jack carries the ground signal.

Phone Jack Connectors

TRS (tip, ring, sleeve) is a balanced phone jack connector. It works the same as a TS connector, but has a ring that carries the cold signal.

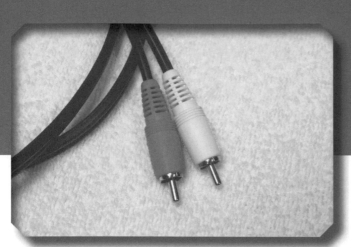
RCA Connectors

RCA Connectors

RCA connectors bear the name of the company that designed them, Radio Corporation of America. Today, these connectors are most commonly found in the consumer audio/video market. RCA connectors have only two conductors and are therefore unbalanced. The pin (or plug) carries the hot signal. The sleeve carries the ground signal.

XLR

XLR connectors are the industry standard for microphone cables. The name is a reference to a model series designed by Canon when these connectors were first developed. Despite the rumors, XLR does not stand for anything. This connector has three conductors.

Pin 1 carries the ground signal.
Pin 2 carries the hot signal.
Pin 3 carries the cold signal.

XLR Connectors

CHAPTER SEVEN

Building a Field Recording Package

Selecting the Right Gear for the Right Price

YOU NEED TO BUILD A package that allows you to work with any location or scenario thrown at you — most times at a moment's notice. As with building anything, budget will dictate quality. Luckily, over the years, high-quality recording equipment has become more and more affordable.

The following are examples of three different recording packages priced from low to high.

Basic Recording Package

A basic recording package consists of:

- A Recorder with Built-In Stereo Microphone
- Batteries
- SD Memory Card
- Headphones

With a street price of around $400, this package gives entry-level recordists the basic tools to record in the field and in the studio. In this price range, the following equipment offers great versatility:

Zoom H4 Field Recorder

The Zoom H4 can be used for covert recording in places where you don't want to stand out and attract attention. The microphone can be used outdoors where there is no wind; however, even with the supplied windscreen, mild gusts of wind will affect the recording. The unit is also handheld, so be sure to limit your movements.

Sony MDR-7502 Headphones

Sony offers great, accurate headphones at just about every price level. This particular pair is a prosumer brand that looks like the kind of headphones commonly used with an MP3 player. These headphones can be paired nicely with the Zoom H4, giving the appearance that you are just listening to music and not recording.

Note: The Zoom H4's microphones make it look like a stun gun. Use caution in public places to prevent people from calling the police.

Basic Field Package

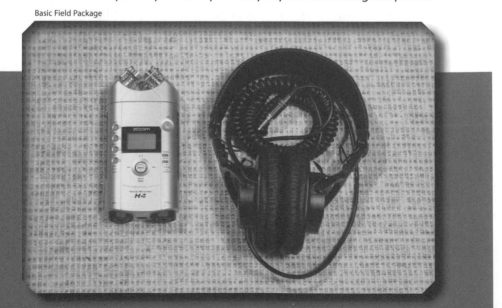

Standard Recording Package

A standard recording package consists of:
- A Field Recorder
- Rechargeable Batteries
- Compact Flash Card/Micro Drive
- Headphones
- Stereo Microphone
- Wind Protection
- Shock Mount
- Microphone Stand
- Mic Stand Adapter (3/8" Male Screw to 5/8" Female Connection)
- Cables

This package has a street price of around $2,000 — considerably more than the basic package, but the results are considerably higher in quality. In this price range, the following equipment offers great quality:

Fostex FR-2 LE Field Recorder

Fostex is one of the most recognized manufacturers of field recorders. The company has set the standards for field recording equipment for decades and has adapted to become a pioneer of new format recorders. The FR-2 LE is the little brother of the FR-2 in a smaller, more affordable package.

Standard Field Package

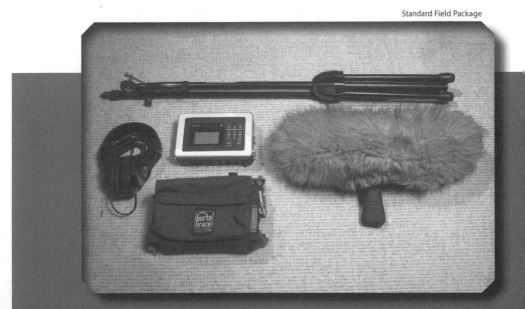

Sony MDR-7506 Headphones

These are the industry standard headphones for film, television, and radio. They have a closed-ear design that stops the sound from getting outside the headphones and back into the mic, and a wide frequency response range.

Rode NT-4 Stereo Microphone

Rode is an Australian manufacturer of high-quality, low-cost microphones. The NT-4 is a perfect stereo field mic that captures rich and faithful reproduction of sound in just about any given location. Though a tad heavy and bulky (the microphone barely fits inside the mounting clips of the Rycote suspension mount), this mic is a perfect stereo workhorse for field production.

Rycote Windshield Kit #4

Rycote makes the best wind protection equipment in the business. They are used on the sets of nearly every film and television show out there. This unit will give your microphone the maximum amount of protection available on the market. The kit includes a modular suspension mount with a pistol grip, a windshield (zeppelin), and a windjammer.

Professional Recording Package

A professional recording package consists of:

- A Field Recorder
- Professional-Grade Rechargeable Batteries
- Compact Flash Card/Micro Drive
- Back-Up Compact Flash Card
- Headphones
- Stereo Microphone
- Wind Protection for Stereo Mic
- Shock Mount for Stereo Mic
- Shotgun Microphone
- Wind Protection for Shotgun Mic
- Shock Mount for Shotgun Mic
- Microphone Stands
- Mic Stand Adapters (3/8" Male Screw to 5/8" Female Connection)

- Boom Pole
- Cables
- Carrying Bag

This package has a street price of around $6,000. The price can easily climb to $10,000 based on microphone and recorder selection, but the equipment listed below will provide high-quality recordings and is commonly found in the tool kits of motion picture and video game sound effects recordists alike. In this price range, the following equipment offers professional results:

Fostex FR-2 Field Recorder

Fostex has set the standard for high-definition digital field recorders with this unit. The microphone preamps are extremely quiet and the unit is very easy to work. All of the major controls are associated with real-world buttons and switches, not hidden deep within soft menus. The recorder also offers pre-record buffering.

NP-1 Batteries with Charger

NP-1 batteries are professional-grade batteries that can last for more than a solid day of recording. They can be purchased with LED status indicators to let you know if the battery is fully charged. I've used NP-1s for years and I've never had one run out of juice in the middle of the day when powering my audio packages. *Note that you will need a special adapter to connect the NP-1 battery to your FR-2 recorder.*

Professional Field Package

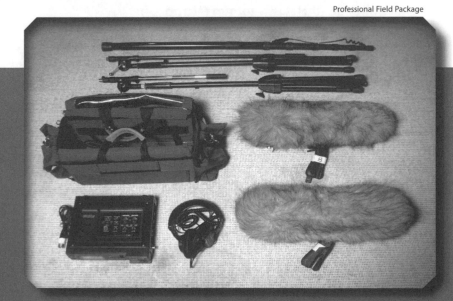

Sony MDR-7509HD Headphones

These are the top-of-the-line Sony High-Definition headphones. They fit around your ears, reducing the amount of leakage. They are great for voice work because the closed-ear design prevents sound spill into the mic. The frequency response range covers everything that any human ear could possibly hear.

Rode NT-4 Stereo Microphone

Despite the option to upgrade, the Rode NT-4 is still a fantastic general purpose stereo microphone that is able to go wherever you go. I have had great service from Rode with microphone damage (caused by me), and their turnaround time will make your head spin. They believe in their customers and it shows in the quality of their mics.

Rycote Windshield Kit #4

The Rycote Windshield Kit #4 will fit both the Rode NT-4 and the Sennheiser MKH-416. However, you will need to use the largest mounting clips to fit the Rode NT-4. Keep in mind that you will be pushing the limits of the mounting clips to fit the mic. It is a good idea to secure the microphone to the mounting clips with cable ties to prevent the mic from falling out of place.

Note that you will need one Rycote Windshield Kit for each microphone.

Sennheiser MKH-416 Shotgun Microphone

This microphone is the most durable shotgun available in the world. The quality is superb and it can withstand extreme temperatures ranging from the hottest desert sun to the coldest winds of the South Pole. The extreme focus of its pickup pattern allows you to zero in on the sound that you are after without picking up much of the surrounding environment. Every professional sound recordist should have this mic.

Porta Brace AR-FR2 Production Bag

Porta Brace is the premier maker of custom equipment bags for the film and television industries. They are easily recognized by their trademark blue corduroy material that can withstand the rigors of fieldwork without showing wear and tear. The Chop Shop owns a half dozen of these bags, and the oldest, which is now ten years old, has yet to see a single rip or tear. They last forever and will keep your gear protected from extreme locations.

Other Goodies

There are many other tools and devices that you can add to your package to make it more roadworthy. One of the best investments that you can make for your gear is cases. This is especially true if you plan to travel with your equipment. This is not a place to skimp. Spend the money to protect your equipment. A great start is a Pelican case. These cases are indestructible and waterproof.

Here is a list of common items found in the packages at the Chop Shop:

- Flashlight
- Leatherman
- Connectors and Adapters
- Gaffer's Tape
- Cans of Air
- Power Invertors
- Headphone Extension Cables
- Walkie-Talkies
- Umbrellas
- Extra Batteries
- Sound Blankets
- Additional Mic Stands
- Sandbags
- Hair Rubber Bands
- Equipment Manuals

The principle behind a well-built field recording package is to keep it portable but still have all the necessary tools to tackle the challenges that the day may bring. Always be prepared.

The Ten Recording Commandments

Go Forth and Record!

OVER THE YEARS, I HAVE kept a record of all of the mistakes I've made while recording. I'm a big fan of not repeating the same mistakes. At the Chop Shop, I have a manual that I give to the recordists and sound designers. The manual includes many of the tips and tricks in this book. Above all, the most important section for recording is the "Ten Recording Commandments."

These ten commandments have proved irrefutable over the years. They are each equally important as individual rules, but even more powerful when used together. The use of these commandments will result in top-notch, professional recordings.

■ TEN RECORDING COMMANDMENTS

1. Thou Shalt Have a Pre-Roll and Post-Roll of Two Seconds on Each Recording
2. Thou Shalt Record More Than You Need
3. Thou Shalt Slate Every Take with as Much Information as Possible
4. Thou Shalt Check Thy Levels Often
5. Thou Shalt Listen to Thy Work by Always Wearing Headphones
6. Thou Shalt Eliminate All Background Noise
7. Thou Shalt Not Interrupt a Take
8. Thou Shalt Point the Microphone at the Sound
9. Thou Shalt Check Thy Equipment Before Going into the Field
10. Thou Shalt Remember the Copyright Laws to Keep Them Unbroken

Commandment 1

Thou Shalt Have a Pre-Roll and Post-Roll of Two Seconds on Each Recording

In the sound recording world, it is helpful to have a few seconds of silence before and after each take. This allows for cleaner fades in the edit and gives a moment of settling time for the recordist/Foley artist to reduce their self-noise and clothes movements before-hand. This also gives the recordist a moment to "confirm the roll." By confirming the roll, the recordist takes note of any recording indicators, such as a red record light, as well as noting the position of the time display counter to verify that the numbers are moving and thus that recording is taking place.

In the old days of analog and digital tape, the sound recordist had to press record and wait for a second or two to allow the record deck to "get up to speed." This brief time allowed the gears and motors of the machine to begin to spin and move in proper sync with each other to reduce an analog glitch known as wow and flut-ter. The same was true for video decks. To ensure a seamless edit, the video editor would allow the deck to roll for a few seconds before and after the edit point to eliminate flicker and glitches. In general, you should always pre-roll and post-roll each take for two seconds.

Pre-rolling the record deck before the event allows for a more graceful recording. Many times when the record button is pressed in a hurry to record the sound, the take can sound cut off at the front or end of the take. This is especially true of sounds that need to settle, such as glass breaking or an object dropped on the ground that continues to bounce or roll for a few seconds before finally coming to rest. Post-rolling past the event ensures that the take will have more than what is actually needed, allowing the sound to be properly edited.

With modern digital recorders, it is now possible to have a pre-record buffer rolling at all times. For example, with the pre-record function on the Fostex FR-2, you can press record and start recording from ten seconds before that time. This can be a powerful tool when you are limited on drive space or need to record something spontaneous.

Imagine that you are recording jets taking off from a nearby Air Force base. You only have four minutes of drive space left, but you still need to record the sound of an F-16. The problem is you don't know when the next one will fly overhead. With a pre-record buffer enabled, you can simply wait to press record until you start to hear the jet. The moment the record button is pressed, the unit saves the ten seconds of pre-recorded sound and continues from that point on.

This is a huge leap forward from the days of DAT recording, when pressing record usually meant you had to wait a second or two before the deck actually began to record. Gone are the days of sitting by the railroad tracks with a handful of two-hour DAT tapes with the deck in record, waiting to capture a passing train.

By knowing when to roll and when to cut, you give yourself more sound to work with. You also help eliminate mistakes such as background noise before a take or cutting off the tail end of a sound.

Commandment 2

Thou Shalt Record More Than You Need

Always record an ample amount of material. There is no such thing as too much when it comes to sound gathering. You never know what you might need in the final edit, and conversely, sometimes the material that you thought was usable can contain flaws. For this reason, record additional takes, variations, perspectives, and safety takes.

Safety Takes

"Safety take" is a film term for an additional take of a scene. After filming a perfect take, a director may say, "Perfect. Let's get one more for safety." Why? There are many reasons, but perhaps the most important is that it's better to be safe than sorry. Directors know that once they are in the edit, they can only cut what they shot. Sometimes even the most vigilant director may overlook an obvious mistake such as an actor saying the wrong line, a continuity error like an actor holding the prop in the wrong hand or an actor walking in off-cue. By rolling a safety take, they give themselves options to work with in post.

When recording at locations that are difficult to schedule, you should record additional takes of the events to ensure that you have the most amount of usable material for editing. A good example is recording additional gunshots, but at lower levels in case there is peaking or other forms of distortion in some of the takes. Another example might be your rich uncle's Lamborghini that he allowed you to record as he begrudgingly revved the engine. If there was an error in the recording like an unnoticed neighbor's car horn in the background, the revving might have been in vain. It's better to roll on one more take than to lose the event altogether.

Another scenario where safety takes are important is when an object or location is about to be permanently altered or destroyed. For example, let's say you are recording the rare antique furnace inside of a vacant house that is about to be destroyed. Of course you are going to stick around to record the demolition, but once the house falls, that great metal squeak that the door to the wood-burning furnace made can never be recorded again. So, while the house is still standing, record as many takes as possible. Keep in mind that safety takes can sometimes be creatively used as source material.

Source Material

Source material is priceless in the hands of a good sound designer. Ruin becomes riches, garbage becomes gold. Save your extra takes and use them as source material. Multiple takes of a door slam might give you a couple of leftover takes that can create beefy wood impacts or become the base for a solid bullet impact into wood. The leftover bins on your hard drive may serve as a smorgasbord of material that can be similarly repurposed. Even mistakes can be a source for something else.

Source material can become virtually anything. The catch is that you have to have source material in order to be able to use it! When working with props, record extra performances that can later be combined to create sounds that are bigger, longer, or more complex than the original sound. Be sure to vary the performance of each sound. The idea here is that each sound is unique by itself but, when combined with other unique sounds, can create something spectacular.

In my experience, the best crashes come from dozens of takes that are layered and designed into one. A small pile of junk that might contain 20 pieces of metal and plastic debris can be recorded smashing and crashing on ten takes. When those takes are combined, the modest pile of junk is transformed into a mountain of debris.

In the television news world, there is a saying: "The best shooters are editors." An editor knows what is usable and what is unusable. Shooters (cameramen) who are not editors might not be familiar with the editing process and shoot way too much footage or not enough. Good sound effects recordists don't just look for practical sounds, they also look for source material. Use your creativity when recording source material, but be sure to find the balance between recording too little and too much. No one wants to sit and edit hundreds of crash elements!

Ambiences

Ambiences are generally edited down to a final sound of about two minutes. This gives an editor more than enough sound to work with or loop without a noticeable loop point. However, there are several advantages to recording more than two minutes' worth of raw material.

The first advantage is that during recording there might be unnoticed background sounds that need to be removed in the final edit. If there is only two minutes' worth of material, then any time removed will shorten the final duration. When recording a crowd inside a mall, for example, the voices might sound like indistinguishable white noise — a sea of nonsensical words — in the headphones. But in the edit there might be a noticeable voice that is mentioning copyrighted or trademarked names, for instance, "I hate shopping at store XYZ because they never have what I'm looking for!" Something like that is unusable because if it was heard in the final production it might lead to a lawsuit.

Ambiences are best created as a bed of sound that identifies a location without being specific. Identifiable words and phrases should be avoided because they would be quite noticeable if the ambience was looped. It might also pull listeners out of the moment as they try to figure out what is being said. Identifying sounds or so-called identifiers should be eliminated so that the ambience will be more versatile for future use. A perfect example of an identifier is my next door neighbor's son, Mac. Let me explain.

Over the years, I have unintentionally recorded my neighbor shouting his son's name dozens of times. Every year on the Fourth of July, my subdivision holds a makeshift fireworks show, and my neighbor Scott and his son, Mac, are always there. All of the neighbors gather while a few intoxicated smokers fumble around in the dark with lit cigarettes trying to ignite highly explosive mortars and rockets for the amusement of the rest of the group. While this is taking place, I am sitting back in my chair next to my sound cart monitoring several recorders taking feeds from well-placed microphones around "ground zero."

These mic placements include 20-foot boom poles, fully extended with microphones pointing straight up into the night sky ready to capture the bombs bursting in air. Without fail, every year, the fireworks show ambiences I record include my neighbor yelling for Mac to get out of the way of the fireworks. As Mac grows older, each year's recordings yield fewer and fewer repetitions of his name. Nonetheless, I always anticipate recording more material of that event than I need to allow me to remove his name in the edit.

The second advantage to recording additional amounts of ambience at a location is to gather extra material for doubling or designing the sound in the edit. This is particularly valuable when recording at locations that sound thin or not very active. For example, a grocery store might allow you to come in and record, but what if that day has a low amount of traffic? Fewer patrons means less sound. However, by recording double or even triple the desired length of time, you can layer the sounds on top of each other to create a busy supermarket ambience out of the small and empty grocery store that you recorded.

Surround Ambiences

Another advantage to recording more than you need might be for fabricating surround material from a stereo source. Surround sound recording in the field is an art form in itself. It is difficult enough to record in one direction as a stereo recording. Finding a location that sounds great in every direction is a virtual impossibility. Stereo sounds can be edited, looped, and cross-faded as needed to eliminate extraneous or unusable sounds. But true surround recordings have six tracks instead of two and are less flexible in the edit.

A less expensive work-around for recording surround sound material is to use a stereo microphone and record twice the amount of material. You can use the first half of the recording in the front left and front right speakers, and the second half of the recording in the rear left and rear right speakers. This can be very helpful when you have a tight budget that does not allow for single-point surround sound microphones such as the Holophone series.

An even better pseudo-surround sound recording trick is to record five minutes of material facing one direction and five minutes of additional material in the opposite direction. Use the first recorded direction in the front left and front right speakers, and the second recorded direction in the rear left and rear right speakers. The results can be very convincing and can sometimes produce a cleaner and more pure-sounding recording than a true surround sound microphone.

Finally, if you have two recorders (or a four-track recorder) and two stereo microphones, you can set up a quadraphonic recording. Place one stereo microphone facing forward and the other stereo microphone in the opposite direction. When using two recorders, clap your hands together to create a sync point in the recording that you can use during the edit.

Record Different Takes with Variation

Avoid recording too much of the *same* type of material. This will only give you redundant takes and waste time. Instead, record additional takes with variations. This will give you more usable material.

Use variations such as:

Duration
Perform the event with short and long takes. Keep in mind that long takes can easily be shortened. Short takes, however, don't give you much to work with. Record a variety to provide flexibility during editing.

Frequency
Recordings can be varied by how frequently events are performed. Changing the timing between events will make the takes different and give you more to work with later.

Impact

How hard or soft you perform an action can evoke emotion (for example, slamming a door) or can imply weight (a hard body fall on wood). When recording, try to vary the force with which you move or strike objects.

Perspective

Where you place the microphone can give you different perspectives on a sound. Try miking footsteps from underneath stairs, a garage door from the inside and the outside, or even door knocks from both sides of a door. Using different perspectives gives you not only different sounds but also source material to use for mixing and designing different effects.

Speed

The speed of an object will affect how it sounds. Recording a car driving by at the same speed five times is only going to give you five takes of one sound. Try recording the car driving by going 15 mph, 35 mph, 55 mph, 75 mph, and 95 mph. This will give you five different sound effects. You can apply the same principle of variation to other sounds (opening and closing doors, typing on a keyboard, fan speeds, and so on).

Record More

Recording additional material will give you the best odds of producing a better ambience track. In the end, it is easier to discard the unused material with a simple press of the delete key than it is to go back to the location and record an extra minute's worth of material. Always record more than you need. Remember, the more you record, the more you have to work with in the edit.

Commandment 3

Thou Shalt Slate Every Take with as Much Information as Possible

A day in the field or on the recording stage can yield hundreds of sounds. It's easy to deceive yourself into thinking that you will remember what every sound was. Without fail, during the edit there will be a host of sounds that you won't recognize or remember where they came from. Many times, the sounds recorded won't be edited for weeks or even months. Therefore, you need to slate each take with as much information as possible.

When I first started researching sound effects recording techniques years ago, I remember one blog noting that the easiest way to remember what you recorded for a particular sound was to record the sounds with a video camera. That way you could see what you were recording and use the audio track on the video for the sound. Even as an amateur at the time, I knew that video cameras would produce far from professional sounds. However, this was the first time I realized that it would be important to somehow log each take with information that could be used in naming and describing each final sound file. But how?

Because I was fresh out of film school, I remembered learning about location sound recordists who record the dialogue for films. It is their practice to write down each take's information: scene name, take number, time code information, and sometimes even the microphones they were using. This is somewhat easy for them because they are usually sitting in front of a sound cart and have a clipboard with log sheets right there. Writing things down isn't practical for sound effects recordists, though, because our days are filled with run-and-gun-style shooting: Paperwork and fieldwork are rarely good bedfellows. However, location sound recordists also slate each take with their voice, recording the same information they write down and giving the editor two points of reference: a written log and a spoken log of each take. This was the answer.

A slate is a spoken description of the event on the same take as the event. The slate should always be on the same take as the event so that the two are never separated; over time, individual files can be separated as they are moved around from folder to folder or across several hard drives. Slates should appear at the front of each take and should be isolated from the actual event. Sound recordings that have talking over them are unusable, so be sure to allow time between the slate and the performance.

Each sound recording should be accompanied with a slated voice indicating:

■ Name of object or location being recorded
■ Specific object or location information
■ Activity being performed

Here are some examples of slates:

"Door knock, hollow wood door using the open palm of my hand"

"Door knock, hard wood door using a closed fist"

"Car drive-by, Pontiac 2007 Grand Am at 45 mph"

"Forest, with a stream nearby"

"Insects, forest ambience"

Other useful and unique information might include:

■ Microphone name
■ Microphone placement
■ Time of day

Here are some additional examples of slates:

"Door knock using knuckles, hollow wood door, miked from outside the door"

"Door knock, hard wood door using a closed fist, miked from down the hall"

"Car driving, interior perspective, Pontiac 2007 Grand Am at 45 mph"

"Forest, stream nearby, stereo mic"

"Insects, forest at night, close-up on the crickets with a shot-gun mic"

It is also a good idea to start each day's recordings by slating the first take with the following information:

■ The date of the recording
■ The name of the sound recordist
■ The names and types of microphones to be used during the day
■ The channels in which the microphones will be used
■ Locations to be recorded

Slate Mics

Many field mixers and recorders have a slate button that activates an onboard microphone. The switch is often labeled "slate" or "talk-back." This internal mic can be very useful when the recording microphone is positioned on a boom pole or on a stand far away from the recordist. If a slate switch is not available on the recorder, be sure to slate the take loudly enough for the microphone to pick it up. Keep in mind, the slate does not have to be recorded at a usable level. The slate only needs to be loud enough to be understood during the edit.

Tail Slates

For takes where a slate would interfere with the take (for example, a train pass-by), use a tail slate, which is simply a slate that is given at the end of the take. In the film world when it is impractical for the camera to film a slate at the start of the take, the actual film slate or clapper would be photographed upside down to let the editor know that the slate belonged to the previous take.

I remember an intern at the Chop Shop who would slate takes during the events, thus rendering them useless. My favorite example was a take at an ice rink in which he recorded for several minutes waiting for the sound of a Zamboni (the vehicle that resurfaces the ice). During the edit, we listened to the take and also patiently waited for the sound of the diesel engine. Suddenly, a roar filled the room as the engine started up and the Zamboni made its way onto the ice. It sounded great, clean, perfect. Then, much to our dismay, there was a voice. In fact, it was the voice of a pirate! "Arrr, here comes the Zamboni!" said the pirate. The take was ruined — and the intern's career as a pirate was over.

Now, I should explain that it is a common practice at the Chop Shop for the recordists to try their best to entertain the editors by using funny voices or accents during take slates. Keep in mind that the editors are locked up in a studio all day chopping away at the endless supply of recorded sounds and have no social life. Every year or so, we compile all of the outtakes into a reel and throw a humorous music bed underneath and sit back and listen to all the fun — both planned and unplanned.

Undoubtedly this particular intern was trying to get his 15 seconds of recorded fame on the outtakes reel, and yes, his voice did end up there with all the others, but the joke was at the expense of a take that was difficult to reschedule. In the end, he learned that all slates should be separate from the events. So remember, if necessary, tail slate the event.

New Objects, New Takes, New Slates

It is also a good idea to record each new object or activity on a different take. While it is easier to simply press record and work for hours on end, you will waste time during the editing process searching through lengthy files that can also take a long time to transfer and load into your DAW. Start each new event with a new take accompanied with an informative slate.

Keep in mind, though, that when working with certain objects (for example, mud or torches), it makes sense to press record and continue to perform events as one long take. In such cases, be sure to slate each separate action. Sometimes it helps to snap your fingers or clap your hands together prior to the slate. This will give the file a visible and audible spike that is easy to locate during the edit. Some field recorders have a button that lets you drop markers in the file while recording.

I am reminded of a special gun Foley session that we lined up with our local sheriff's department. A recordist was given access to the gun vault and recorded hours of gun Foley (loading and unloading weapons, cocking, locking, and other various handling movements). Despite their high-quality sounds, the bulk of the recordings were unusable.

The problem was that the recordist only slated the beginning of each take with the name of the weapon before performing dozens of actions. Weeks later, the editor sat puzzled as to what action was being performed. They tried to decipher the dozens of clicks and mechanical sounds of each gun, but to no avail. Ultimately, the sounds were unusable. There was no way of determining what each action was. The editor needed to know the precise information for labeling and metadata purposes. The recordist could have prevented this loss by simply slating each specific action (for example, "Smith and Wesson, 9mm Pistol, Loading a Full Magazine").

In the end, takes that are properly slated will give you all the information you need to properly describe your sound. You can then create an accurate and detailed database of searchable keywords to retrieve the sounds that you spent so much time and energy to record.

Commandment 4
Thou Shalt Check Your Levels Often

It is imperative that you check the levels on your recorder — both recording meters and physical knob positions — as often as possible. In the film world, the camera department usually "checks the gate" of the camera every time the camera is moved or whenever they break a location for an extended period of time. Sometimes hair, dust, or other debris can work its way into the gate of the camera and leave imprints or scratches on the film. Checking the gate often saves the film crew from having to redo an entire day's work. The same concept applies to sound recording.

Knobs and Faders
The arduous conditions and the constant running and gunning of field recording can cause knobs to get bumped and moved, resulting in levels being turned up or down accidentally. There is nothing more frustrating than wrapping up for the day only to look at the recorder and find out that you've been working at unusable levels of audio; just the thought of it gives me a sick feeling in the pit of my stomach. Check your knobs and faders every time you press record, every time you wrap a location, and every time you set up at a new location.

Meters

There is an old saying in the wonderful world of recording: "The meters never lie." Assuming that your meters are properly calibrated, this is a very true statement. Always rely on your meters to inform you of when a recording is too hot or too low, and then make the necessary adjustments. Never make a *volume* adjustment based on your ears.

I'm reminded of Luke Skywalker's Jedi training on board the Millennium Falcon when he was wearing a helmet that shielded his eyes. His task was to use a light saber to protect himself from harmless but painful laser beams being shot at him from a hovering remote. He complained to his Jedi trainer, Obi Wan Kenobi, that he could not see anything with the blast shield covering his eyes. The wise old master calmly replied, "Your eyes can deceive you. Don't trust them." Luke complained with a sigh, but sure enough in time he was able to deflect the laser beams. He was shocked to learn that he could use the Force in place of his eyes to "see" his enemy.

Back to reality: Your ears can deceive you. Don't trust them.

Headphone amplifiers can deceive your ears into thinking that a particular recording's volume is too loud, but in actuality the headphone's volume may be too loud; turning down your microphone's level would result in a low level and possibly unusable recording. If the recording level is too low to start with but your headphone's volume is too high, the microphone level might not be raised to a usable level because your ears are telling you that the level is appropriate. Always monitor your levels with your *eyes*.

Digital Zero

As we discussed in Chapter Six, analog and digital recorders work differently, and clipping should be avoided at all costs. Analog meters usually show +6dB of headroom above zero. With digital meters, zero is the absolute highest level that the sound can go. When setting your levels on a digital meter, you should use -18dB as a digital reference to analog zero. This will give you +18dB of headroom should the sound peak.

There is no industry standard for a digital zero reference. Some digital devices such as hard disk field recorders and cameras read it as -18dB, while others read it as -20dB. Regardless, the principle remains the same: Leave headroom for peaks. Impacts and sounds with sharp attacks will read all the way up to -1dB. This is fine, as long as they don't go over the digital zero mark. The idea is to **record the signal as hot as possible without clipping**.

Commandment 5

Thou Shalt Listen to Thy Work by Always Wearing Headphones

Always monitor your sound quality and mic positioning with headphones. While the recording deck's meters monitor the recording's level, the headphones monitor the "picture" of sound that you are taking. There are many aspects to the recording that meters cannot indicate.

So monitor your levels with your eyes, but listen with your ears.

For example, if you are recording the interior of a car being driven down the road, you might look at your meters and see that the recording levels are acceptable — only to find when putting on your headphones that the microphone is picking up an excessive amount of low-end rumble from the engine. With headphones on, you can move the microphone and discover a position that captures the sound you want more clearly. You might find that the levels are lower in the new position and need to be adjusted, which is fine. But never make a mic position adjustment based on your levels — make it with your ears first by wearing headphones, then adjust your levels.

You will be amazed at the sounds professional microphones can pick up. Great mics can give insane clarity to what might otherwise seem a sonic desert. Foley artists often wear headphones on professional sound stages not only to monitor the sounds they are performing but also to listen for any sounds that might happen accidentally, such as self-noise.

Humans become sonically blind to their environment very quickly, especially the sounds their own bodies make. It's not unusual to be able to hear breathing during exceptionally quiet sounds or even in loud sounds like crashes if the Foley artist is physically involved in the performance, throwing heavy objects around and the like; this is especially noticeable after several takes, when the breathing becomes labored. One of the practices we use at the Chop Shop is to hold our breaths during takes to reduce the chances of being heard by the microphones.

I remember a winter when one of our recordists had a vicious cold that lasted for more than a week. During that time, his nose made a slight whistling sound that was heard at 2.5KHz in most of his recordings. I am quite certain of the frequency, because that was the setting I used on the paragraphic equalizer to notch out the sound of his nose! Needless to say, he wasn't wearing headphones on the Foley stage and didn't notice himself breathing.

Recording without headphones is like taking a picture with your eyes closed. Sure, you will get an image, but will it be artistic or spectacular? Probably not. Always wear headphones when recording. Let your eyes monitor the levels, but let your ears monitor the sound.

Microphones Hear Differently Than Ears

It is important to realize that there is a difference between what you hear during recording and what you will hear during playback. Impacts that sound huge and thunderous may turn out as weak smacks during playback. This has to do with the physiology of hearing, which involves not just the sound waves reaching your eardrums, but also the vibrations received by the rest of your body. Together, these perceptions help your brain determine the size or weight of the sound. The microphone does not always translate size and weight as accurately. Do not fret. There are some editing tricks, such as pitch shifting, that can replenish these effects.

Commandment 6

Thou Shalt Eliminate All Background Noise

The key to recording clean sounds is to have a clean sonic environment. Critical listening must be used when recording. To be honest, half of the time that I am recording, I am listening for the things I am not supposed to record rather than what I am recording. Train your ears to be hypersensitive to the things that are not prominent in the sound field around you. Those are the sounds that will be blaring in your ears when you start editing your material.

In my days as a location sound mixer for movies and television shows, directors would often ask me to repeat what was just said by the talent. I would usually respond that I had no idea. They would always get confused at that point, wondering why one of the only guys in the room with headphones on, whose sole job was to record the audio, couldn't remember what was just said. I would simply tell them that I was listening to what was being recorded, not what was being said. There is a big difference. It is just as important to focus on the background sounds as on the main element being recorded.

Air conditioning hum, traffic, and planes flying overhead are just some of the most frequent challenges that recordists face when searching for a good location to record. The earth is becoming an increasingly noisy planet. Silence is golden because it's just as rare. Here are a few tips for dealing with these problems:

AC Buzz/Hum

Nearly all location recording equipment is designed to be battery operated. This is obviously to allow for portability, but it also reduces the risk of inducing a 60Hz AC buzz or hum. The most common causes of this buzz are faulty ground connections, light dimmers, and air conditioners on the same circuit.

Equipment manufacturers have produced great solutions for this problem. One of the most popular and economical is Ebtech's Hum Eliminator. The Hum Eliminator miraculously filters out AC noise without coloring or affecting the sound. The Chop Shop has a Hum Eliminator in each studio and they work like champs.

On location, it is best to stick with battery-powered equipment. Batteries will keep you portable and reduce the stress and headache of figuring out how to stop the buzz. However, XLR cables can still induce the dreaded AC hum if placed too close to an extension cord, power strip, or other electrical device. If you have to cross an XLR cable with a power cord, be sure to run the cables perpendicular and never parallel to each other; parallel lines can induce hum. Crossing the AC cord perpendicularly will reduce the chances of inducing buzz.

It's also important to point out that connecting any AC-powered gear to your battery-powered equipment can introduce hum. This includes headphone amplifiers and feeds from sound cards, mixers, and video cameras.

Air Conditioning/Heating Rumble

Some locations will allow you to disable their heating and cooling systems to provide a noise-free environment for recording. It never hurts to ask. If you are working in an industrial building or office complex, the management will probably turn you down because these designs have multiple zones on the same heating and cooling system. If it is not possible to turn off the system, try blocking the air ducts with sound blankets or coats to reduce the low rumble. If this is not an option, try using a shotgun mic pointed away from the source.

Automobiles

When working outdoors, sometimes the settling sound of the vehicle that you drove to the location can be the source of background noise. I first noticed this while recording nature ambiences during the middle of the night. It was early August and the insects were screaming at the top of their lungs. I arrived at a thick forest in the middle of nowhere. It was dark and spooky. There was no moon, so the sky was jet black.

After quickly rolling down my window enough to inspect the sound quality of the location, I sprang from my car and pointed my microphone into the endless sea of branches and leaves. Then it happened: a sound that was not natural. First one sound, then another.... What was it? A moment or two later, I recognized the sound. It was the metal of the underbelly of my car buckling as the vehicle began to cool. The car kept babbling during the take. It was useless. I hopped in my car and drove about a quarter of a mile away before walking back to the spot I had found.

When working outside be sure to keep recently driven vehicles away from the recording site. Unfortunately, there is no other work-around for this as time is the only thing that will cool off your vehicle.

Clocks
Clocks are deceiving sources of background noise. Even with a trained ear, I still find myself several takes into a location before I notice the faint tick-tock of a wall clock. A quick solution is to remove the clock's battery or take the clock off the wall and place it under a couch cushion or coat. Listen carefully to see if your make-shift sound dampener worked before continuing with your session.

Fluorescent Lights/Ballast Hum
When possible, try to have any ballast-based lights turned off at the location. The droning sounds they make are easy to get used to but are very noticeable during playback. It is a good idea to bring a work light to locations, such as a gymnasium, that will be dark once the lights overhead are turned off. If turning off the lights is not an option, try using a directional microphone facing away from the lights. See *Room Tone* below to learn about sampling sounds for noise reduction.

Insects
These little guys can quickly ruin a location. Insects are difficult to work around because they usually produce constant noise for a few minutes, then pause, then make noise again. Using a para-graphic equalizer in the editing process can reduce or eliminate their chirping altogether, but not always. For this reason, I try to line up locations that are free of bugs, or I wait until September or October when they have died off or gone into hibernation. If you must resort to equalizing to reduce a cricket's chirping, start with a notch filter around 8KHz. The frequency of the cricket will

be very precise, so keep the bandwidth small once you have found the offending frequency. Keep in mind that the farther away the crickets are, the lower the frequency will be.

Planes

When a plane flies overhead during recording, it is best to cut the take and wait for the plane to leave the area, which can take several minutes. It never seems to work to the advantage of the recordist. The plane is either too far away to record or just close enough to spoil a take. Avoid recording near major airports, where the noise will be virtually constant. Also, be aware that weekends are the most popular time for pilots to go joyriding in propeller aircraft, which tend to fly low enough to be heard.

Refrigerators

When working in a house, disable the refrigerator so that the compressor does not kick on in the middle of a take. A good trick is to leave your car keys inside the refrigerator to remind you to turn it back on before you leave. You are unlikely to leave in your car without remembering where your keys are! I say unlikely, because I have a short story to tell.

I was recording a fireplace at my dad's house one day when his refrigerator kicked on. He was reluctant to disable the fridge because he didn't want to forget to turn it back on. I confidently told him not to worry and that I had a trick for that. I turned the fridge off and placed my keys on the top shelf inside. I recorded for several hours. When it came time to leave, I forgot where I put my keys! Of course, my dad forgot, too!

After a long search, I was certain that the keys had been accidentally thrown in the fire among all of the materials I had brought to burn. I spent a good 20 minutes searching through the ashes, listening carefully for the jingle of the keys as I poked around with a stick. No luck. I called my wife and had her drive to my dad's house with a spare set of keys. On my way home, I got a call from my dad, who was drinking an ice-cold soda that he had just pulled from the refrigerator along with my keys. Needless to say, we had a good laugh.

Reverb

While not truly background noise, this is a good time to mention reducing reverb. Try to select locations to record that do not have opposing flat surfaces that could generate reverb. Bring sound blankets or other sound-absorbing material to help tame the room and make it as usable as possible.

When all else fails and you have to record in a reverb-heavy room, be sure to wait until the reverb tail is completely settled before performing the next take. The reverb tails from the previous action can affect and color the next sounds that you record. It also helps to record all of the reverb tail in environments where reverb is practical, such as a gymnasium or racquetball court.

Room Tone

In the film world, it is common practice for the sound mixer to record the sound of a room or environment for up to a minute. This sound is called room tone and is very useful for an editor who is splicing different pieces of dialogue together that were shot at different times, locations, or perspectives. Without room tone, the backgrounds of all the clips of dialogue might sound different from each other. The result can be unnatural-sounding dialogue that pulls the audience out of the story. To prevent this, the editor takes the recorded room tone, loops it, and places it underneath all of the dialogue in the scene. The effect is a natural and flowing dialogue track.

Apart from being a very useful sound effect by itself, room tone can help mask breaks in silence heard in sounds that have been cut together. But the best use for room tone in sound effects recording is as a source sample for noise reduction. Noise reduction programs can learn the sonic characteristics and frequencies of the room tone or other static noise. Then the program can actually remove that sound from beneath the rest of the sound, leaving only the pure sound effect. Although programs like Sony's Noise Reduction are very easy to use, there is an art to working with noise and removing it from a sound. The best way to learn how to properly reduce background noise from tracks is to practice. And remember, less is more.

Television Sets

Televisions and some professional monitors give off a specific 15KHz buzz. The easiest and simple fix is to turn off the television (I know, I'm a genius). However, there are times when turning off the unit is not an option, such as in public locations or when working with a video feed during a sound-for-picture Foley session. One solution is to put a sound blanket over the television. You may need to experiment with the position of the blanket, but generally you need to cover the back and top of the unit. The high frequency is too weak to travel through the fabric and this will usually eliminate the sound entirely.

When a blanket is not an option, try using a directional mic pointed away from the television. Also, try muting the television set; sometimes even the lowest volume setting will still produce a high-pitch signal. During the edit, use a paragraphic equalizer with a notch filter set at 15KHz to remove the offending frequency. As with insects, this frequency is very precise, so keep the bandwidth tight. This will usually not affect the rest of the audio.

Traffic

If there is a specific location that you need to record and traffic is very noticeable, try recording the location during off hours, such as in the middle of the night. If the location is an exterior, try recording with a directional mic, such as a shotgun facing away from the traffic. Keep in mind that traffic noise might be reflected off buildings or trees in the opposite direction. If the location is indoors, try to avoid recording near windows.

Although it is not optimal, a solution to recording at locations with noticeable traffic noise is to use equalization during the editing process. Traffic is most noticeable in the low mid range around 400Hz. Take care not to color your sound with too much equalization. The goal of recording should be to faithfully reproduce the sound, not necessarily to artificially manufacture it.

Commandment 7
Thou Shalt Not Interrupt a Take

Keep Rolling

Once you press record and are in the middle of a take, it is best to let the take happen naturally. Avoid making any changes to the recorder, the microphone, or anything else that will be noticed in the recording. This includes mistakes and gaffes. Even accidents can be used in the final edit.

I remember one day when a recordist informed me that he had broken one of the overhead lights on the Foley stage by hitting it with a wood stick during a take. Of course this was a complete accident. It should also be said, though, that this particular recordist was an accident magnet: If something was broken, he was usually the one with a sheepish, guilty smirk on his face. But the damage was done and I was more interested in listening to the take to hear if the crash was usable.

We went into one of the nearby studios and cued up the track. After several attempts at a whip sound with a wood dowel rod, we heard the lightbulb shatter into dozens of pieces that trickled down the recordist's body, creating some cool debris. But the sound was unusable: After the moment of impact, the recordist began to say, "Ah, man. I broke the light!" The lesson he learned from this accident was never interrupt a take. The lightbulb was already broken and there was nothing he could say or do to stop the event from happening. In these cases, let the event unfold and deal with the aftermath once you have stopped recording.

Keep Your Levels Consistent

You should also refrain from changing recording levels during a take. A change in level is very noticeable and it is nearly impossible to correct in the edit. It can also affect the background noise, making the sound inconsistent from the start to the end of the take. Instead, after the event, do another take with the levels corrected. You will be surprised how many bad takes turn out to be usable in whole or in part.

There's an important exception to this rule. When recording events that permit only one take, such as a launch of the space shuttle or a building demolition, adjustments may become necessary. If the event is long and constant, like a train passing by, and the levels are distorted, you have no choice but to correct your levels to salvage at least some of the take. Make such adjustments quickly to capture the rest of the event as cleanly as possible. In the edit, you may be able to remove the section that is distorted and still have a usable sound effect.

Talk with Your Hands

Never interrupt a take by talking or giving directions. Sometimes recordists will work in the same room as Foley artists and give them direction on their performance. At the Chop Shop, we have created hand signals to communicate various directions, such as:

1. Rolling (i.e., we're recording)
2. Action
3. Keep going
4. Settle
5. Watch your movement/self-noise
6. Wrap it up
7. Do one more

These signals are very helpful when working with another person. You should never "step" on a person's performance with words. It is very easy to let this go unnoticed until the edit, when you realize that you talked over the event. Instead, use hand signals to indicate direction or let the Foley artist finish the performance and redirect afterwards.

It is better to continue to roll on a bad take than to interrupt a take that might work out after all. Remember, you can always set the bad takes aside for source material.

Commandment 8

Thou Shalt Point the Microphone at the Sound

As obvious as this may seem, it never ceases to amaze me how many sound effects I hear that are off-center or have moving stereo images and microphone movement. Think of the microphone as a camera. The camera can only "see" where you point it. The same is true of a microphone. It can only "hear" where you point it. When taking a picture of a friend at the beach, you position the camera so that your friend is framed properly (the head isn't cut off, but centered). Microphones work the same way. Frame your recordings with your microphone — the sonic camera.

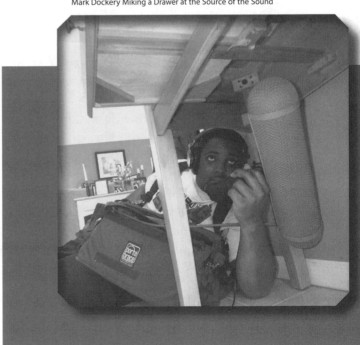

Mark Dockery Miking a Drawer at the Source of the Sound

Center the Microphone to the Sound Source

When recording an object, find the source of the sound that is being produced. This is called the sound source and should be the center of the microphone's focus. If you are recording a door creak, then point the mic where the sound is coming from. For instance, a door produces a creak when there is stress on the hinges. So point the microphone at the hinge that makes the loudest creak. Simply pointing the microphone directly at the door will not give you the best recording. Find the sound source of the object and start there. Then be creative and try miking the object from different perspectives and directions.

The Stereo Image

If there were such a thing as dimensions in sound, they would be as follows:

First Dimension — Mono
Second Dimension — Stereo
Third Dimension — Surround

These dimensions affect how we perceive sound in terms of direction and location. In stereo, your ears hear the balance between left and right. When we move our heads to look around our environment, we don't notice drastic changes in sound. This is because our brains have developed a sort of sonic equilibrium with the atmosphere around us. When you turn your head, the sound of your environment shifts with the movement. This shift usually appears natural and isn't always noticeable because your ears are also using the third dimension of surround. Your ears can help you locate sounds behind you, so when you move your head, any sounds you already heard simply change position.

Stereo sound works differently. Microphones are cold, calculated devices that are very subjective in terms of direction. Moving a stereo microphone back and forth or in one direction can give a seasick or wobbly feeling to the sound. This is especially noticeable in static sounds like ambiences. There are always exceptions to the rule, such as experimentation, but generally you should avoid moving stereo microphones during a recording.

Preserve the Stereo Field

When you are capturing the ambience of a specific location, find the key identifying sounds and center the microphone on those sounds. This might lead you to create multiple recordings for different identifying sounds. For instance, if you are recording inside a convenience store with coolers, record the environment with the microphones centered in front of the coolers. Next, record the opposite direction (for example, the front counter), with your back centered on the coolers. This will result in an even stereo field for both recordings and give you more uses for your sounds.

Let's say, for example, that you are using the convenience store ambience in a movie soundtrack and the scene shows the coolers centered in the background. If your ambience was recorded in a subjective manner that positions the coolers in only the right speaker, then your sound effect would not be usable. More than likely, a scene like this would incorporate multiple shots from different perspectives, resulting in changing positions of the coolers relative to each shot. If you recorded an objective ambience, then you can simply add a background track that is universal for the scene.

Another option is to shift perspectives in the soundtrack by toggling back and forth between the front counter ambience and the coolers for various cuts. You can also mix the two sounds together and gentle fade one perspective up and down to suggest location within the scene. Recording both perspectives with an even stereo field gives you greater flexibility in the edit.

The stereo field should also be preserved when recording stationary objects. For example, if you are recording a car engine in stereo, the sound should appear even between the left and right channels. This means that the sound is balanced in your headphones and in both of the meters (left and right). Remember to listen with your ears and not your eyes. The center of the sound might be different from the physical location of the sound. If a certain part of the engine is louder than another, your sound will appear off balance. Try miking the engine from a different position to correct this.

Stereo Pass-Bys

When recording pass-bys in stereo, leave the mic centered to both directions (left and right). It is not necessary to observe polarity when recording. If the scene calls for a car to pass from left to right, you can use a right to left recording and swap the channels in your DAW. By swapping the channels, your left becomes your right and vice versa. Keep this in mind when recording. Focus on the stereo field as whole, but don't worry about left to right and right to left.

Don't Move the Microphone

The microphone and mic stand should never be moved during a take. A good example of how this affects a take comes from a lesson learned by the intern pirate. While recording nature ambience in a forest, the intern realized that nature was giving him a call. He decided to continue to record and simply point the microphone in a different direction.

At first, the editor did not fully realize what was going on — all he heard was the perspective of the stereo image shifting from left to right. The editor listened more closely. Suddenly there was a zipper sound. Then there was the sound of liquid splattering on dry leaves. The editor's eyes widened.

Apart from thinking that his actions weren't being picked up on the recording, the intern assumed that he could simply point the microphone in a different direction without affecting the take. This is not the case, especially when working in stereo. It is now years later and we are still laughing about that one. Arrr!

Moving the Microphone to Follow Action

The exception to microphone movement is when you are following an action (for example, a skateboard pass-by) with the microphone on a handheld pistol grip or on a boom pole. In these cases, be aware of microphone handling noise, cable rustling, and wind sound. Hold the pistol grip or boom pole gently and allow your arm to be loose. Don't hold the microphone tightly as this can introduce movement sounds. It should also be noted that it's best to use a directional microphone like a shotgun when moving a microphone to follow action. Using a stereo microphone will shift the image of the background in addition to the action and give undesirable results.

Commandment 9

Thou Shalt Check Thy Equipment Before Going into the Field

Working in the field is like going camping — you only have what you bring with you. Therefore, a recordist needs to adopt the famous Boy Scout motto: "Always Be Prepared."

When I first started out, I worked a lot of ENG shoots doing television shows. I was amazed at how prepared the crews were. Everyone was ready for anything at any time. In fact, the "airplane crash tape" was a common reference that shooters used for a blank tape that they had stashed somewhere in their truck in case they drove by a crash. This would ensure that they had something to record on in the case of an emergency. Others had food and beverages kept in coolers for late-night news vigils for court case verdicts, celebrity prisoner releases, rock band arrivals, and the like.

I quickly learned that Murphy's Law was in full effect and was in fact the governing rule of fieldwork. It seemed that whatever you didn't bring to the set was what was needed, and what you brought was never used. I can remember dozens of times when being prepared saved the shoot and even more times when not being prepared could have cost the shoot.

During the 2000 presidential campaign, my friend Wes Heath and I worked for MSNBC. During one of our assignments, we followed Vice President Al Gore as he traveled down the Mississippi River. Wes ran the camera, while I took care of the audio duties. We threw two of everything we could think of into Wes' trusty red van and headed down the campaign trail. We would arrive at each of the day's several press events and set up for live shots of the vice president giving his usual speech that Wes and I had memorized after weeks of hearing it over and over again.

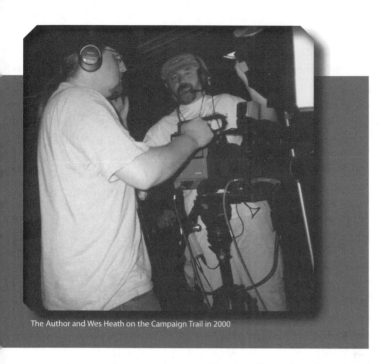
The Author and Wes Heath on the Campaign Trail in 2000

In one city, we were ready to go live when I noticed my sound mixer's batteries were running low. Rather than risk the live shot, I reached into my handy bag and pulled out a brand new case of batteries that I had brought and swapped out the old with the new. Nothing! The new batteries were dead. The campaign theme song began to play, cluing the audience that Mr. Gore was soon approaching. As fast as I could, I swapped out the batteries again. Nothing!

I would soon find out that the entire case of new batteries were defective. Game over. A fellow sound mixer witnessed my plight and quickly tossed me a fresh set of batteries. I was back in business. As soon as I turned my mixer on, Mr. Gore took the stage. You can never be too prepared.

Incidentally, Al Gore stepped on my mixer later that week. It's a long story, but I wasn't worried because I had a back-up mixer in Wes' van.

For the most part, recording situations are planned and controlled. There will be a location lined up, things to record, and a timeframe to work with. However, what happens when you're sitting in your car at a train crossing and a train comes barreling down the tracks? You'll record it, of course! This scenario has happened to me more than once. And every time, I'm ready to record.

When I'm out field recording, I usually keep the record deck on and strapped into the front seat of my car. The mic cable is spooled out for easy access and the headphones are lying outside the bag for me to grab. On one occasion, I heard an ambulance siren behind my car. I pulled my vehicle onto the shoulder, pressed record, grabbed my headphones, and stuck the microphone outside my car window. As a result of my preparedness, I captured a very difficult sound: an emergency vehicle pass-by.

When I first started The Detroit Chop Shop, I decided that there was great wisdom in the ENG mindset of "bring it all and pray you don't have to use it." Shooters always had a fresh battery on the back of their camera and a beta tape loaded up with bars and tone, ready to roll. So it is policy at the Chop Shop to have a fresh battery ready and loaded on the recorders with a newly formatted compact flash card. At the start of the day, the recorders are turned on, the microphones are plugged in, and a test track is recorded and played back. Then the recordists leave the shop with the headphones and a microphone plugged into the recorders. They have extra cables, mic stands, back-up batteries and extra compact flash cards that we fondly call the "airplane crash cards" — only to be used in case of an emergency.

Having your gear prepped and ready to go before you leave for your location saves time and stress once you arrive. Not to mention, having a record deck ready to roll at any second allows you the flexibility of recording spontaneous and unplanned sounds. Following this simple rule has produced helicopter pass-bys, Air Force fighter jet flybys, motorcycles, sirens, and more. In fact, a month ago one of our recordists got another sound of a train from his driver's seat ... because he was prepared.

Commandment 10
Remember the Copyright Laws to Keep Them Unbroken

Copyrighted material should never be recorded without written permission from the holder of the copyright. There are no exceptions to this rule. Breaking this commandment could result in serious legal problems. There are several aspects to this commandment. The first involves the most obvious: copyrighted music.

Music
Music can make ambience recording very difficult. Malls, restaurants, and department stores have nonstop loops of music gently playing throughout their buildings, making it impossible to record without infringing on copyright laws. Many of these establishments will readily allow you access to record there but are often very reluctant to turn off their music. Major-league sporting events, if you are lucky enough to gain access (or crafty enough to sneak in a recorder), are littered with music and sound clips from movies and other copyrighted material.

Unfortunately, if you can hear any amount of the music, the location is a bust. Don't even bother trying to record. If someone can hear the music in one of your recordings and reports it, you will be liable for breaking copyright laws. In order to use copyrighted material, you must receive permission from the holder of the copyright.

But the laws are a little trickier than you might think. For example, receiving permission from a local high school to record their marching band does not mean that you have permission from the copyright holder of the music they are playing — unless, of course, the band instructor is the composer of the song and gave you permission. If this is the case, be sure to get the permission in writing because this will be your only proof if there is a dispute later on.

Some music does not have a copyright holder and is considered to be in the public domain. This includes traditional songs such as "We Wish You a Merry Christmas" or music by Ludwig van Beethoven and the like. You can make your own recordings of these songs and use them any way you want. However, you cannot use someone else's recordings without their permission.

Movie Soundtracks, Radio and Television Broadcasts

Soundtracks and broadcasts should be treated like copyrighted music. Even free broadcasts of sporting events are copyrighted and are unusable without permission. You cannot record the sound of your television while a broadcast is being played. If you are recording ambience on a public beach and there is a radio playing, even if it is only the disc jockeys talking, you cannot use the material. You cannot use one-liners or scenes from movies, nor their music soundtrack and sound effects. Copyrighted sounds also include ringtones and sounds from arcade games and video games. Keep in mind, even a few seconds of use could result in a lawsuit against you.

Voiceover Artists

When working with voice talent, make sure that you obtain a signed release form giving you permission to use the person's voice for your production. Failure to do so might result in a messy legal dispute over royalties or use altogether. This includes working with family members and friends. Always cover your bases legally. There is no such thing as being too safe.

Make sure to obtain the release before the recording begins. It's all too easy to forget afterwards, and it also sets a clear understanding of the agreement that you are entering into with the artist. As a back-up, also have the artist give an oral release at the start of the first track that you record. It can be something along the lines of:

"My name is (so-and-so) and I give (such-and-such) the right to use this recording of my voice however they see fit, including the use of my voice in commercial productions."

Here is an example of a general release form that we use at The Detroit Chop Shop:

VOICE ARTIST RELEASE FORM

I hereby give and grant The Detroit Chop Shop the right to use my name and/or the right to photograph my physical likeness in any manner you desire and/or the right to reproduce and record my voice and other sound effects made by me, and I hereby consent to the use of my name and/or said photographs, likenesses and any reproductions thereof and/or the recordings and reproductions of my voice and other sound effects, by you, your licensees, successors and assigns, in or in connection with any productions, exhibitions, distributions, advertising and exploitations and/or other use of any of your photoplays and/or otherwise.

This document is signed and dated by the artist, along with the artist's full legal name, address, and social security number.

Copyrighting Your Own Work

Make sure that your own work is protected from others using it without permission. There is no worse feeling than hearing your work being played over the radio or watching it being shown on the silver screen without your permission. It has happened to me countless times. They were hard lessons, but I have learned to protect my work by filing the appropriate copyrights. Hiring a lawyer and filing the appropriate documents can be costly, but in the end it's well worth it.

Legal matters are very serious in the entertainment world. It's called show business because it is the *business* of show. Protect yourself and those you work with by being up-front about your intentions for using the recordings. Put everything in writing and have it signed by both parties. In addition, make sure that you protect your own material by faithfully documenting and filing copyrights with the Library of Congress.

Don't Steal Someone's Thunder

The saying '"They stole my thunder" is actually a sound effects reference. In the early 1700s, a playwright named John Dennis developed a sound effects device to recreate thunder for a play he wrote called *Appius and Virginia*. The play had a short, unsuccessful run, after which the theater replaced it with *Macbeth*.

Dennis attended one of the performances of Shakespeare's play and was shocked to hear his sound effect being used during the production. He was quoted as saying "That is my thunder, by God; the villains will play my thunder, but not my play." His remarks evolved into the phrase "steal one's thunder."

Take pride in your own work. Create fresh, original material. If you use someone else's material, do so with permission and give credit where credit is due. You should never take credit for work that you didn't do yourself. I can count numerous times when my work was stolen, used as someone else's idea, or flat out ripped off. I even have copies of magazine articles, pictures, and radio promos where people have taken credit for my work. It's disheartening and frustrating for you, and unprofessional of them. Don't steal someone's thunder!

Sound Effects Gathering

Location, Location, Location

Finding the Right Location

Without question, location recording is the most difficult part of the process of making sound effects. Selecting the right location is just as important as what you are going to record there. Environments shape your sound. Be sure to select a location with your ears and not with your eyes. A great-looking location may not be a great-sounding location.

Here are a few things to consider when selecting a location:

The Time of Day to Record

Each time of day has its perks and downfalls. Night recordings are usually optimal, but locations that might be willing to let you record may not be willing to join you for all of the fun at two in the morning — and they probably won't give you permission to roam free on their property without supervision. Morning recordings in urban settings are subject to traffic noise; in rural settings, there are insects and birds to worry about. It is best to scout a location during the time of day that you plan to record. This will give you a sense of what you may have to deal with, so you can plan accordingly.

Exotic Locations Can Offer Isolation and Unique Sounds

The Traffic Conditions

Questions should be asked, such as:

> Are there any active railroad tracks in the area?
> What are the flight paths of air traffic in the area?
> Are there any major highways or roads nearby?

Heavy traffic areas pose major problems for recording. Traffic usually gives off a steady drone of roaring engines in the distance, and trains and planes will pop up unannounced and possibly ruin a take. Try selecting a location that gives you the best of both worlds. Planes and trains are easier to contend with than traffic because they're sporadic. If you don't have a choice, be sure to wait until the noise has passed before you continue to record.

Contact Information

I've had locations like auto shops give me permission to come in and record their tools and other machinery. Simple enough, right? But when I show up, there is always some disgruntled worker there who was not informed of my visit. And they're not backwards about letting you know that you're not welcome, often responding unkindly to requests to turn a stereo off or to refrain from talking or moving while you record. I've had some employees deliberately interrupt takes so that I would leave.

When dealing with the owner or person in charge of the location, ask straightforward questions so that you don't waste each other's time. Inform them that you will need them to turn off any music, and ask if it's possible to disable their heating and cooling systems. If you are working in a room with loud halogen ballasts, ask if the lights can be turned off (and be sure to bring a work light with you when it's time to record). And most importantly, get the name and phone number of your contact in case nobody knows who you are when you show up.

Authorization

Agree on boundaries for what you are allowed to do at the location. This is especially important when destruction is on the menu. Be sure to let the owner know if you plan on using flammable materials, firearms, explosives, or anything out of the ordinary. When working with junkyards, make sure you know what is okay to smash and what is not.

I will never forget an experience I had at a junkyard near Port Huron, Michigan. I spotted the salvage yard when I was out scouting for isolated places to record. It was a great location, with piles of junk and scrap everywhere. There were cars stacked four and five high that made up walls that went on for hundreds of feet. I knew this location would give me just the material I needed for some great car crash sound effects.

I walked into the small white building that served as the office. I was introduced to the owner, Ron, who was more than happy to let me record there. But they had a crane that operated throughout the day. Ron was not willing to shut down long enough for me to gather the material I needed, but he was fine with me coming after hours, when no one was there.

We agreed to me coming at 4 a.m. the next morning, before his crew arrived at 8 a.m. This would give me four hours, which was more than enough time. Before I left, I made sure to tell him I was bringing a friend with a sledgehammer and would be recording various crashes and impacts with the vehicles on his property. He smiled and told me that it was all junk anyway and to have fun.

The next morning, my friend and I spent hours busting every wind-shield, headlight, bumper, fender, grill, hood, and side mirror that we could find. We even found an abandoned RV that we went inside and completely obliterated. There was nothing left by the time we were done.

I brought the takes back and spent days chopping up all of the thousands of sounds that we had recorded. The material was beyond belief. That session became the source for all of the car crash material on the sound effects library "Crash and Burn" from Sound Ideas. I was very proud of the results.

Months later, another project came along and I needed to head back to the junkyard. I called Ron to set up a day and time. He very politely declined. I could sense hesitancy in his voice. I was certain that my friend and I were very respectful of his property (outside of total demolishing more than 75 cars). Ron then told me that the last time I was there, he'd had a car parked in the back of the yard that he was planning on fixing up for himself.

My heart sank. I knew exactly which car he meant. I remembered asking myself why a Trans Am with a body that was still in good shape was being junked, but I also remembered Ron clearly telling me that I had free reign over anything on his property. He was very gracious and admitted that it was his own fault for telling me that I could destroy anything I wanted. I avoided a potentially huge mess because I was up-front and open about my intentions.

Make sure that you fully disclose everything you plan on doing at a location.

Call 911

Inform the local police department if you will be working late at night doing anything that might be seen as suspicious activity by anyone driving by. I've had the police call on me dozens of times for suspicious activity that just turned out to be me and my micro-phone. The police are usually cordial as long as you are up-front and honest about what you are doing.

Remember, trespassing is illegal. Even if you are just standing inside the edge of the property to record ambience, you are still on the property and the police have the right to arrest you or at least issue you a citation. You are, however, allowed to stand on public property, such as sidewalks. Although this might not get you close enough to the action to record some sounds, public areas are typically great for recording airplanes, Air Force jets, boats passing in a harbor, and so on.

Isolation or Environment?

Isolation is probably the most important factor when gathering the majority of sound effects. In photography, you can take any picture and crop it, frame it, cut it out, and paste it on a different background — your options are endless. Sound is much more finicky. To ensure the same editing options as with a photograph, the original sound source must be pure and free of background sounds. This includes room sounds and acoustic signatures. Be very picky about where you choose to record. Your location will affect your sounds.

For The Hollywood Edge's *High Impact* series, I gained access to the Kresge mansion in Detroit, Michigan. I was first there working on a film and befriended the caretaker, who arranged for me to come back and spend a day recording. This mansion was originally the

The Kresge Mansion in Detroit, Michigan

home of Sebastian Kresge, the founder of the retail chain that bore his name until becoming K-Mart. The massive home was built in the early 1900s and features amazing furniture, rooms, dumbwaiters, and other turn-of-the-century technology.

I returned with Chop Shop recordist Brian Kaurich, armed with mics and recorders. We were amazed at what we heard. The sounds of the basement, the attic, the long hallways for the servants' quarters all gave the sound effects character. They were amazing. Locations like this can offer acoustic detail that is worth recording. Isolation is preferred, but authentic environments occasionally have something unique to offer.

Everything Makes Sound

One thing that I have learned after creating hundreds of thousands of sound effects is that everything makes sound. With the advent of DAWs and the countless number of plug-ins available, just about any sound can be used to create something new and fantastic. If you find yourself scratching your head wondering what to record next, experiment. Sometimes you'll find new and exciting sounds. Other times, you won't realize what you discovered until you start editing. Be creative. Try everything.

Nik Drankoski Getting Crazy on Location

When working in the field or on a Foley stage, create a gather list of things to record. Use this list as a guide and try to get as many sounds as possible. But also allow yourself to be creative and stray from the list when ingenuity strikes. Nothing is more frustrating than having more than $10,000 of sound equipment strapped to your body, a full tank of a gas, and more than eight hours at your disposal, only to realize that you have no idea what to record.

It can be helpful to spend time breaking down your mind's paradigms of certain sound effects. Just because a spaceship sounds a certain way in a movie does not mean that's the best way that it can sound. Push the envelope. Try new things. Never stop experimenting. Some of the coolest sounds come from the most common sources.

Over the years, I've taken time for nonsensical play and experimentation with recording. I've used barn door leafs from movie lights to create the buckling sounds of the metal walls inside a submarine. I've used electronic equipment like CD tray motors as the basis for space doors opening and closing. And I've taken pigs grunting at a feeding trough and reversed the sound pitched down to create the spine-tingling shrieks of demonic creatures.

You never know what you will discover in the field or in the edit. A perfect example of this happened during a training session at the Chop Shop. I was showing some new recruits the ropes of Sony's Sound Forge. I challenged them that anything could be used to make great, usable sound. At first they disagreed, but I taught them what I now refer to as the "cat effect."

We were editing some household sounds (doors, I think). In the background of one of the takes I could faintly hear the sound of my cat, Princess, meowing. I told the recruits to watch and learn. I cut up the sound and normalized it. There was hiss and background noise. Clearly the sound was useless, but after some looping, pitching, and processing, I came up with two dozen awesome science fiction sounds in a matter of minutes. They sat in disbelief as I simply said, "Everything makes sound."

Remember, sound recording is highly technical, but great sound recording is highly creative. Don't allow your mind to put your concept of a certain sound effect inside a box. Take it out of the box. Kick the box out of the way. In fact, record the sound of the box being kicked. Then try something different.

CHAPTER TEN

Building a Foley Stage
for a Home Studio

Designing and Building a Place to Record

Jack Foley

Foley is the art of performing sound effects. This art bears the name of the sound effects pioneer, Jack Foley, who worked at Universal Pictures during the 1930s. Traditionally, Foley artists perform while watching images on a screen. Today the term Foley describes general sound effects performed by humans, but not necessarily to picture. This includes sounds that are pulled from a sound effects library, commonly known as canned sounds.

The term "canned sounds" comes from the days when sound effects were recorded on magnetic tape reels and stored inside protective tin cans. A well-known example of a canned sound is the laugh tracks that used to play under television shows like *Happy Days*. Sound effects libraries are great resources for sound designers because they can provide useful material to build from. They also provide sounds that are difficult to record or get access to, like the sound of an F-16 canopy closing.

The term "Foley stage" was originally a reference to Jack Foley's workroom where he recorded his sound effects at Universal. People would call it "Foley's room" or "Foley's stage." Soon sound departments in other film companies started building their own Foley rooms and the name stuck. Jack's work spanned more than 30 years, but despite all he contributed to the film industry, he was never given on-screen credit for his unique sound effects work.

Jack held to his philosophy that the sounds had to be performed as if the actor on the screen was performing them. He focused on being the character and not just stepping whenever the character stepped. Foley work is truly an art form that needs to be practiced in order to be perfected.

Construction

Recording on a Foley stage carries the fundamental principle of location recording: The key to great recordings is a great environment to record them in. After all, the goal of recording an event is the sound of the event and not the surroundings (a dog barking or a train whistle in the background). And the greatest environment is a sanctuary of silence in which to record your masterpieces.

In the film world, a sound stage is a room that has been designed to be isolated from its environment, both visually and acoustically. High-end sound stages in Hollywood are not only sealed off from all sources of light, but also specially treated to reduce sound reverberations from inside and built with sound-deadening materials to eliminate sound leakage from outside. Foley's stage, Stage 10 at Universal Pictures, was originally a shooting stage. Of course back then pictures were silent and the stages weren't called sound stages, yet. Since the inception of the talkies, shooting stages converted to sound stages. Today many sound stages have gone to the extent of "floating" the floors by pouring concrete slabs that are isolated from the surrounding ground to reduce low-end vibrations that could travel through adjacent floors.

For the rest of us, we need to treat an existing room both to greatly reduce sound transmission to and from the outside (both for our sake and our neighbors') and to reduce reverberation inside. An ideal room can be as simple as a garage or a basement. A garage can work nicely if it has high ceilings, which provide ample space for movement, and a cargo door for bringing in large materials to record like cars. But cargo doors allow extraneous sounds to penetrate and they tend to rattle during heavy winds. On the other hand, a basement has walls surrounded by earth, which can greatly help in reducing exterior sounds. The drawbacks include footsteps coming from upstairs, limited access for large materials to record, and lower ceilings. We'll analyze how to treat both.

Designing a Foley Stage in a Garage

The goal of your Foley stage is to seal the room acoustically. Understand that you will not be able to do this completely without breaking the bank. You can, however, reduce the effects of your environment enough to allow you to have a suitable place to record.

Isolation

First, eliminate primary sources of noise infiltration by locating acoustic holes. Remember that sound is the movement of air. If air movement is possible, then sound is possible. Turn the lights off in your garage. If you can see daylight other than through a window itself, then you will be able to hear sound leaking in from the same place. Check around windows, doorframes, and utility ports. Solid garage doors work best; panel doors have holes at the seams.

Walls and Ceiling

Next, let's deal with the walls. In the case of thin wood walls, you will need to beef up the shell of your room by adding layers of insulation. Sound is acoustic energy that diminishes when it passes through substances that have high absorption qualities. The thicker the insulation you use, the better results you'll get. Don't forget the ceiling. You may need to place a layer of insulation in the attic or overhead crawlspace to cut down on noise coming through vents or other holes.

Acoustics

Now that you've dealt with the shell, treat the inside walls with sound-deadening fabrics. Place a layer of sound blankets — a.k.a. furniture-moving pads — over all of the walls and the ceiling. This will help reduce reverberation as well as isolating the room. Suitable pads can be purchased at your local furniture store, moving supply store, or online at places such as *Markertek.com* or *BHPhotovideo.com*.

In addition to the sound blankets, you'll need a layer of sound foam to help deaden the room. Sound foam can be purchased at any guitar store or online sources such as *www.usafoam.com*. Because sound will continue to bounce off surfaces until it loses energy, you need to place absorptive material on all of the walls *and* the ceiling. Keep in mind, not every inch needs to be covered to reduce the reverb, but a combination of sound blankets and foam panels will give you the best results short of bringing in a professional architect or acoustician. As with insulation, the thicker the material, the better the results.

The Garage Door

You may need to use some elbow grease and ingenuity to prevent a garage's cargo door from shaking — and therefore rattling — during sudden gusts of wind. Solutions include placing large, heavy items against the door, affixing it to the garage walls with clamps, and using bungee cords to tighten it down. For sound treatment, use a layer or two of sound blankets before using foam to help deaden the door.

Flooring

A thick piece of carpet works great for the floor. It helps stop reflected sound from bouncing off the floor and entering the microphone milliseconds after the direct sound is recorded. Don't nail or glue the carpet down because you will want to be able to expose the bare concrete underneath sometimes so you can record footsteps and other movements, or smash fruits and vegetables to produce realistic splattering sounds, as well as more destructive sounds such as crashes and other impacts.

You can never really overdo it with sound reduction for a Foley stage. If you've done your job right, your ears should be ringing from the absence of sound. Keep in mind, loud sounds like car horns and truck rumbles may still leak into your room. Just stop between recordings and wait for the sound to pass.

Designing a Foley Stage in a Basement

The typical basement has natural insulation from outside noises in the form of its solid concrete walls and especially the surrounding encasement of earth. If you can, situate your Foley room in a corner so that you can take advantage of two existing outer walls. Pick a spot that is away from active rooms above like the kitchen or living room. And try to stay away from utilities like the sump pump, the furnace, or the washer and dryer. Under an infrequently used dining room or spare bedroom is best.

Walls

To start with, you need to frame the entire room you're creating. Although two of the walls already exist if you're able to be in a corner, you still need to build four walls so that insulation can

Framing the Walls of a Studio

Adding the Insulation in the Walls

be placed inside the walls. Use 2 x 6 studs for framing to allow for thicker amounts of insulation. Seal each wall by running a bead of caulk along the floor joint to help prevent sound leakage into the room.

If your budget allows, build a double wall for each of the two walls facing the inside of your basement to maximize the isolation of

your room. For the best results, stagger the studs between the two layers of wall. A dual layer of drywall can also help keep outside sound from entering your room. Stagger the layers of drywall as well; for example, one layer would be horizontal and the other layer vertical. You'll treat the walls later with a heavy layer of sound-absorbing material, so it's not necessary to mud and tape the drywall.

Ceiling

Now you need to build a ceiling that's separate from the floor above. Be sure to use solid materials; drop ceilings offer little separation from outside sounds and can rattle or vibrate. Drywall is a good solution — but realize that you are sealing off access to the basement ceiling itself. Avoid sealing off areas with pipes, gas and water valves, and wiring you might need to be able to get to. If necessary, put a removable access panel into your new ceiling.

The main sound source that you have to contend with is vibrations from upstairs foot traffic, so try to float the stage ceiling from the basement ceiling. If this is not an option, use a judicious amount of insulation in the ceiling and double up on the drywall layers.

Air Conditioning

Your next task is to contend with the necessary evil of an air conditioning vent. Without one, you're building a room that has no airflow whatsoever — it's going to get hot in there really fast. So make sure that you include a vent to send cool air into the room. You can place foam inside the vent to help reduce the noise of the air conditioning unit as well as whistling air sounds created by the vent itself.

Acoustics

Now let's deal with taming the reverb of the room. As with a garage, you'll want to cover a concrete floor with carpet to prevent unwanted sound reflections, but remember to keep it removable so you can utilize bare concrete for certain effects. Cover the walls and ceiling with a double layer of sound blankets, then place foam panels over the sound blankets. You can get large, 2 1/2-inch-thick egg crate foam panels that are 72 x 80 to help cover the large surfaces. Note that this is acoustic foam, not actual egg crates. Real egg crate will do nothing for your room acoustically except to disperse high frequencies. Use 3-inch roofing nails to affix the foam to the walls. Avoid using drywall screws, which tend to twist up the foam. Once the walls are covered, the room will seem to suck the sound away from your ears. Your stage is almost ready.

Doors

Lastly, choose a door that is made of solid wood. This will provide the best defense against sounds that would normally transmit through a hollow door. Weather stripping is perfect for sealing the edges of the door. Foam should be mounted to the inside of the door to reduce reflections inside the room.

Remember, you will not be able to create a vacuum, but if you follow these steps, you will end up with a Foley stage that is very versatile and shielded from the majority of outside noise.

CHAPTER ELEVEN

The Art of Foley

Tips, Tricks, and Tools of the Trade

FOLEY ARTISTS ARE MUSICIANS OF sorts, but instead of using traditional instruments, they use common household items and materials typically found in a junkyard to create their art. Every Foley artist performs differently. They each have their own style, developed over time and with experience. The best way to perfect your craft is to keep doing it.

Recording Techniques

For the most part, Foley is recorded using close miking techniques, which help bring the sound into focus and reduce the effects of the room. You should always record sounds dry (no effects). Compression and reverb should always be added afterwards.

The Pits of Working Foley

A professional Foley stage has Foley pits consisting of various surfaces to perform sound effects on. These surfaces generally include concrete, hollow wood, solid wood, dirt or earth, marble, and gravel. The sizes and shapes of pits vary, but a good, usable size is 4′ x 4′. These pits are primarily for recording footsteps but can be used for much more. Creating these surfaces can be a bit tricky. The main challenge is containing and isolating your surface, even from the concrete floor.

Here are some tips for creating homemade Foley pits:

Making a Solid Wood Foley Pit

A good solid wood Foley pit can be relatively easy to make. To start, build a 4' x 4' frame with 2 x 6 boards. Then cut sheets of plywood down to four panels that are 4' x 4' and place them inside the frame. Be sure to glue them together to eliminate any movement they might make. Next you'll need to isolate the bottom of the pit from the concrete floor. This can be done by tacking a piece of carpet or a sound blanket to the bottom.

This pit will give you a flat wood sound. You can modify the design and add hardwood flooring on top of the plywood for a different texture. You can also use a piece of carpet on top of the pit for a realistic household floor surface.

Solid Wood Foley Pit

Making a Boardwalk Foley Pit

Boardwalks help sell the sound of walking on a wood deck or the wood surfaces of the Old West. Build a 4' x 4' with 2 x 6 boards, and place 1 x 4 boards across the frame. Use screws to attach the boards. The screws can later be loosened to allow the wood to creak or tightened to give a standard wood floor sound. Attach a piece of carpet or a sound blanket underneath to help isolate the pit from a concrete floor.

Boardwalk Foley Pit

Making a Hollow Wood Foley Pit

For resonating wood sounds, build a 4' x 4' frame with 2 x 6 boards and cap the top and bottom with sheets of plywood. This leaves six inches of empty space between the top and bottom for the sound to reverberate. Again, place carpet or a sound blanket underneath.

Hollow Wood Foley Pit

Making a Gravel, Dirt, or Earth Pit

This is where the fun starts. Professional Foley stages have earth and gravel pits dug out of the ground in their stage floor. This is probably not an option for budgetary reasons, so let's look at alternatives. If you don't mind the mess, simply place a large amount of gravel on a thick layer of carpet or sound blankets. The thicker the layer of carpet, the less solid an impact you'll get from the cement. The catch with this setup is that you'll have to clean it up. You can use a large tub to store your gravel for future use.

The same method can be applied to dirt. You will need to use a considerably thick layer of dirt for it to sound convincing and to reduce the sound of the surface underneath. For grittier-sounding textures, add straw and leaves to the dirt. If the dirt kicks up a lot of dust, spray it down with a light mist of water. For a mud pit, simply add more water.

Earth Surfaces

If you can afford to lose floor space, a perfect scenario would be to make a 4' x 4' concrete frame and line it with carpet or sound blankets. Then pour in your dirt or gravel. To be space-efficient, you could throw a sheet of plywood on top of the concrete frame and make that your hollow wood pit.

In a pinch, a wood frame can be used to hold in dirt or gravel, but the wood will resonate. Heavy layering of carpet and sound blankets may help reduce the sound of the wood. Start with a 4' x 4' wood frame with 2 x 6 boards. Attach a sheet of plywood underneath. Use multiple layers of sound blankets inside the pit and attach carpet underneath. Record some tests with your pit and make adjustments as needed.

Foley Materials and Props

While you're out in the field, keep your eyes open for the next cool surface or prop to bring back to the studio. Become a pack rat at home. Don't throw anything out without asking yourself if it can be used as a Foley prop. You'll be surprised how much stuff you'll keep. Glass bottles, pill containers, boxes, and magazines are among the many things you can use in Foley. Ask your friends and family members to pitch in. You'll get some weird looks, but in the end, the sounds will justify the means.

Props!

Over the years, the Chop Shop has gathered thousands of props and dozens of surfaces. After a while, your Foley stage will start to look like Fred Sanford's living room. But these are the tools of the trade. Remember, microphones and recorders are useless if you don't have something to record.

Prop Room Shelf

Junkyards are gold mines for props. Most junkyards are willing to part with a damaged hood or fender that you can bring back to your stage. Be sure to wash off the props before you bring them inside as they may have stowaways such as insects and other creatures.

Find props that are worn in. Older objects tend to be more vocal. Metal creaks and squeaks can be produced by soaking a door hinge in a cup of water and letting it rust. Wood pallets, like those found on loading docks and at construction sites and grocery stores are great for wood surfaces that sound aged. A stack of wood pallets can make a great surface to walk on. Creaks and other stressed sounds can be created by offsetting the top pallet.

Surface Props

Home Improvement Stores

Another good source for props is the local home improvement store. You will have to pay for the material found there, of course, but the cost can be well worth it. You'll find everything from surfaces to crash material. A Foley shopping list at these stores might look like this:

Bricks
Cinderblocks
Dirt
Dowel Rods
Gravel
Patio Blocks
Plywood
Rocks
Sand
Sheet Metal
Shims
Wood Panels
Wood Planks (2 x 4s, 2 x 6s, etc.)

Dollar Stores

Perhaps the best source for props is your local dollar store. I consider these stores to be America's prop house. And the best part: Everything is only a buck! This can mean a lot when you need to load up on glass that you intend to break. I've made a deal with the dollar store near me and they save all of their glass that ships to the store damaged. They sell the b-stock to me at half price, which saves both of us money. Many of these stores now sell food products. While probably not the best choice for consumption, these food products can make great sources for sound effects.

Spend some time at a dollar store and walk around touching and moving the products on the shelves. You will get looks from fellow shoppers and mothers will try to protect their children from you, but it's better to know what something sounds like before you decide to buy it. This exercise will help open your mind to common items that you might already have at home. Half the battle of recording sound effects is finding things to record. You can find thousands of items and ideas under one roof at these thrift stores.

Debris

Whether you bought your material for full price at a hardware store or found a bargain price at a dollar store, you'll get the best bang for your buck if you save the debris created from your crashes. Separate each material into its own bin. Glass should be separated into different bins based on the type of glass. For example, glass panes from picture frames make a completely different sound from the glass debris of lightbulbs. You can even create a junk bin that contains more than one type of material for crashes.

Foley Tips

It never ceases to amaze me that there are no books that deal with the black art of Foley. Perhaps that's because the magicians don't want their secrets getting out. I'm not sure. But I do know that the art of Foley is a big subject — much bigger than the scope of this book. So here are some quick tips and tricks to get you started working in Foley.

Find the Sound with Your Eyes Closed

I really can't emphasize this enough. Record with your ears and not with your eyes. When looking for a sound prop, don't think of the object that you're after; instead, think of the *sound* that you're after. Some props might be impossible to find or may not even exist — a Klingon phaser, for example. When you get a new prop, twist it, turn it, shake it, drop it, and rub it up against other props. Learn the sound of the prop. Forget what it looks like. The listener won't care what color it is, only what it sounds like.

Handle with Care

Where you hold the prop can affect how it sounds. Start with the edges and work from there. Holding props in the middle can some-times mute the sound. Other times, holding a prop in the center will allow the rest of it to make the sound. Experiment by getting your hands on the prop and test-handling it in different places.

How you hold the prop can affect the sound as well. Lightly holding a prop allows it to resonate or vibrate more. Firmly holding a prop will deaden the sound. Stressing props is a great way of producing sound. Some props seem to come to life when you move them more slowly, while others need faster movements to produce more interesting sounds. Again, experiment.

Safety Equipment

Safety equipment should be worn when necessary. Wear a dust mask during crash sessions that can produce harmful dust and debris. Protective eye wear (safety glasses or goggles) should be worn to shield your eyes from flying debris. There are times when you'll need to wear gloves to protect your hands from glass, splinters, and other sharp objects. Cotton gloves are quieter than leather ones but won't fully protect your hands from cuts.

The Foley Dress Code

The purpose of a good Foley stage is to have an isolated environment to work in, one that enables you to record only the props or movements without any external noise. With a room that is completely separated from outside noise, there is only one potential source of unwanted sound: you. Always be aware of the noise that you make. Wear quiet clothing.

Choose clothes that do not have noisy zippers or vinyl fabrics that make sound every time you move. Sweat pants are preferred, but blue jeans will do fine. The idea is to have loose clothing that will allow you to move freely without affecting the recording. Wear shoes that are comfortable but not big and bulky. You may need to tuck in long shoelaces that can bounce off your shoes when you move around. It is not uncommon to see Foley artists at the Chop Shop walking around with gaffer's tape on their clothing or shoes.

Also, refrain from wearing jewelry that will jingle or rub up against the props (watches, rings, necklaces, and the like). I have fond thoughts of my friend the Foley artist Aaron Golematis, who always wears a homemade necklace. This necklace consists of a dog chain that has a huge cross at the end of it (think Mr. T). That necklace, along with his all-black outfit including a long leather coat (even during summer months) and an even longer pony tail, makes up the persona that is Aaron. Of course, he grumbles when he has to take the necklace off during recording sessions, but jewelry and recording don't mix.

The Amazing Aaron Golematis Performing Foley

Don't Go to Work Hungry

Avoid performing Foley on an empty stomach. The microphones are very sensitive and will pick up the gurgling and gaseous cries from deep within. If you're working late and don't have time for a break, try some crackers and water to settle your stomach — that is, of course, after you've recorded your stomach growling.

Silence Is Golden

Turn your cell phone completely off. Cell phones create interference in recording equipment. This happens even when they are on vibrate. When you are ready to roll, turn off your phone. If you have to leave your phone on, place it away from the recording gear.

Sound Dampeners

Towels, rags, foam, and sound blankets can all be used as dampeners to reduce vibrations in the props you are working with. They can also be used to separate the props from the surfaces that you work on. Putting a towel inside a prop to deaden the resonance works on the same principle as placing a towel inside a kick drum.

If placing a dampener on top of a prop doesn't give you the results you want, try placing a weight on top of the dampener. C-clamps and other fasteners can be used to help tighten down dampeners on props as well.

Perform the Sound

A good Foley artist uses props to perform sound. They are not merely moving objects. In my experience, musicians make the best Foley artists, because they understand how movement and sound coexist. If you are not a musician, don't be discouraged. Study musicians and how they perform. It might even help to have a musician come in and give you a hand recording. Despite my many years doing Foley, I still think that Aaron Golematis (an insanely talented musician) is ten times the Foley artist I am. I try to bring him into the studio whenever I can.

Foley Supplies

Here is a list of tools and supplies to have on your Foley stage:

Ax	Rags
Baseball Bat	Rope
Broom/Dustpan	Rubber Bands
Buckets	Rubber Gloves
Can of Air	Rubber Mallet
Carpenter's Hammer	Safety Goggles
C-Clamps	Sandbags
Cotton Gloves	Sledgehammer
Dust Masks	Sound Blankets
Gaffer's Tape	Spring Clamps
Knife	Towels
Leather Gloves	Weights
Mop	

CHAPTER TWELVE

Digital Audio

Making Sense of Ones and Zeros

DIGITAL AUDIO IS NOTHING MORE than ones and zeros. The process of turning analog information into digital information is called digitizing. An audio signal is analyzed by an A/D (analog to digital) converter that translates the analog audio signal into digital information. Conversely, a D/A (digital to analog) converter takes the digital information and translates it into an analog audio signal. Both converters are found inside digital field recorders and sound cards.

Sample Rate

The A/D converter analyzes the waveform of an analog signal and samples that wave a predetermined number of times per second, known as the sample rate. For example, a sample rate of 48KHz means that the waveform is analyzed 48,000 times per second. Higher sample rates equal a higher resolution of frequency.

Sample Rates

The more sampling points (higher sampling rate), the more accurate the digital representation of the original waveform.

A. This represents how a low sample rate, such as 22KHz, would recreate the sound wave digitally.

B. This represents how a standard definition sample rate, such as 44.1KHz, would recreate the sound wave digitally.

C. This represents how a high definition sample rate, such as 96KHz, would recreate the sound wave digitally.

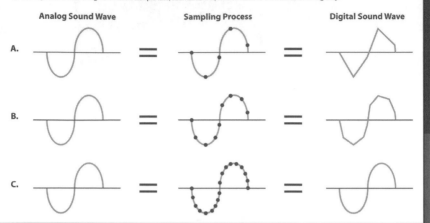

Analog Sound Wave   Sampling Process   Digital Sound Wave

The Nyquist Theorem

The Nyquist theorem, named after engineer Harry Nyquist, states that the sample rate must be twice as high as the highest desired frequency to be sampled. If the sample rate is less than the highest frequency, a phenomenon called aliasing, which distorts some frequencies, can occur during the conversion process. The human ear is capable of hearing frequencies up to 20KHz, so a frequency of 20KHz would need to be sampled 40,000 times.

However, researchers discovered that when frequencies were present above the highest desired frequency, the conversion would still result in aliasing. So a low-pass filter was placed in the chain before the A/D converter to stop any frequencies above 20KHz. Low-pass filters are not absolute brick walls that can stop all the frequencies precisely at a certain point — a slight roll-off occurs. This sloping effect tapers off the frequencies above 20KHz. To compensate for this sloping, the sample rate was adjusted to allow for a highest recorded frequency of 22,050Hz. This provided more than ample room for the A/D converter to sample the signal with no noticeable aliasing. The result was the standard CD audio sample rate of 44.1KHz.

Quantization or Bit Depth

Bit depth refers to the measurement or sampling of a sound wave's amplitude. On a graph, the sample rate is a horizontal measurement and the bit depth is a vertical measurement. A bit depth of 16 uses 65,536 steps to measure the volume. A bit depth of 24 uses 16,777,216 steps. As you can see, 24 bit has 256 times more resolution than 16 bit. Therefore, 24 bit gives the better representation of the volume of a waveform. Higher bit depths equal a higher resolution of amplitude.

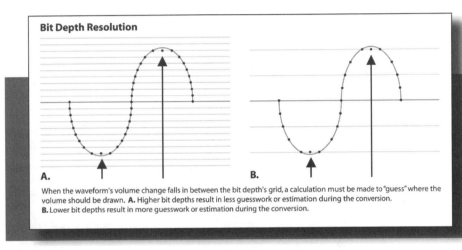

Bit Depth Resolution

A.

B.

When the waveform's volume change falls in between the bit depth's grid, a calculation must be made to "guess" where the volume should be drawn. **A.** Higher bit depths result in less guesswork or estimation during the conversion. **B.** Lower bit depths result in more guesswork or estimation during the conversion.

Digital Audio Files

A digital audio file contains all of the data gathered by the A/D converter. The size of the audio file is based on three factors: sample rate, bit depth, and time.

Sample Rate Size

The difference in file size between 48KHz and 96KHz is 200%. For example, a digital audio file that has a sample rate of 96KHz is twice the file size of an audio file of the same length and bit depth with a sample rate of 48KHz.

Bit Depth Size

The difference in file size between 16 bit and 24 bit is 300%. For example, a digital audio file that has a bit depth of 24 is three times the file size of an audio file of the same length and sample rate with a bit depth of 16.

The resolution of the audio file will determine how much computing your digital audio workstation (DAW) will need to do when working with the file. If you have a high-resolution audio file, then your DAW will need to handle more processing. For some systems, this can mean longer render times and jittery playback when playing multiple files at the same time. As CPU speeds increase exponentially, it will soon be commonplace for a home computer to be able to handle dozens and dozens of high-definition audio tracks with no external processing.

Audio File Overview

Here is an example of an audio file in Sony's Sound Forge.

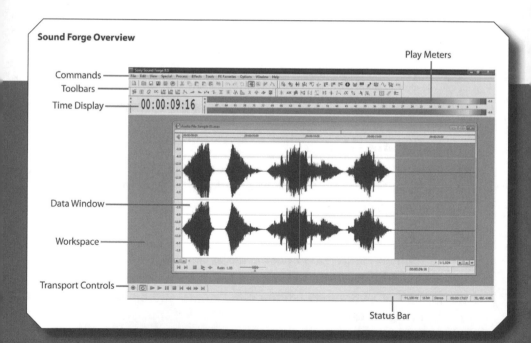

The data window displays the waveform of the audio file. This example is a stereo file, so it shows two waveforms. The top waveform is the left channel. The bottom waveform is the right channel. The numbers to the left of the waveform indicate the amplitude of the file. The numbers at the top of the file indicate duration or time. The cursor indicates which part of the audio file is being played.

The solid line in the center of the waveform is known as the zero line. This represents no change in air pressure. This is the point where there is no audio; it's also known as the baseline. If a section of the audio file is muted or silence has been inserted, you will see that the sample points of the waveform are still drawn at the sample rate intervals but all appear on this line.

Professional Audio File Formats

In the professional audio world there are three main audio file formats that are used. These file formats use uncompressed PCM (pulse code modulation) and deliver the maximum quality in audio files. Nearly all professional audio software is capable of handling these files. Here is an overview:

.AIFF Files
(Audio Interchange File Format)
Developed by Apple

.WAV Files
(Waveform Audio Format)
Developed by Microsoft

.BWF Files (or sometimes .BWAV)
(Broadcast Wave Format)
Created by the European Broadcast Union

The BWF is the next generation of the WAV file. This file format is now considered to be the new industry standard for professional audio files. The file structure allows for the inclusion of metadata, time code stamping, and interleaved files. These are basically standard WAV files with extension chunks of data.

MP3 Files

MP3 is a compressed audio file format that is very popular in the consumer market. These files are used for audio file sharing over the Internet and in MP3 players and also video games. The MP3's compression ratio allows for files to be a tenth of the size while maintaining a reasonable level of quality. Most people cannot distinguish the quality differences between .WAV files and .MP3 files. For a professional sound engineer the differences are like nails on a chalkboard. Although your final delivery method in making sound effects might be MP3 files, you'll obtain immeasurably better results by recording, editing, and mastering in WAV format and then converting to MP3.

Time Code

SMPTE time code is a time stamping system that gives each frame in video and film a certain time address. There are 30 frames per second (fps) in video and 24 fps in film. The most commonly used time code is 29.97NDF (non drop frame). Drop frame time code drops frames periodically to account for lost time that originated when television first started to broadcast in color. This is not incredibly important to the sound world, except that when working to picture, you should be sure your audio matches the frame rate of the video.

MIDI

Founded by David Smith in the early 1980s, MIDI (Musical Instrument Digital Interface) is a protocol designed to allow computers and musical equipment to communicate and synchronize. No audio is transmitted through the MIDI cables. Instead, digital messages are sent through their 5 pin DIN cables. The same holds true for the newer protocols Firewire and USB.

MIDI equipment and interfaces allow you to connect synthesizers and other equipment to your DAW so that you can play modules in your software via a real-world keyboard. The effect is an organic-sounding performance with a digital instrument.

SPDIF

SPDIF (Sony/Phillips Digital Interface) is a protocol for transmitting digital audio. RCA is the most common connector used for SPDIF. This format appears on both professional and consumer equipment including home theater electronics. In the days of DAT recorders, SPDIF cables were used to import digital audio from DAT into a DAW. This resulted in a clean transfer of the audio, because the transfer was strictly digital and there was no digitizing or re-recording of the audio.

CHAPTER THIRTEEN

Studio Equipment

Choosing the Right Equipment

NOW THAT YOU UNDERSTAND THE basic principles of recording and DAWs, let's look at what equipment you'll need for a studio. First let's look at the vital parts of a digital audio workstation. There are five main components in a computer-based digital audio workstation:

1. DAW
2. Plug-Ins
3. Sound Card/Audio Interface
4. Monitors
5. Storage

DAWs (Digital Audio Workstations)

Digital audio workstations are where all the magic happens. An audio file can be opened, processed, and manipulated in just about every conceivable way. There are standalone workstations that do not require the use of a computer as a host system, but a computer-based system with software will provide the best results with the most versatility. Computer-based DAWs work off the processing power of the host computer and are RAM intensive.

Before selecting your software, be sure that you have a fast and reliable computer with plenty of room to add on more RAM. Each workstation has different computer requirements that you should refer to before purchasing. The exception to host processing is Pro Tools HD. This software uses outboard processors to handle all of the audio and only utilizes the computer to control the software. These systems are the industry standard for professional film and music production.

Non-Destructive Editing

In the days of analog tape, an edit meant that you physically cut the tape with a razor and spliced it to another section of the tape. This seemingly barbaric process was very tedious and time-consuming, not to mention destructive. With a digital audio workstation, you are merely referencing an audio file. These references make up an edit decision list.

In the digital audio workstation, the edit decision list (EDL) is called a session. When you splice files together or fade them in and out, you are creating a complex playlist in which the workstation uses the timeline to determine when to play the file and the track list to determine which file to play. There are many other factors that are included in this list, such as volume and pan settings, effects or plug-in settings, and automation. All of this data is stored in the session file. The original audio files remain unchanged, despite any changes or modifications made in the session.

Digital editing programs like Sound Forge work a little differently. Your changes are non-destructive until you save the file. When the file is saved, the original content in the audio file is affected. Up until saving the file, your edits and other changes are stored either in RAM or in a scratch folder on your hard drive. As you play the file, the editor points to the temporary files and seamlessly plays back the audio.

Types of Workstations

DAW software comes in all shapes and sizes. DAWs fall into three main categories:

Editing Workstations
Loop-Based Workstations
Multitrack Workstations

All three types offer unique solutions for working with digital audio. Below is a brief description of each:

Editing Workstations

Often referred to as editors or wave editors, these workstations usually offer two-track audio editing. Recently Sony raised the bar by offering a multitrack version with Sound Forge 9. An editor lets you handle all of the processing and mastering of your audio file. Newer editors allow you to insert a plug-in chain so you can run numerous plug-ins in real time simultaneously to hear their effects in concert with each other. Although most editors allow you to apply cross fading and limited mixing techniques, you'll find a looping or multitrack station works better for these processes.

Loop-Based Workstations

Workstations such as Abelton's Live, Apple's Garage Band, and Sony's Acid provide an interface that allows you to take existing audio files and loop them on a timeline. Grids can be used to indicate musical measures, enabling you to place your loops in perfect timing with each other in relation to a beat. This is most useful for music creation, but it can also give you a whole suite of toys to play with when it comes to sound design.

Looping programs are great for creating synthetic sounds and science fiction material. Pitch shifting is very easy, allowing you to layer the same sound on different tracks but in different pitches. Most looping software also allows you to use it as a multitrack recorder, adding even more flexibility. The possibilities are endless.

Multitrack Workstations

These workstations are designed to record and mix multiple tracks in the same way that the original two-inch analog tape recorders did. The difference is the infinite level of flexibility that a digital multitrack system offers. Tracks can be moved, cross-faded, or even reversed with the simple click of a mouse. Multitrack workstations function as both recorder and mixer, with the same features of analog mixing systems such as inserts, subgroups, and master faders. The added advantage is that all of the aspects of the workstation can be completely automated, giving you precise control over your mix.

Software Choices

The software is the central hub of your DAW. It is, in fact, the workstation itself. The type of workstation that you choose will depend on your needs. For straightforward editing, an editor like Sound Forge will work perfectly. For sound design, a looping or multitrack workstation will work better.

If your budget allows, a combination of the three will give you the most options and tools for working with sound. If you have to choose between a multitrack workstation and a looping workstation for the purposes of sound design, you are probably better off with a looping station. You can use the looping functions of the software and still have your cake and eat it too with the multitrack recording functions.

Plug-Ins

In the days of analog audio production, outboard processors were physically patched into the signal chain of a sound board to help shape the audio. DAWs work in the same manner but with plug-ins. Plug-ins are basically mathematical processes or algorithms that are applied to the data in an audio file. Because plug-ins are software, they exist in the digital world only and there is no patching or expensive hardware components. This technological advance has brought lower-priced, higher-quality tools to the project studio.

With the computer processing power now available, it is possible to apply plug-ins to your audio files in real time. This works much the same as outboard processors worked in analog systems. The signal (albeit ones and zeros) is routed to a processor (or plug-in), and the signal is processed and sent back to the main mix. As with analog, the levels to and from the processors need to be adjusted to prevent overloading or clipping the signal.

There are several types of software plug-ins:

DirectX (Microsoft)
RTAS — Real Time Audio Suite (Digidesign)
VST — Virtual Studio Technology (Steinberg)

Most popular DAWs will support all three formats, but you should double-check a plug-in's compatibility with software manufacturers before purchasing. Remember, plug-ins are software and cannot be returned to the store once they have been opened. To prevent software piracy, some manufacturers, such as Audio Ease, require the use of a dongle to activate the software. A widely used dongle is the iLok. This USB key stores the licenses for all of your favorite software and is made by PACE, an anti-piracy company.

New outboard processing technologies are being developed for plug-ins. Manufacturers such as TC Electronics and Universal Audio are now offering plug-ins that are processed through external processors that are connected to your computer via a PCI slot or through Firewire. Digidesign's ProTools offers TDM (time-division multiplexing) plug-ins that run on proprietary DSP (digital signal processing) chips. This outboard processing frees up your CPU and allows your computer to focus on playing the files rather than performing the complex calculations of the plug-ins.

Here is a breakdown of the most commonly used types of plug-ins:

Analog Simulators
The main complaint that audiophiles have with digital audio is that it sounds cold and brittle. The analog process naturally warmed

the sound during processing with real-world circuitry, a step that doesn't happen in the digital process. For this reason, software developers have created plug-ins that recreate the warm sound of analog processing. Analog simulators add a warm character to digital sound. The PSP Vintage Warmer

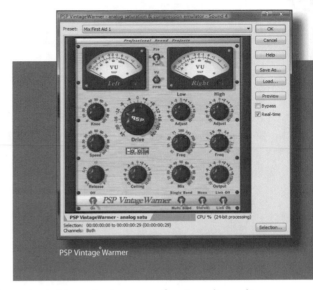

PSP Vintage Warmer

is among my favorites. You can achieve instant, professional results with their presets or make adjustments and experiment to get the sound you're looking for.

Auto Trim/Crop

Most DAWs come with a set of tools to start you on your way to editing. An auto trim/crop tool allows you to remove silence from a file and automatically fade the beginning and end points based on given parameters. This can be helpful for removing clicks and pops that may occur at the beginning and end of files when the waveform does not start and finish on the zero line.

Auto Trim/Crop Plug-In

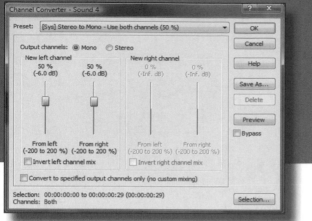

Channel Converter Plug-In

Channel Converter

A channel converter allows you to convert a mono file into a stereo file and vice versa. It also enables you to perform panning effects as well as swapping channels.

Compressor

A compressor automatically controls the levels of a signal, which helps to prevent overloading and to maintain a consistent volume level. A makeup gain is often inserted at the end of a compressor's chain to increase the volume of the compressed signal. Compression is very

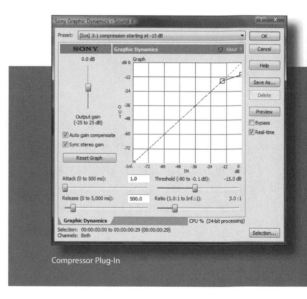

Compressor Plug-In

useful for controlling the overall balance of a sound especially when mixing several tracks together.

Equalizer — Graphic

A graphic equalizer features bands of frequencies that can be increased or decreased to help shape the overall color of a sound. These bands can come in any number, the most common being 5, 10, 20 and 30 bands. The more bands the equalizer has, the narrower each bandwidth becomes.

Equalizer Graphic Plug-In

Equalizer Graphic Plug-In

Equalizer — Paragraphic

A paragraphic equalizer offers greater control over frequency selection and bandwidth than the graphic equalizer. It allows you to increase or decrease the gain of a specific frequency with little or no effect on the surrounding frequencies. These equalizers are perfect for notching out a certain frequency, such as the 15KHz buzz from a television set.

Equalizer Paragraphic Plug-In

Gate

A gate allows sound that is above a certain level, called a threshold, to pass through and be heard. When this happens, the gate is considered to be open. Sound levels below the threshold are muted and remain unheard, and the gate is considered to be closed. Gates reduce background noise automatically. Care should be taken in setting the parameters of the gate. If the settings are too extreme, the sound can appear to be cut off.

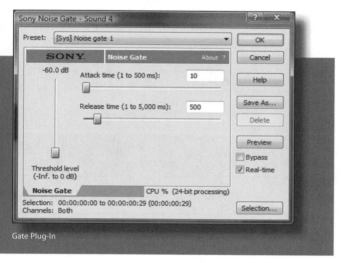

Gate Plug-In

Insert Silence

Inserting silence into an audio file means placing a predetermined amount of time anywhere in the audio file, which can be useful for timing a sound effect. For example, let's say you have the single tick of a clock. You can prepare that sample by reducing background noise and with compression and normalization. Now that the sample is pure, you can insert silence to allow the tick to be looped, giving the effect of a clock ticking. If the sample is 10 frames, you would insert 20 frames (remember, there are 30 frames in a second) at the end of the file. This gives you a one-second sample to loop to create a time-accurate sound effect of a ticking clock.

Some plug-ins, such as reverbs and delays, will extend the sound after the actual audio file. If there is no silence at the end of the file for this to occur, the sound would simply stop at the end of the file. This can sound like a mistake because the sound is cut off before it can finish. In such a case you need to insert enough silence at the end of the file to allow the delay or reverb tail to fade into natural silence.

Fifteen frames (or one-half second) of silence should be inserted at the beginning of a track that is being prepped for an audio CD. This allows the CD player enough time to read the track before it plays. Failure to add this silence can result in the track being cut off for a fraction of a second when the CD player advances to that track. This usually occurs when using the "previous" and "next" buttons.

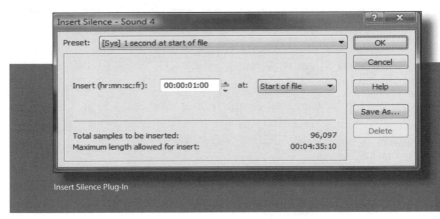

Insert Silence Plug-In

Limiter

Limiting is basically a form of compression with an extremely high or infinite compression ratio. All compressors have the ability to function as a limiter. Limiting is most practical on devices like field recorders; it prevents the signal from peaking or clipping when you're recording.

Compressor Plug-In Acting As a Limiter

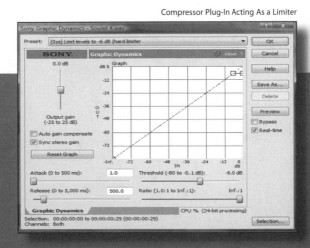

Noise Reduction

Noise reduction plug-ins process the audio by scanning, detecting, and removing noise. FFT (Fast Fourier Transform) noise reduction allows you to take a "snapshot" of a section of the noise in the audio. This snapshot serves as a reference of what to remove from the entire file. The software then uses intense mathematical processes to analyze the rest of the audio and remove or reduce that particular sound signature from the file. When selecting your snapshot sample, be sure to find a section of audio that contains only the noise. This will yield the best results.

Noise reduction plug-ins are very powerful tools but should be used in moderation. Overprocessing a sound to remove noise can cause warble and digital hiccup-sounding artifacts. High-frequency noise is much more noticeable than low-frequency noise. If you can't find a good balance with your plug-in, try equalizing the higher frequencies. Again, moderation is the key.

Noise Reduction Plug-In

Normalizer

A normalizer allows you to set the maximum level of an audio file. Using this setting, the plug-in raises or lowers the amplitude of the entire file to the predetermined point, increasing or decreasing the amplitude equally without affecting the dynamics of the file. Normalizing files exactly to digital zero can still cause the audio to clip in some applications and CD players. For this reason, you should normalize the audio to -.5dB below digital zero.

A normalizer should be used during the MP3 conversion process to avoid clipping. Generally, you should set the normalizer between -1dB and -2dB before converting the file to MP3. You should check your file after the conversion to ensure that no clipping occurred.

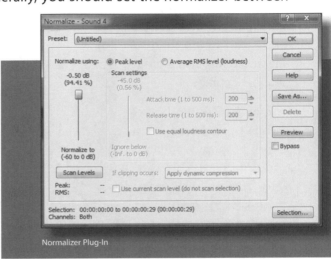

Normalizer Plug-In

Pitch Shift

Pitch shifting is a powerful plug-in that increases or decreases the pitch of your sound. Traditionally, the sound is shortened when the pitch is raised and lengthened when the pitch is lowered. Pitch shifting is one of the primary techniques used in sound design. Lowering the pitch of a sound can instantly give it more weight, making it sound bigger.

Some pitch shift plug-ins allow you to raise or lower the pitch but maintain the duration of the sound. This effect is not that noticeable when used in moderation. In extreme amounts, it can produce a digital distortion effect similar to sounds heard in *The Matrix*.

Pitch Shift Plug-In

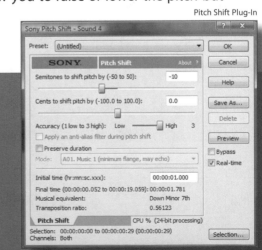

Reverb

Reverb plug-ins add the characteristics of a particular environment, such as a hall, a church, or a sewer. These plug-ins have
become very sophisticated over the years. Today, there are convolution reverbs that allow you to sample the IRs (impulse responses)
of a location or room.
Once it is sampled, the
acoustic response of that
space can be applied to
any audio file with a great
deal of accuracy.

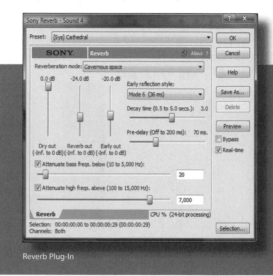

One of the best and most
widely used convolution
reverb plug-ins is Altiverb
by Audio Ease. This soft-
ware comes with loads
of presets, as well as an
impulse response disc
that allows you to go out
in the field and record

Reverb Plug-In

your own IRs and apply them to your sounds. Audio Ease has an
open-community-based library where you can share your IRs with
other users. Unique IRs that exist in the Altiverb library include
metal pipes, helicopter cockpits, speakerphones, and even trash
cans. Altiverb is a must-have for serious sound designers.

Spectrum Analyzer

This scope allows you to view a real-time graph of your audio file's
frequencies and their respective levels in your audio file. This tool

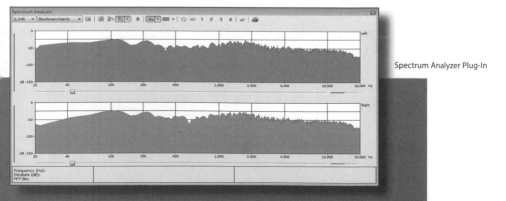

Spectrum Analyzer Plug-In

can be used to find offensive frequencies and see how they relate to the rest of the frequency spectrum in terms of amplitude.

Time Stretch or Time Compression

Time stretch allows you to extend or shorten an audio file without affecting its pitch. When used sparingly, time stretch can work without being noticed. This can be an

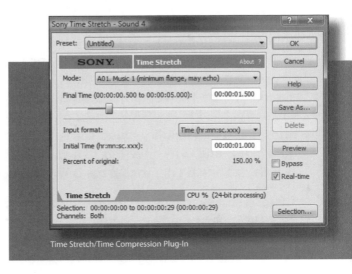

Time Stretch/Time Compression Plug-In

extremely useful tool when you need to fit a sound into a specific amount of time.

Plug-In Chains

A plug-in chain is a series of processors that are daisy-chained together to create a complete effect at one time. In setting up a chain, you must set the levels properly so that a plug-in doesn't distort or raise the level too high for the input of the next processor. Unless you are going for a special effect, it's best to use effects sparingly as too much effect will wash out the original sound. On most effects processors you will find a dry/wet knob. This lets you select between having the effect wet (completely processed), dry (not processed), or a mix between the two.

Where you place a processor in the chain will affect the processors before and after it. If you place a reverb plug-in at the end of the chain, then all of the plug-ins before it will be processed through the reverb. Placing the reverb at the front of the chain will mean that the reverb sound will also be processed by the plug-ins after it. A reverb plug-in is usually at the end of the chain.

Putting reverb before a heavy compressor will make the reverb tail pump or warble.

Sound Cards and Audio Interfaces

Sound cards and audio interfaces are the devices used by the software to bring sound in and out of the DAW. A sound card is physically placed inside the computer in an available PCI slot. An audio interface is an external device that connects via a USB or Firewire cable. While a DAW has its own set of maximum resolutions that it can handle, sound cards and audio interfaces have built-in A/D and D/A converters that will determine the maximum sample rate and bit depth that the DAW can use.

There are many makes and models of sound devices to use with your DAW. Most modern computers come with a built-in sound card that can handle high-definition audio. These consumer devices can offer reasonable levels of quality for audio playback, but that does not necessarily mean accuracy. Sound cards and audio interfaces are similar to headphone amplifiers on a field recorder in that they do not affect the quality of the actual audio — only the way it is perceived. The inputs of these devices, however, directly affect the quality of your recording.

Sound cards can sometimes add noise from your computer in the recordings. For this reason, break-out boxes (BOBs) are used to separate the input jacks from the sound card. Audio interfaces do not encounter this problem because they are only connected to the computer through a digital cable that only transmits data.

When choosing such a device, consider the following:

Will you be recording directly into the computer?

Do you need XLR and 1/4" connectors?

How many channels of output do you need (for example, 5.1 surround sound mixing)?

Do you need a headphone jack and volume control?

Do you need SPDIF connectors?

Do you need a MIDI interface?

Will you use the device with more than one computer (laptop and desktop)?

Do you need high-resolution sample rates?

These questions will help you decide if you need a sound card or an audio interface and give you direction on which card might be right for you.

Monitors

Monitors are the name given to professional speakers that are designed and constructed to have a flat response when reproducing sound. "Speakers" generally refers to consumer-level speakers, which may sound good but are not well suited for professional use. The difference between a professional monitor and a consumer speaker is accuracy.

Monitors are the last link in the recording chain. It is vital for critical listening to be able to reproduce the sound as accurately as possible. A monitor that colors the sound can deceive the editor into thinking the sound needs to be corrected in some fashion. For example, a consumer speaker may have a boost in the low frequencies. This boost artificially enhances the actual sound. If you use these speakers professionally, you may think that the low frequencies need to be managed through equalization, when in actuality the low frequencies are fine.

Like a professional microphone, a professional monitor should have a wide and flat frequency response range. While some microphones are enhanced at certain frequencies, this is not desirable for monitors. All professional monitors have a flat frequency response range of 20Hz to 20KHz or greater. Keep this in mind when selecting your monitors.

Active and Passive Monitors

Monitors come in two flavors: active and passive. Active monitors (powered) have an amplifier built into each speaker cabinet that drives the speaker. When using active monitors, you need to match the output level of each speaker to ensure a true stereo balance of the sound. This is done with volume control knobs on each cabinet. Passive monitors do not have an internal amplifier and therefore need amplification.

Placement

Where you place your monitors in relation to your ears is important to how you hear the sound. There are three ways to monitor the sound: far field, near field, and headphones.

Far field monitors are large (usually starting at 2' x 3') and are usually mounted inside a false wall or soffit in the studio. These monitors produce accurate sound at high volume levels. Because they are positioned far away from the listener, they are greatly affected by the room's acoustics. Far field monitors are generally used in music and movie soundtrack mixing and can be very expensive.

Near field monitors are smaller in size (usually smaller than 2' x 2') and are placed closer to the listener. Because they are closer, they are less affected by the room's acoustics and can therefore give a more accurate reproduction of the sound. Near field monitors are less expensive than far field monitors and are more practical for the home or project studio. They should be placed a foot or more away from the wall and should not be in the corners of the room to prevent the low-frequency buildup that can occur in corners and against walls. You can place them on a desk or on stands. Use isolation pads to reduce the vibrations that a monitor transmits when placed on top of a desk.

Subwoofers are often used with near field monitors to assist in reproducing the low frequencies that most near field monitors struggle with. These frequencies are usually in the 20Hz to 80Hz range. Subwoofers are usually placed in the corner of the room. A great technique for isolating the subwoofer from the floor is to use feet that are cone shaped and come to a fine point. The point is placed on the floor and helps minimize the bass absorption that the floor, walls, and ceiling conduct.

Headphones are the most accurate way to critically listen to sound. They are the stethoscope of the audio engineer. They allow the listener to hear only the sound because the room's acoustics and environmental sounds (birds through a window, air conditioners, etc.) are completely taken out of the picture. It should be noted that extreme low frequencies (50Hz and less) are difficult to accurately reproduce with headphones, because those frequencies are more felt than heard. But headphones still give you the most accurate reproduction. It's a good idea to always have a pair of headphones in your studio.

Positioning

Ideally monitors should be positioned at ear level. Having them higher or lower will adversely affect the way the sound is heard. They should also be symmetrically balanced in an equilateral triangle in relation to the listener. The listener's position on the triangle is known as

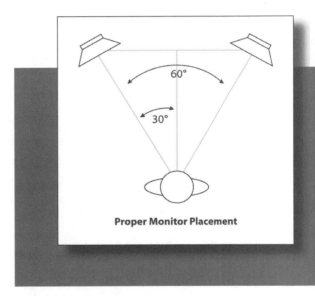

Proper Monitor Placement

the *sweet spot*. This is the optimum listening position, where sound from both speakers can be heard equally. This positioning is paramount for accurately reproducing a true stereo image.

Playback Reference

In the music world, it is not uncommon to record a song in a multimillion-dollar studio and then reference that recording in a car or even a $50 stereo system. This practice has been used for decades and is intended to let the professional hear the mix the same way the audience will hear it. Multimillion-dollar stereo systems are not what the average listener will use to hear the song. Instead, they'll hear it in their cars, out at the beach on a portable stereo, or nowadays over their cell phone. Television professionals employ the same practice; TV broadcast trucks use limited-range mono speakers to reference the mix to ensure that it will sound good on the average television set.

In the film world, there are two approaches to referencing the mix. The first is to mix and monitor the film in a studio that has been set up like a movie theater. These studios are known as dubbing stages or mixdown stages. They allow the engineer to sit where the audience would sit and listen to the film the way they would listen to it. The second method uses home theater systems to monitor films being mixed specifically for DVD release. Disney is the first major studio to offer home theater remixes of their theatrical releases, cleverly called a Disney 5.1 Enhanced Home Theatre Mix.

Listening to your sounds, music, or other audio on multiple systems allows you to better understand your mix. Every system sounds different, including professional systems. To help correct this, companies like THX have set up standards for what movie theaters and home entertainment systems should sound like. As these standards become more widely used, the overall quality of the entertainment experience will increase.

I remember watching *Star Wars* for the first time. I was sitting in a lawn chair at a drive-in theater. A single, mono speaker was hanging off my dad's car window. As a child the sound seemed amazing to me. However, the director, George Lucas, was disappointed that the sound mix he had meticulously worked on did not translate well over substandard equipment. It was for this reason that he birthed THX (Tomlinson Holman Experiment), which is named after the lead developer.

THX certifies both movie theaters and home theater equipment. Although THX covers both picture and sound, it is best known for its sound research. Theaters bearing the THX certification have met strict standards for the theater's acoustics, playback system, and overall noise level. This includes noises produced by air conditioning systems, the movie projector, and the soundtrack from the theater next door. THX-certified home theater equipment guarantees the listener that the program's material will be reproduced with a high level of accuracy. The goal of THX is to allow the audience to hear the mix the way the filmmakers intended it to sound.

Playback Volume

Overall, your playback volume should remain at a consistent level. There are times when you will have files that are quiet and the monitoring volume will need to be raised to enable you to listen for noise or other background elements. After listening at this level, it is a good practice to return the monitoring volume back to the original level. This helps train your ears to a certain average volume between the files.

Most professional studios monitor playback at an average volume of 80dB. You can properly calibrate your studio monitors by using a sound level meter that can be purchased at any electronics store, such as Radio Shack. Once your monitors are set up, use music CDs and movie DVDs to get used to the sound of your room. The more you understand how your monitors reproduce your sound, the easier it will be to work with them.

Be aware that prolonged exposure to high volumes can cause ear fatigue and ultimately ear damage.

Deaf to the Mix

Even when listening at moderate levels, you should take a break every couple of hours to let your ears rest. A common occurrence in monitoring sound is when the engineer becomes "deaf to the mix." This phenomenon happens when your ears have heard the same sound or song over and over again and you lose your ability to distinguish what sounds good. It is a cross between your ears getting tired and your brain losing focus. When this happens, walk away and revisit the mix the next day or a couple of days later. This will give you a fresh perspective. You'll be surprised what you'll hear.

Turning Monitors On and Off

Your monitors should always be the last thing turned on when powering up your studio. They should also be the first thing turned off when powering down. Doing so will protect the speakers from the harmful audio spikes that occur when shutting down the rest of the equipment. Turning your monitors on or off at the same time as the rest of your gear (i.e., all of the equipment on one switch) can still cause damage. Having all of your monitors plugged in to the same power supply or power strip can make this task easy.

Storage

Regardless of the DAW you select, one rule should always be followed: Be sure to keep your media on a different hard drive from your local C drive. The C drive of your computer is where the operating system and application information is stored. When you place media on the C drive, you are forcing the computer to access multiple portions of that hard drive at one time. This results in slower response times and problems with playback.

By using a separate hard drive to handle the playback responsibilities, you allow the C drive to focus solely on the operating system and the application. Storing your media on a separate hard drive also prevents possible data loss or damage if the C drive or operating system becomes unstable. If you have to reinstall your operating system or it crashes altogether, you will lose all of the data that was on that drive. Be safe. Keep your media on a separate hard drive and back up the files on that drive to a solid-state medium (CDs or DVDs) often.

When purchasing a storage drive, look for speeds of 7200 rpm or greater. This speed refers to how fast the drive spins and searches for information. Fast speeds are essential when playing multiple files in real time. A raid setup can help boost speeds as well, but a good old-fashioned hard drive can provide great results.

Defragging your hard drive helps reduce data traffic jams when accessing information. Perform monthly cleanups of your drive. To free up space, back up and delete old information. Like a computer, the hard drive will function better in cooler conditions and will run slower and eventually burn out in extreme heat.

Gear Envy

In days past, a home studio might look like a small control room for NASA. It was littered with cables, patch bays, racks full of gear, and a thousand points of light. Today, a laptop and a good pair of headphones can give you professional results. That said; don't give in to "rack envy," a phenomenon that occurs among gearheads. It's the desire to have more gear.

Today, Racks of Gear Do Not Necessarily Mean Better Sound

While having loads of gear gives you more tools to use, odds are that you won't master them all. It is better to have fewer pieces of gear that you are great at using than tons of gear that you have no idea how to use properly. There is always another cool piece of gear to buy. I'm as guilty as the next guy. Be selective. Your wallet and your mix will thank you.

We've discussed the basic requirements for studio gear, so now let's look at some of the extras to help sweeten up the room.

Control Surfaces

DAWs keep everything inside the computer. All of the major functions, such as record, play, stop, and fader movement are handled by the software. During the initial transition from analog to digital, old-school engineers complained that they couldn't get their "hands" on the mix. These seasoned veterans were used to physically moving a fader in order to control the level.

In response, manufacturers began to research and produce control surfaces that connected to the digital audio workstation via MIDI cables. These surfaces brought the mix out of the computer and back into the hands of the engineer. One of the pioneers of the control surface was Mackie. Their HUI protocol is supported by most major DAWs and is still used today as the protocol foundation in products from manufacturers like Alesis, SSL, and Tascam.

Since its inception, the HUI has evolved into the Mackie Control Universal. This is arguably the most commonly used control surface in home, project, and professional studios. This expandable unit controls nearly all of the major functions of the DAW. It gives a more natural feel to working with the audio. There are many more control surfaces on the market today. Referred to in some DAWs as external control, the more modern control surfaces connect via Firewire and USB connections.

Control surfaces are not necessary, but at the same time they're irreplaceable. Automation, the process of programming a mix to repeat performed functions (for example, fade and pan), is simplified with a control surface. Once you get your hands on the mix, you won't want to mix with a mouse anymore. Be warned: Control surfaces are addictive.

Monitor Management

The volume of your DAW's output can be controlled through the audio interface's internal menus or through a control knob on the front of the unit. However, audio interfaces don't always offer all the functionality that you might need when trying to control how you hear the sound. Monitor management devices like the Big Knob from Mackie or the PreSonus Central Station give you more flexibility with your monitors.

Monitor management systems feature a variety of controls and functions, including talkback, dimming, mono mixdown, muting, headphone cues, input selection, and monitor selection. Here is an overview of these functions:

Talkback

Talkback is communication between a control room and a recording booth. This is done through an internal mic on the talkback device or an external mic. The communication is sent via control room monitors or a headphone mix and does not appear in the recording. This allows direction and feedback to be given to and from the talent. Talkback systems appear on some monitor management units and mixers. On some units, the signal can be routed to the recorder (often called 2 Track — for two-track recorder) for the purpose of slating takes.

Dimming

A dim switch allows you to attenuate the mix (for example, -20dB) with the push of a button. When the switch is released, the mix is heard at full volume.

Mono Mixdown

When working in stereo, it is a good practice to test the mix in mono so that you can check for phasing issues.

Muting

The mute button is simple enough to understand. It can be very helpful when feedback or extremely loud sounds play unexpectedly.

Headphone Cues

Headphone cues allow you to determine what is sent to the headphones and also include a volume control.

Input Selection

This can be useful when switching between sources, such as a CD player, keyboard, or other audio inputs.

Monitor Selection

Having more than one pair of monitors allows you to check the mix through different sources. A monitor selection switch routes the audio signal between monitors with a button instead of requiring manual patching.

Power Conditioners

Plugging all of your gear into a power conditioner can help filter out noise within AC lines. This will improve the quality of your audio while providing surge protection for your equipment. Of course, it is also nice to have a single power switch to turn off all of your equipment at the end of the day. Remember to turn your monitors off first!

CHAPTER FOURTEEN

Designing Your Own Studio

Creating the Environment to Work In

A STUDIO IS, BY DEFINITION, A space where an artist exercises his or her creativity. A good studio is a balance of environment, inspiration, and technology. If you are working in your home, choose a room that is as far away as possible from the chaos of everyday living. Think escape. Think paradise. Now come back to reality and work with what you have.

The editing studio will affect the way you hear sound. The acoustics of the room will need to be treated to provide a well-balanced listening environment. In addition, you will want to have a room that isolates your ears from the outside world.

I remember working on an ambience track with the window open one day. I was frustrated because there were too many birds chirping in the background of the sound I was working on. I kept looking for clean sections of the track to work with. It wasn't until I pressed stop for a moment that I realized I wasn't hearing birds from the track, but rather through my open window. I felt like the Three Stooges trying to remove a spot from a painting that turns out to be a beam of sunlight. I closed the window and finished the track.

Studio A at the Chop Shop

Studio D at the Chop Shop

It is important to have a room that can keep outside influences and distractions on the other side of the door. It's equally important that you keep the sound from the room on your side of the door. Let's look at two different rooms for a home editing suite: building a basement studio from scratch and converting a bedroom into a studio.

Basement Studio

In a perfect world, you have the space and budget to build a room. If you've built a Foley stage in your basement, it would be convenient to build your studio on the other side of one wall and to have a window between the two spaces. This would allow you to record on one side of the glass while someone else performs on the other side. Take extra steps to separate the rooms acoustically. A double wall with an 18-inch space in between is optimal.

Window

Plexiglass can be used for a window to give you a view of what is going on in the Foley stage. A plastics or window factory can provide a custom piece for about the same price as a normal window. If you

Studio Window Under Construction

installed a double wall, place a 1-inch-thick plexiglass window on each wall to help reduce sound transmission. Pitching one of the windows at a slight angle will reduce the chances of a standing wave building up between the windows.

Cable Ports

You can design ports to allow you to pass cables back and forth between the rooms, but some sound leakage will undoubtedly occur. Try separating the ports from each other by placing one a few feet away from the other. Wall plates or panels with custom jacks soldered at both ends work great, but be sure to keep your audio wires away from your electrical wires. Also, place the panels a few feet apart on the walls as with the ports. Even though there is a wall plate or panel, sound can still leak through. Extra insulation can help.

Acoustic Treatment

In general, the room does not have to be as acoustically sealed off as the Foley stage. If you can afford it, you should use the same steps given in Chapter Ten for building Foley stages and follow the same construction tips for the door, walls, and ceiling. It's not necessary to cover every inch of the walls with sound-absorbing material. Instead, mud and tape the drywall as usual and paint the surface. Next, use acoustic foam to help tame the reverb of the room. Acoustic foam panels come in various sizes. Panels that are 2 inches thick and 2' x 4' work great and can add a nice design touch to the room.

Electrical

If you are building a room from scratch, be sure to run an electrical supply from a separate breaker. If possible, also run a separate electrical ground to the room to isolate your electric from the rest of the house. This will eliminate buzzes and hums that can occur when air conditioners, fans, and refrigerators are running. Avoid using dimmers on the light switches. If you do, be sure to place them on a separate circuit from the rest of the room; otherwise, they will introduce a buzz into your audio.

Bedroom Studio

If your space and budget are limited, a spare bedroom can still provide usable results. Unfortunately, bedrooms usually have four walls that face each other: Reverb builds faster and stronger in rooms that have parallel walls. You will need to treat the walls with some acoustic foam to reduce the room's reverb.

Acoustic Treatment

Use acoustic panels (2 inches thick and 2' x 4') on some or all of the walls. It's not necessary to cover the entire surface — the goal is to avoid leaving blank surfaces facing each other. Try staggering the foam on each wall; this will help considerably. Carpet or at least a throw rug can help reduce reflections from the ceiling. A couch or chairs with fabric can also reduce upper mid frequency build-up.

Door

Replacing the bedroom door with a solid wood door will reduce the amount of sound leaving and entering the room. A door with weather stripping will be the most effective, although not the most esthetically pleasing.

Furniture

Try to avoid using desks or furniture that vibrates, rattles, or gives off a metallic ring when sound is played through your speakers. The purpose of your studio is to give your ears the most accurate representation of the sound your room allows. Even the slightest resonance from furniture or metallic objects may adversely affect how your ears are hearing the true sound.

Place sound-absorptive materials inside large empty cabinets or furniture to help reduce low-frequency build-up. This includes empty closets, which allow the sound to enter and resonate. Dampen metallic surfaces with cloth or large, heavy knickknacks. Also avoid glass shelves and tables that can rattle when low frequencies are played.

Noise Control inside the Studio

Now that you've done your best to reduce the amount of sound coming from outside the room, let's discuss the sounds produced inside the room. Computer fans are almost always an issue. The white noise they generate can be lulling, but they can often mask sounds from your monitors. This is especially true of hiss and background noise. The listening environment should be kept as pure as possible.

Where you place your computer might address the problem. Placing it underneath the desk helps reduce the direct sound and still gives access to the disk drive and USB ports. A closet will eliminate the sound altogether, but the computer can overheat from being in an enclosed space with little or no ventilation; you also have to deal with blocked access to the disk drive and potentially long cable runs for the computer's monitor, keyboard, and mouse.

A professional solution would be to use an isolation cabinet, like those made from AcoustiLok (*www.norenproducts.com*). These cabinets completely eliminate the sound of the computer but still give access to all the necessary ports and cables. Be careful when selecting an isolation cabinet: Some manufacturers do not take proper airflow and ventilation into account. Higher-end models offer temperature gauges to show the heat inside the cabinet and include internal fans to pull heat away from the computer.

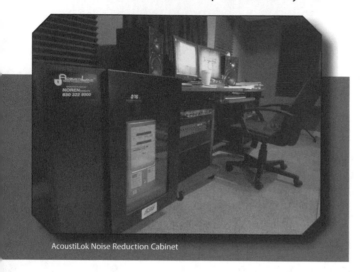

AcoustiLok Noise Reduction Cabinet

Lighting

What does light have to do with sound? Your body operates with a balance of your senses; limiting or disabling one of your senses will cause the others to become more sensitive. When dealing with sound, you want to heighten your sense of hearing, and one way to do this is by working in areas with low lighting. It helps your ears focus. Indirect lighting works best to set the right mood and also to reduce unwanted glare from your computer monitors.

The Ten Sound Editing Commandments

Go Forth and Edit!

SOUND EDITING IS THE PROCESS of trimming, cutting, and preparing audio. In addition to keeping a list of all the recording mistakes I've made over the years, I've also kept a list of my editing mistakes. Here are the Ten Sound Editing Commandments for editing sound effects:

■ TEN SOUND EDITING COMMANDMENTS

1. Thou Shalt Name Thy Sound
2. Thou Shalt Save Often
3. Thou Shalt Work Non-Destructively
4. Thou Shalt Copy Thy Media Files from Thy Sessions
5. Thou Shalt Crop Thy Sound
6. Thou Shalt Honor the Stereo Field to Keep It Even
7. Thou Shalt Not Cut Off Thy Sound
8. Thou Shalt Remove Unholy Clicks and Pops from Thy Sound
9. Thou Shalt Use Wisdom in Making Thy Cut
10. Thou Shalt Protect Thy Ears

Commandment 1

Thou Shalt Name Thy Sound

Every sound needs a descriptive name. There is no visual reference — such as a thumbnail picture — to indicate the sound inside a file. Your only reference will be the file name. Be as descriptive as you can when naming the file, but try to keep the name down to a few words or abbreviations. Long file names do not always translate across platforms and disc-burning software. Metadata has given sound editors a whole new way to search for sounds beyond the file names, but we'll discuss that in the next chapter.

When editing sound effects, you should name the sound what it is and not what it was. You will undoubtedly find material that doesn't sound like what was recorded but instead sounds like it should be called something else. Name the file based on what it sounds like. For example, if you record a bulldozer with large treads and it sounds like a military tank rolling by, name the sound TANK. Or even better, name the file BULLDOZER, TANK.

Remember, the brain can't see what was recorded. It can only interpret what it hears based on its memories of other sounds. This concept is your first step into the world of sound design. As you deprogram your mind to forget what it sees with your eyes and reprogram it to see with your ears, you will find a whole new dimension to the sound effects recording process. After some experience with editing files using this principle, you'll find yourself thinking differently while recording. And more importantly, you'll start hearing differently.

Commandment 2

Thou Shalt Save Often

In the computer world, everyone is very familiar with the word "crash." Just typing the word sends shivers up my fingers. There is nothing more frustrating than creating the right mix or building the right sound … and then the program freezes up, or even worse the computer shuts down. We've all been there. And if you haven't, take warning: It *will* happen. I've lost hundreds of sound effects and mixes to computer and software crashes.

Your best defense against losing your work is to save as often as you can. This commandment applies more to looping and multi-track workstations. A good habit to get into is to save (CTRL+S in most applications) every time you make a significant change to the session. This could include major level changes, plug-in adjustments, or rearrangements of the tracks.

Some workstations offer automatic saving features and can create back-up sessions for you. Although this is great start, it's not always a failsafe solution. Anytime you've reached a milestone in your work, make sure you save.

Note: Saving a file in an audio editor can sometimes prevent you from using all of your levels of undos.

Commandment 3
Thou Shalt Work Non-Destructively

Looping and multitrack workstations offer a completely non-destructive environment to work in. Sometimes, however, you are given the option to open a file from the workstation into an audio editor to make changes. The changes that you make to the file in your editor will be permanent upon saving the file and, therefore, destructive. Some workstations offer you the option of opening a copy of the file in the audio editor. The copied file is then saved to your hard drive with the same name as the original file, but usually with a suffix such as "Take 2."

Always Work with a Copy
In an audio editor, you are working with the original file. Copy the file, paste it into a new data window, and experiment from there so that you leave your original file unchanged. You can also use the "Save As" feature in your workstation to save changes to your audio without affecting the original file. "Save As" closes the original file (leaving it unchanged) and opens a saved copy of the file.

At the Chop Shop, we never edit the original files that we record. To begin with, the recorded files are backed up on network servers and also burned to DVDs at the end of each day. Next the files are opened in Sound Forge; then the editor selects the sound to work with and copies and pastes it into a new data window (pasting a file into a new window can be done in Sound Forge with the short-cut CTRL+E). The new file is saved as the final edited sound effect. Finally, a marker is placed on the section of the original file that was copied to keep track of what sounds were used.

Save Different Versions of Your Sessions

When working with looping and multitrack workstations, save different session files for different mixes. This leaves a back door for revisiting a previous mix in case you head in a wrong direction. For example, if you have a mix of sound effects for a military battle scene and would like to change the perspective on some of the sounds, you should save the current session, then save a copy of the session and add an identifying tag to the name.

For example:
AMBIENCE BATTLEFIELD CLOSE PERSPECTIVE 01
AMBIENCE BATTLEFIELD DISTANT PERSPECTIVE 01

In the case of different versions of the same type of sound, you can just increase the session file number by one.

For example:
GUNSHOT PISTOL 9MM EXTERIOR 01
GUNSHOT PISTOL 9MM EXTERIOR 02

Commandment 4

Thou Shalt Copy Thy Media Files from Thy Sessions

Some looping and multitrack workstations give you the option of copying the media used in a session and saving it in the same folder as the session file. This can be very useful for a number of reasons. Hard drives can quickly become cluttered with files, folders, temp files, scratch sounds, and other digital clutter. As a result, you might inadvertently delete files that were used in your session the next time you clean out your hard drive.

Remember, a session file is just an edit list — it only points to where the files are stored on your hard drive. By copying the used media to the same folder as your session file, you are keeping together all of the necessary components for working with that session again. This also provides one convenient location from which to burn a back-up disc of the session with all of the media.

When taking a session to another workstation or someone else's studio, you must bring the media files as well. But sharing or transporting sessions is a little more complicated than that. First you need to make sure that you are not using a session file that has been saved in a version of the software that is newer than the software of the studio or workstation you're moving to. For instance, although a session from Vegas 6.0 will work in Vegas 7.0, a session from Vegas 7.0 will not work in Vegas 6.0. You also need to verify that the other studio or workstation has the same plug-ins that you used in the session. If not, you won't be able to use those plug-ins or effects.

Copying media files from sessions is a perfect way of future-proofing your mix. You'll be able to tweak the session or even add or remove tracks at a later date. And with 5.1 surround sound becoming more and more popular, you never know when you might want to revisit an old stereo session and remix it into a surround mix.

Commandment 5
Thou Shalt Crop Thy Sound

When saving your sound effects as an audio file, be sure to remove any silence from the beginning and end of the file. This will save hard drive space and ensure that when the file is loaded into a session's edit point, the sound starts immediately. Also, clicks and pops can occur when a file's first or last sample is above or below the zero line. Use an auto trim/crop function to ensure that the head and tail of a file start at zero.

Multiple takes of a sound effect should be saved as separate, individual files. In the days of CD audio sound effects, multiple sounds were placed on the same track with indexes that marked where each sound started. When the files were ripped into a workstation, all the sounds of a track would appear in one file. This would create an extra step in laying the sound into a session because you would have to trim or cut the file to start at the sound you wanted and trim or cut the remaining sounds in the file. With CD-ROM, DVD-ROM, and hard drive sound effects collections becoming more and more standard, each sound effect is now produced as an individual file.

There are a few ground rules for what constitutes an individual file. Sound effects in a sequence, such as a dishwasher that starts, runs, and stops, would be saved as one sound effect in one file.

For example:
DISHWASHER TURN ON RUN OFF 01.WAV

A loop of a dishwasher running could be pulled from this sound effect and created as a separate file.

For example:
DISHWASHER RUN LOOP 01.WAV

A door that opens and closes would be saved as two files:

For example:
DOOR OPEN 01.WAV
DOOR CLOSE 01.WAV

A key inserted into a door that opens, after which someone walks through the doorway and then closes the door, would be saved as one file:

For example:
DOOR KEY UNLOCK OPEN WALK THROUGH CLOSE 01.WAV

A shotgun firing three shots in succession (i.e., overlapping sound) would be saved as a single file.

For example:
SHOTGUN BENELLI 12 GAUGE THREE SHOTS 01.WAV

The same shotgun firing three single shots (i.e., shot, pause, shot) would be saved as three files.

For example:
SHOTGUN BENELLI 12 GAUGE SINGLE SHOT 01.WAV
SHOTGUN BENELLI 12 GAUGE SINGLE SHOT 02.WAV
SHOTGUN BENELLI 12 GAUGE SINGLE SHOT 03.WAV

Keeping your sound effects as separate files will speed up the process of searching for and retrieving sounds and laying them into your sessions.

Commandment 6

Thou Shalt Honor the Stereo Field to Keep It Even

When editing stereo sounds, make sure that the stereo field is balanced. Ambiences and other continuous sounds can sound lopsided if the stereo field is off balance. If the sound appears more in the left channel, lower the left channel's volume so that it is balanced with the right channel or vice versa. This will result in a naturally balanced sound.

For other off-balance sounds where the stereo aspect is not critically important, you can convert the file from stereo to mono. Use a channel conversion tool or simply select the channel that you wish to keep and copy it to the other channel. Keep in mind, the exact same sound will now be on both channels. Even though there are two channels (left and right), the sound is now mono. When mixing the two channels together using a channel conversion tool, be sure to check for phasing problems.

Off-balance sounds can be used with corresponding images in cinema. They can also be used as an effect like a force field's energy modulation continuously panning from left to right. But typically it is best to keep the sound centered and balanced. This will give you greater control over how the sound is used later on.

Commandment 7

Thou Shalt Not Cut Off Thy Sound

Sound effects should have a natural start and finish. Cutting off the sound on either side will draw attention to the fact that it was edited. The best edit is one that is not noticed. It takes practice, but in time you will begin to develop a sixth sense for finding a natural point to begin and end the sound effect.

Starting Points

For the start of the sound, find the point where the sound begins. This can be tricky when you are working with sounds that have a slow build to them. You can use fades in moderation at the beginning to ramp the sound, but it's best to keep these ramps short. For impacts, gunshots, or other sounds with an obvious starting point, make the cut right before the spike in the waveform.

When dealing with sounds that have errors or undesirable material at the beginning, start a short fade after the imperfection in the sound. For example, let's say you have a recording of someone running on ice and then sliding with their feet. If you only want to keep the sliding sound, you'll need to cut out the footsteps, but there might be the sound of one last step at the start of the slide. To correct this, begin a short fade after the step for a clean ice scrape/slide sound.

Ending Points

Finding a good starting point is relatively easy. The ending point is where things can get a little hairy. The general rule here is to allow the sound to finish, then cut or fade. For example, if you break a glass, let the debris settle before you cut. You'll be surprised how long a single piece of debris can keep moving.

Some sounds do not end or go on too long, such as a Jet Ski pass-by. The sound you want might last for only a few seconds, but you'll probably still be able to hear the sound of the motor receding into the distance for another minute and the background of the environment (waves splashing, other boats, etc.) starts to become noticeable. Let the event happen and then fade the sound for a few seconds so that it sends the Jet Ski off into infinity. Doing this will reduce any noticeable background sounds and still keep the main focal point of the sound effect.

If you have a sound that never ends, find a suitable length for the sound and then start your fade. Sound effects fades are much different from music fades. A song might fade for anywhere from eight to 20 seconds. A normal fade for a sound effect is one to four seconds. If you are working with the sound of a machine that has no start-up or shut-off, fade the sound up for one second, give the sound a duration of a minute or two (or longer if you need), and then fade the sound out for four seconds.

Avoid conflicting sounds during your fades. If you are fading a sound and during the fade another sound is heard, the fade becomes noticeable. For example, if you start to fade a crowd clapping and just before the end of the fade someone whistles, the effect of the fade is lost. Keep your fades clean and free of last-second sounds.

Sound effects should be edited so they can be used more than once. Don't just think of the immediate use for the sound effect. Try to keep the sound as objective as possible. This will give you more control over its use in your production.

Commandment 8
Thou Shalt Remove Unholy Clicks and Pops from Thy Sound

In the analog days of editing, edit points were easy to mask. In the digital age, it's all about the math. Because the waveform is made up of numbers (namely sample rates), you need to make your cuts in the right spots on the mathematical grid. Make sure that your sound is free of digital hiccups and glitches.

Clicks and Pops
Always make your cuts at the zero line. It's imperative. Clicks and pops occur when the waveform is cut at any other point. Higher sample rates have greater resolutions and therefore more sample

points where you can perform edits. This gives you a little grace to make your edits at points slightly above or below the zero line — but not much.

Low frequencies are more difficult to cut around than higher frequencies. Because they are larger waves with peaks farther apart, they have fewer crossings at the zero line. Higher frequencies are thinner, their peaks closer together, so they have more crossings at the zero line.

Cross Fading

Cross fading is a technique that can reduce unwanted clicks and pops. Some digital editors allow you to select a portion of the waveform and insert it at another point. During the insertion, the two edges are cross-faded to eliminate any clicks and pops. You can manually determine how fast and steep the cross fades will be.

Digital Click Removal

There are plug-ins that automatically search for and remove clicks from an audio file. These plug-ins can be helpful but are not 100% accurate. They can also cause aliasing at the restored click point. The best defense against clicks is to make the cut at the zero line.

Digital Errors

Digital errors can occur when recording to a tape format like DAT or when digitizing the material off the DAT tape into your workstation. Hard disk recordings now offer fewer errors than their tape-based predecessors. File corruption can also account for glitches in digital audio. You may need to go back to the original source to correct these glitches, or edit them out altogether.

Commandment 9

Thou Shalt Use Wisdom in Making Thy Cut

Knowing where to make the cut is what will make you a great editor. There are many things to consider, such as pacing, context, and removing mistakes. What comes before and after the cut can also determine how the cut should be made. The idea behind an edit is to join two sections together by removing or inserting another section. Remember, the cut only works if it goes unnoticed.

Pacing for Time

Timing within the sound effect can give a sense of grace, urgency, or even a feeling of momentum. The recording itself most often determines a sound's timing, but good editing can take a recording and alter the pace. When there is more than one component to the sound effect, it's also important to decide the appropriate duration for each component relative to the others.

If there is silence before and after the cut point, all you need to worry about is the timing between the sections. For example, pulling the pin from a grenade, tossing the grenade, and the explosion are essentially three separate sounds that make up one event. If you are joining separate pre-edited sounds to create one sound, pacing becomes the issue. Simply cutting these sounds back to back can make them rushed and like a cartoon sound or cheap video game.

A short duration between the pin being pulled and the grenade being thrown creates a sense of urgency. A longer duration can appear more dramatic and calculated. The duration between the throw and the landing of the grenade communicates distance. A short duration makes it sound like the grenade landed nearby, and a longer duration naturally suggests a much longer toss. The timing of when the grenade explodes can also add suspense.

You can use pace to indicate speed. For example, the recording of a single fan blade swoosh can be copied and the copies placed close together to create the sense of a fast speed — or farther apart for a slowed-down effect. With footsteps, you can edit to communicate tempo. You can make the person sound in a hurry, relaxed, or even injured. Timing is everything.

All of these things should be considered when cutting for pace. Don't rush your sounds unless it's for an effect. Have a flow to your edits within a single sound effect.

Dealing with Mistakes

Mistakes naturally occur during the recording process. Sometimes the mistake falls in the middle of the sound, but the beginning and end of the file are fine. Rather than discard the entire sound, you can remove the unwanted content.

For example, if you drop a ceramic bowl and one of the pieces of debris hits a metallic object nearby that is clearly not part of the effect, you will need to remove that metallic hit to make your sound effect pure. Play the sound until you hear the unwanted impact, which will appear as a spike in the waveform. Select the audio with the metallic hit and delete it. Next, check the edit point for clicks and pops. Some audio editors allow you to make a selection and preview the edit by skipping the selection during playback. This can be very useful when you're trying to determine where to best cut a sound.

Another example of a mistake could be a car horn honking in the background. If the take is a constant sound effect (for example, an ambience), you can cut out the section with the car horn and cross-fade the two remaining sections. This will blend the cut and make it more natural. If the sound is not constant (for example, a plane flying overhead), you'll have to get a little more crafty.

Recently I recorded the sound of a bowling ball being smashed into a television set. The sound was great, but the television set rolled over and hit the mic stand during the take, making the second half of the sound unusable. To correct this, I recorded a couple of additional takes of the television being smashed. In the edit, I kept the first half of the original recording where the ball broke through the face of the television. I then added one of the additional takes of the smash to the second half. The sound effect became one seamless sound.

Doppler Effect

When a plane or other vehicle passes by, there is a change in pitch known as the Doppler effect. Named after its discoverer, Australian physicist Christian Doppler, this effect is the result of a build-up of high frequencies from an approaching object and a transition to lower frequencies as the object passes. This is similar to when a boat passes in the water. The boat pushes small waves in front of its bow and large waves in its wake. A sound's "bow wave" and wake are similar.

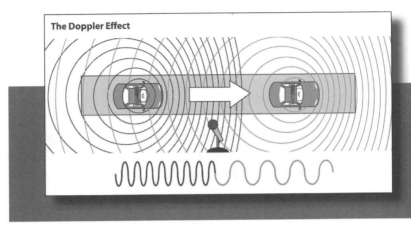

The Doppler Effect

In this diagram, we can see that when a car approaches a point, higher than normal frequencies are heard first. As the vehicle passes, there is a sudden shift to lower frequencies. We're probably all most aware of the Doppler effect when we hear the change in pitch of a siren as a police car or ambulance speeds by.

Cutting a sound during the Doppler effect can expose the cut point. A straight cut would result in two different pitches being joined together and the sound would jump from one pitch to the next — a noticeable error. In some cases, a gradual cross fade can mask the cut and help blend the two pitches to sound like one smooth, constant change in pitch. However, cross fading during the Doppler effect is not always successful.

Commandment 10

Thou Shalt Protect Thy Ears

It's all fun and games until you lose your hearing. Then the game is over.

When I first got out of college, I found work installing a sound system for a church. This church was huge! It sat more than 10,000 people, and we used over 20 miles of cable to wire up the speakers and the sound board. One day, my supervisor's digital watch alarm went off. He didn't seem fazed by it. After about ten seconds of the alarm, I asked if he was going to turn it off. He smiled, turned it off, and told me that he had a hard time hearing his alarm. Turns out, as a seasoned audio professional and musician he had exposed his ears to dangerously loud levels over the years. As a result, he had hearing loss around 4KHz — the same frequency as his watch's alarm.

Long-term exposure to high volumes will damage your ears permanently. Once you lose your hearing, you can never get it back. If you are serious about being in the recording industry for a long time, you'll need to protect ears. Louder does not equal better. Always listen at moderate levels.

How Loud Is Too Loud?

Good question. Unfortunately, there really is no answer. There is no specification for how "loud" a digital audio file should be. You can certainly tell when a sound is overcompressed and has no dynamics. Sounds that contain noticeable audible hiss when the volume is increased should be lowered in volume. But there is no magic number — more of a guideline.

Loud is an irrelevant term during the editing process. Level is a far more important term. Peak meters help you determine whether or not the sound is clipping, but VU meters really come into play when

Dorrough Meters in Action

you're trying to find the overall volume of the sound. Playback meters on your DAW can help you understand where the sound's volume is, but they are not always 100% accurate. Nothing beats a real-world set of analog meters. Perhaps the most respected name in analog metering is Dorrough. Their meters are found in professional studios around the world and offer simultaneous peak and VU metering, as well as phase indication.

You can edit at a moderate volume and still deal with sounds that have intense levels, like explosions. Don't listen to every sound at full volume. High-pitch frequencies do not need to be normalized to appear as loud as a normalized gunshot. If you edit for long periods of time and your ears begin to hurt (even when you're not working), you are listening at dangerous volumes. When in doubt, turn it down.

How Loud Should a Sound Effect Be?
When creating sound effects, you should maintain a good dynamic range in the sound. Keep this dynamic range and normalize to zero (provided that normalizing does not increase the noise level). The sound effects can later be balanced with the rest of the audio in your productions.

It's a good idea to look at the waveforms of DVD movies and music CDs. The waveform of a film is not what you would expect: It is considerably smaller than the waveforms of music albums. Sound effects like a gunshot sound very loud in a film, but they appear in the waveform at much lower levels than, say, a snare drum hit from a pop song. This is due to a healthy balance of dynamics and compression.

The Waveform of the Film *Star Wars*

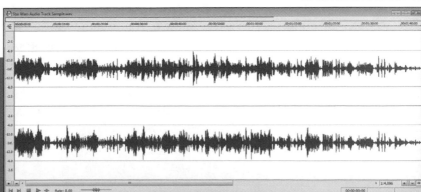

It's interesting to note that if you compare the waveform of a song recorded in the 1980s to the waveform of a song recorded in the 2000s, you'll see a huge difference in levels. That difference is a loss of dynamics. And that loss is a result of what is called the Loudness War.

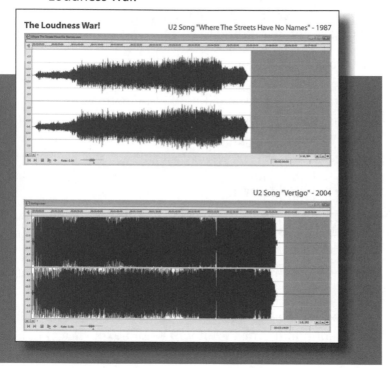

Loudness War

In the early 1990s, engineers started to push the limits of digital recording by using up the entire range of CD audio. This meant that the songs were compressed and mastered all the way up to zero. What followed was a series of record producers asking engineers to push the compression limits to make their records sound louder over the radio than other records. In the end, the record producers made their money at the expense of the music's quality.

Unfortunately, there is no set standard for overall volume. Some television networks and radio stations sound louder than others. The same is true with DVD movies and music CDs. If anything, there is an average range of acceptable level. But it's all relative.

Using the Ten Sound Editing Commandments

In every studio at the Chop Shop there is a piece of paper with a single word: LISTEN. This is the editing mantra. It is the encapsulation of all ten sound editing commandments. Listen to the sound by applying the following steps and you will end up with great sound effects.

The Editing Mantra

L – I – S – T – E – N

L - Listen Critically
I - Identify Clicks, Pops, and Errors
S - Signal Process (EQ and Compression)
T - Trim/Crop the File
E - Examine Fade-Ins/Fade-Outs at the Zero Line
N - Normalize/Name File

When editing a sound file, this acronym can come in handy to help you remember the basic processes involved in preparing audio files.

Listen Critically
Start by listening to the file for sonic integrity. Ask the simple question "does this sound good?" "Is this sound useful or practical?" If the answer is 'no', then do not use the sound.

Identify Clicks, Pops, and Errors
If there are noticeable clicks, pops, or errors, edit the waveform to correct them. Every sound must be free of these imperfections.

Signal Process (EQ and Compression)
Apply equalization to balance the sound. Generally, subtractive equalization is used to reduce unwanted background noise or intrusive frequencies. Additive equalization is used to boost or enhance frequencies that are lacking or to give a particular effect (for example, bass rumble). Light compression should be used to keep the sound balanced in terms of amplitude.

Trim/Crop the File

Each file should start immediately and end when the sound is finished. Use a trim/crop function to automatically perform this operation, or fade the file in and out manually.

Examine Fade-Ins/Fade-Outs at the Zero Line

After trimming/cropping or fading the file, examine the very first sample at the start and end of each file. This will allow you to identify clicks and pops that can occur when the file starts or ends above or below the zero line. Fade the offending samples to the zero line to correct this.

Normalize/Name File

Normalize the audio to -.5dB. You don't need to normalize ambiences or sound beds; peak points anywhere from -18dB to -6dB are acceptable for these types of sounds. Finally, name the sound as descriptively as possible and embed the file with metadata using expressive keywords.

CHAPTER SIXTEEN

File Naming and Metadata

The Importance of a Detailed Database

O NCE YOU BEGIN RECORDING AND editing sound effects, you'll be surprised how many sounds start to pile up on your hard drive. Soon you'll notice how difficult it can be to find the right sound amongst a sea of file names. For this reason, you should use a good file naming system and incorporate metadata into your files.

File Name Structure

A file name structure enables files to be grouped alphabetically/categorically and can offer vital information at a glance. It is imperative that this information be extremely descriptive and precise. A good file structure will let you find the file you're looking quickly and easily. Think of playing 20 Questions, but only use a couple of key words.

There are three main file naming systems that are commonly used today:
- Category-Based File Names
- Effect-Based File Names
- Numeric-Based Files Names

In the end, you'll have to find what works best for you. Here is a closer look at the file structures:

Category-Based File Names

Most sound effects are grouped into top-level categories. Professional sound effects libraries vary from one to the next and there is no standard for categories. A category should define all of the sounds that could be found under its heading.

In a category-based file name, the file is named in the following order:

1. Category
2. Noun
3. Verb
4. Description
5. Number (Zero-Filled)*

Zero-filled numbers have a zero in front of single-digit numbers (for example, 5 = 05). This addresses operating systems and search engines that would place the numbers out of order based on the first digit.

For example: 1,10,11,12,13,14,15,16,17,18,19,2,20,21,22, etc.

Placing a zero in front of each single-digit number corrects this.
For example: 01,02,03,04,05,06,07,08,09,10,11,12,etc.

The noun should be a single word or two- or three-word phrase for the main object creating the sound. In general, you should use simple present tense for verbs (for example, "run" instead of "running"). Also, avoid conjunctions and prepositions (and, with, of, from, etc.). The description should be limited to as few words as possible and should fill in any important information to be considered when searching for the file.

Here are some examples of category-based file names:

TECHNOLOGY BUTTON PRESS DVD PLAYER EJECT TRAY OPEN 01
TECHNOLOGY BUTTON PRESS DVD PLAYER EJECT TRAY CLOSE 01

FOOTSTEPS TENNIS SHOE SINGLE STEP LEFT HARD WOOD FLOOR 01
FOOTSTEPS TENNIS SHOE RUN HARD WOOD FLOOR 01
CRASH METAL POTS PANS 01
IMPACT BULLET HIT METAL 01
FOLEY LID UNSCREW PLASTIC BOTTLE 01

Category-based file names can offer the most logical solution for manual searches. The names are inherently long but can offer key information at a single glance. Once you have established your own categories, you could shorten file names by using abbreviations. Here are some examples of category names and abbreviations:

AMBIENCE — AMB
ANIMALS — ANM
CARTOONS — CAR
CRASHES — CRASH
CROWDS — CRWD
EMERGENCY — EMER
ELECTRONIC — ELEC
EXPLOSIONS — EXP
FIRE — FIR
FOLEY — FOL
FOOTSTEPS — FOOT
HORROR — HOR
HOUSEHOLD — HOU
HUMANS — HUM
IMPACTS — IMP
INDUSTRY — IND
MULTIMEDIA — MULT
MUSICAL — MUS
OFFICE — OFC
SCIENCE FICTION — SCIFI
SPORTS & LEISURE — SPL
TECHNOLOGY — TECH
TRANSPORTATION — TRAN
WARFARE — WAR
WATER — WAT
WEATHER — WEA

For example:
AMB KITCHEN INDUSTRIAL
EXP BOMB DEBRIS
IMP ANVIL METAL

You can also use underscores "_" to separate the fields.

For example:
AMB_KITCHEN_INDUSTRIAL 01
EXP_BOMB_DEBRIS 01
IMP_ANVIL_METAL 01

You should decide on a letter case for your file names and keep all of your files consistent:

All Caps:
HOR_MONSTER_GROWL 01
MUS_DRUMROLL_SNARE 01
WEA_LIGHTNING_CRASH 01

Lowercase:
hor_monster_growl 01
mus_drumroll_snare 01
wea_lightning_crash 01

Title Case:
Hor_Monster_Growl 01
Mus_Drumroll_Snare 01
Wea_Lightning_Crash 01

Mixing up the letter cases can make reading the names difficult, especially when you are dealing with hundreds or thousands of files.

For example:
technology button press dvd player eject tray open 01
Technology Button Press Dvd Player Eject Tray Close 01
FOOTSTEPS TENNIS SHOE SINGLE STEP LEFT HARD WOOD FLOOR 01
footsteps tennis shoe run hard wood floor 01
CRASH METAL POTS PANS 01
Impact Metal Bullet 01
foley lid unscrew plastic bottle 01

Effect-Based File Names

Effect-based file names place the noun (i.e., the effect or prop) first. This can be useful when sorting through category folders but can slow down the manual search process if all of the sound effects are in one folder. You would, for example, end up with ambience files throughout the folder rather than grouped together in one place.

In an effect-based file name, the file is named in the following order:

1. Noun
2. Verb
3. Description
4. Number (Zero-Filled)

Here are some examples of effect-based file names:
BUTTON PRESS DVD PLAYER EJECT TRAY OPEN 01
BUTTON PRESS DVD PLAYER EJECT TRAY CLOSE 01
TENNIS SHOE SINGLE STEP LEFT HARD WOOD FLOOR 01
TENNIS SHOE RUN HARD WOOD FLOOR 01
METAL CRASH POTS PANS 01
METAL IMPACT BULLET 01
LID UNSCREW PLASTIC BOTTLE 01

Note that the Crash and Impact file names are changed so that the category is now the action.

Placing the noun first groups effects that are not in the same category. This can result in confusing manual searches.

For example:
DOOR OPEN CARGO BAY WAREHOUSE 01
DOOR OPEN OVEN 01
DOOR OPEN SPACESHIP ESCAPE HATCH 01
DOOR OPEN HOUSEHOLD 01

All "door" effects are grouped together, but the group is a mix of categories, include Household, Industrial, and Science Fiction.

You should avoid naming files with the verb first. In this case, unrelated objects will be grouped together simply because the basic action is similar.

For example:
OPEN CAR DOOR 01
OPEN JAR PICKLE 01
OPEN LAPTOP COMPUTER 01
OPEN LETTER MAIL PAPER 01

As with nouns, the verb grouping mixes several categories, including Household, Office, Technology, and Vehicles.

Numeric-Based File Names

Numeric-based file names are used to reference a data sheet or track list. They can also be used when metadata is the primary source of searchable information. There are two schools of thought for naming these files. The first includes an abbreviation of the category or effect.

For example:
HUMAN LAUGH FEMALE ADULT GIGGLE 19
would become
HUM_LAUGH 0019 or HUM 0019

The second approach is simply a number for the file name.

For example:
HUMAN LAUGH FEMALE ADULT GIGGLE 19
would simply become
0019

The first approach provides clues as to the sound effect in the file. The second approach is commonly used in stock photography and clip art but isn't very prevalent in the professional audio world. Numbers don't mean anything to an editor who has a project open with hundreds of files that have no descriptive elements in their file names.

Metadata

The inclusion of metadata has drastically changed sound effects search engines and other file management programs. NetMix and Soundminer are the two companies that are blazing the trail in metadata embedding and searching for audio files. Metadata is stored as header information in BWAV files. Any WAV can be turned into a BWAV by simply adding metadata to the file. Some DAWs allow you to search for metadata inside their software, while others work in tandem with external search software.

When inputting keywords into the metadata description field, be sure to use as many words as you can to best describe the sound effect. The search software will look not only at the description as a whole, but also at individual words. A search for the word "CHAIR" would retrieve all files with the word "CHAIR" in the description field.

For example:
EMERGENCY WHEEL **CHAIR** ROLL BY 01
HORROR ELECTRIC **CHAIR** ZAPS 01
HOUSEHOLD **CHAIR** SLIDE TILE FLOOR 01

This can be helpful if you're looking for variations of a sound that appears in more than one effect. The word "SPLASH" would return the following:

WATER **SPLASH** ANCHOR DROP BOAT 01
WATER **SPLASH** DIVE HUMAN 01
WATER **SPLASH** DOLPHIN JUMP 01

In short, metadata has improved search capabilities immensely. It allows you to use more information to describe the file but at the same time keep your file names shorter. File names now play a less significant role, because manual searches are now replaced with advanced search engines based on metadata.

CHAPTER SEVENTEEN

Sound Design

Faders, Plug-Ins, and Fairy Dust

RECORDING IS VERY TECHNICAL AND more science than art. Sound design and mixing, however, are far more art than science.

Sound design is all about creativity. Period. There is no right way, only better ways. Let your imagination run wild when trying to figure out solutions for different sounds. You've reached the apex of your creativity when you can think of a sound in your head (never heard before by human ears) and recreate that same sound using real-world elements. Until then, let's get you started with some basic principles.

Start with the Freshest Ingredients

Working with clean source material is the secret to great sound design. The work that you've done during the recording and editing processes will really pay off here. At this point, you have all of your elements recorded, edited, and named. Now you have all of the paints you need to create your masterpiece.

Complicated events, like a twister ravaging a trailer park, contain hundreds of intricate sounds playing in a symphony of destruction. These effects are recorded as separate, isolated sounds to be mixed and combined in the design process. It is far too difficult, not to mention dangerous, to record a real tornado. Even if you did achieve a safe recording of the event, you would find that the real sound is less dynamic than a sound that has been designed using pre-recorded effects blended together. The result can be pure magic: sounds whirling around, metal scraping, glass crashing, and chest-pounding rumbles.

Source material for sound design should be sounds that are free of background noise, clicks, pops, and mistakes. If these are in the files, they will show up in the sound that you are designing. I've done many mixes where I had more than a hundred elements playing at once. Just when the mix is close to being finished, I notice a click or a glitch in the sound. The problem is — which element?

With a grimace, I go back and solo each track until I find the offender. I've learned my lesson over the years. Now I make sure that every sound is perfect before I experiment with it. Beware in particular of hiss and noise that might be in your elements. If each element has noise, that noise will compound as more elements are stacked on top of each other.

Dynamics

Dynamics is the relationship between high volumes and low volumes. Good dynamics means that there is a natural high point and low point, that there is a difference between soft and loud. Compression should be used sparingly so as to retain the dynamics of the sound effect.

Sound effects for movies do not need to be nearly as loud or compressed as sound effects for radio. In a film's soundtrack, a myriad of sound effects are playing in harmony with one another. There is balance and dynamics to the mix. Sound effects for film should retain as much dynamics as possible. Heavy compression is not needed here. Leave any compression up to the re-recording mixer during the final mix of the film.

In radio land, the sound effect will probably be played by itself, with nothing to mask the noise in the background of the sound.

So these sound effects should be clean and have a good level of compression to them. In addition, radio stations heavily compress their signals to help compete with car noise, traffic, and work environments that the listener may be exposed to. This heavy compression will cause the sound effect to become squashed, resulting in a greater loss of dynamics. From the listener's perspective, this is not as noticeable on the radio as it would be in a movie theater.

Understand that once heavy compression is applied to a sound, it cannot be taken out. However, if a sound effect has good dynamics to begin with, it can be used with those dynamics or compressed further if needed in a mix. It is a knee-jerk reaction for some editors to overcompress their sound effects. Avoid this pitfall. Less is more.

Scratch Tracks

Getting the sound you're after might require the use of scratch tracks. A scratch track is a track used for referencing and timing but not intended for the final mix. Scratch tracks are fairly commonplace in music recording. A vocalist might lay down a scratch track of a song's vocals to help guide the rest of the musicians through the song during tracking. Later, the scratch track is replaced with a final, more polished track. Scratch tracks are useful for timing out effects or sequences when the correct sound effect is not yet finished. They can save time and improve workflow by allowing the creative process to continue without necessitating that one track be completely finished before moving forward.

Temp Mixes/Bouncing Tracks

The practice of bouncing tracks comes from a limitation caused by multitrack recorders with a set number of tracks. This is not as common in the digital age, but some DAWs still set a limit on the number of tracks you can work with. When you run out of tracks to record to, you can mix some of the tracks down to one track to free up tracks. For example, if you have an eight-track recorder (do these exist anymore?) and you've used up tracks one through seven for drums, you can mix those seven tracks down to the eighth track. Now you have freed up seven tracks to lay down guitars, bass, vocals, etc.

Bouncing tracks can be helpful when working with complex sound effects that have hundreds of elements. Even if empty tracks are still available, you might need to render out multiple tracks to a single track because of the complexity of the mix or as a result of CPU overload. Either way, bouncing tracks simplifies the mixing process.

Select tracks that are similar. If you are working on a haunted house sound effect, try mixing all of the wood creaks to a single track. Then mix ghost sounds to another track. Continue doing this until you have grouped all like sounds to new tracks. Now, instead of dealing with a hundred tracks, you might be down to a dozen or even fewer. Remember to save your temp mix sessions so that you can make adjustments and re-render if necessary.

Subgroups

Subgroups are another way of managing multiple tracks. Instead of rendering temp mixes, you bus the tracks to a subgroup, where a single fader will now control the level of the entire group. With subgroups, you'll still need to create submixes within the group. For instance, a drum kit can be subgrouped as a whole, but if the snare is too loud, the snare track has to be dealt with, not the subgroup.

Exaggeration Versus Reproduction

Sound design is not about faithfully reproducing a sound — that's why it's called design. Recording is more about faithful reproduction. Sound design is about creating a new sound or group of sounds, such as an entire film soundtrack. Designed sounds are usually exaggerated for effect, but that doesn't always mean over the top. Sometimes a sound is exaggerated with silence or muted sounds.

Shifting focus is a common sound design technique. The responsibility for this falls more to the mixer of the film, but a sound designer can zero in on a specific sound the same way that a cinematographer can shift the focus of the camera. The sound's volume itself does not necessarily need to be increased. The effect can be achieved by merely lowering the volume of the accompanying tracks.

Layering

Sounds can be layered on top of themselves to make them sound bigger or busier. You can also layer a sound and change the pitch of some of the layers to suggest depth or for a special effect. Layering can also be used to build environments or sounds that are difficult to record (like that tornado).

Using different or like sounds together allows you to create the impossible. Sounds that might not seem to fit together can be mixed to make a fantastic sound effect. One of my favorite types of sounds to make is steam punk creations (i.e. Jules Verne style inventions). Often I'll go through my junk folders and grab odd sound effects that might be fairly useless by themselves, like belt buckle clinks, small metal creaks, and wood stresses. I throw all of the files into ACID and build some of the coolest-sounding inventions. It's amazing what a little elbow grease and imagination can produce.

Layering in Sony's Vegas

Layering sounds adds a third dimension to the sound effects process. Understanding that you can layer sounds in post will allow you to think differently when you are recording in the field.

Offset Layering

Using the same sound on multiple tracks at the same time will only make the same sound louder. To create layers using the same sound, you need to offset the audio on each track. For example, if you have a one-minute sound clip, cut the clip at ten-second intervals. Now copy the sound clip to additional tracks; in this case we will copy the sound clip to six tracks since we have six cuts. Use those cuts as the start of the audio on the different tracks. Extend the sounds on the tracks so that they each contain a full minute before looping.

Below is how it should be laid out. Each sound clip is placed at the beginning of each track, but each sound clip is cut so that it starts in the file ten seconds later than the previous track.

Track 1 — the sound clip starts 0 seconds into the file.
Track 2 — the sound clip starts 10 seconds into the file.
Track 3 — the sound clip starts 20 seconds into the file.
Track 4 — the sound clip starts 30 seconds into the file.
Track 5 — the sound clip starts 40 seconds into the file.
Track 6 — the sound clip starts 50 seconds into the file.

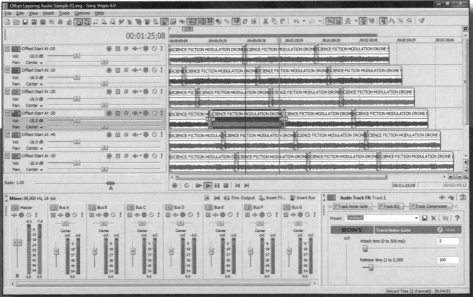

Offset Layering in Sony's Vegas

The result is one sound clip playing on six tracks at six completely different places in the audio file.

Offset layering will allow you to produce richer and more complex sounds from single sources, giving depth and fullness to an otherwise boring sound. It can also create complex sources for ambiences, science fiction, water, and other sounds.

Cross Fading

Sometimes you might have a sound effect that needs to be extended but you don't want to change the pitch of the sound. Time compression can help, but only in small amounts. Try copying and cross-fading the sound. Pay attention to the cross fade and select a point where it will seem natural. Cross fading can also quickly blend two different sounds together.

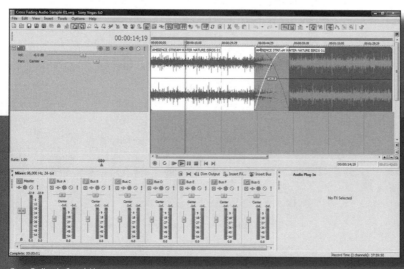

Cross Fading in Sony's Vegas

Looping

Looping is popular in music creation. A single measure of a drum beat and bass line can be looped over and over to create an entire section of a song. In the sound effects world, looping has many uses. It can extend sound samples that may have been shortened because of errors. It also helps create motors, engines, and other repeating sounds.

Loops do not have fades. Instead, the sound starts and ends in such a way that when it is looped there is no edit point. Care must be taken in selecting the start and end points of a sound to be looped. Loops should be perfect. The looping point should never be noticeable. When a proper loop is created, the sound will go on for as many times as it is looped, allowing you to determine just how long you want the sound to play.

Be sure to eliminate clicks and pops by starting and ending the waveform on the zero line. These points should complement each other. If the starting point is at the beginning of a peak, then the ending point should be at the end of the peak.

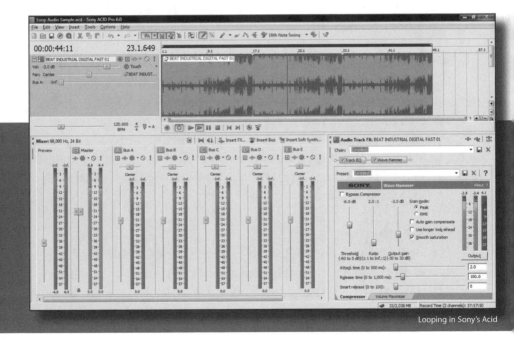

Looping in Sony's Acid

Pay attention to pitch and frequency when finding the loop points of engines and machines. Although these sounds might seem to be consistent, they may actually waver in their tone and pitch. When looped, these slight variations become noticeable and counteract the looping effect. You may need to experiment with your selection to determine a good loop point.

Mono sounds are easier to loop than stereo sounds because a mono sound is a single track and stereo sounds are two mono tracks. With stereo files, you need to find a point in time where both channels cross the zero line. Some audio editors have a snap-to-zero function that automatically searches the audio file to find the nearest point where the waveform intersects the zero line.

Cross-Fade Looping

Cross-fading a loop is sometimes necessary when a seamless loop point cannot be achieved. You will need to manually copy, paste, and cross-fade the loop each time you want the sound to repeat. Be sure to cross-fade the loops for the exact same duration to keep your sound timed properly. This technique is perfect for long, ethereal drones or beds that do not have natural loop points.

Key Framing

Key framing allows you to place anchor points on an envelope (also called a rubber band). In DAWs, these envelopes are used to automate volume, pan, mute, and bus sends. Using key frames gives you unlimited, precise control over your mix. Twenty years ago, this simple technology was only available on multimillion-dollar sound boards. Today, this technology is available for less than $100 at your local guitar store.

Reversing

Playing a sound in reverse usually produces a noticeably unnatural sound. However, if combined with a series of sounds or processed correctly, a reversed sound becomes believable. Reversing is great for creating a suction effect or a sound that pulls the listener in. For example, an explosion can be copied, reversed, and cross-faded with the original explosion to create the effect of a swelling or building effect before the actual blast. Fireballs, spaceship pass-bys, and arrow impacts can also benefit from this technique.

Looping a sound forward and reversed can be useful for creating drones or electronic beds. For these effects, use longer pieces (as much as 30 seconds) and cross-fade the reversed section completely on top of the forward section. The sound is heard forward and reversed at the same time.

Science fiction sounds can also be created this way. Instead of a long section, try shorter sections. This time, don't cross-fade the sound; instead, keep a hard cut for the loop point. The result — a wobbling back and forth from forward to reverse — can make a convincing generator, energy field, or other modulations. Shorter loop sections will result in higher-pitched sounds. Really short sections (think milliseconds) will create incredible buzzes and generator sounds when looped.

Vocalizing

Many sound designers keep a microphone nearby in the editing suite to record their voice and add it to the sound. This is called vocalizing. You can create a sound with your voice alone or vocalize to help sweeten another sound. If you're in a pinch and can't seem to find the right prop to create a specific sound you're looking for, grab a mic and experiment. Incidentally, Ben Burtt used this technique to create the foundation for R2-D2's voice. Never underestimate the sounds that your mouth can make.

Pitch Shifting

Lowering the pitch of a sound instantly gives it more weight and can help beef up explosions or gunshots. Pitching a sound insanely low, say -50 semitones, will create unearthly sounds. This is a popular technique for science fiction and horror effects.

For real-world sounds, pitch shifting should be used in moderation. Too much pitching is noticeable and ruins the effect. Great sound design is like great editing — it only works if it isn't noticed.

Be aware that when you lower the pitch of a sound, you are also lowering the high frequencies of that sound, which can result in a dull sound. Conversely, when you raise the pitch of a sound, you affect its low frequencies, making it sound thin and small.

Pitch Layering

One of my favorite sound design tricks is to pitch-layer a sound. To do this, take a sound into a loop-based DAW and copy the sound on multiple tracks — for the purposes of this example, we'll use four tracks. Leave Track 1 unchanged. Pitch-shift Track 2 by -3 semitones. Pitch-shift Track 3 by -6 semitones. Pitch-shift Track 4 by -9 semitones. Now play the file. The effect is a hybrid of the Doppler shift and can be used to extend and strengthen sounds. Now imagine 20 copies of the same sound that are pitch-layered.

Extreme amounts of this technique can create explosions that trail away into infinity; small amounts can suggest movement or passbys. Keep in mind that all of the files don't have to start at the same time. You can offset the tracks or even loop them for really cool science fiction pulses or modulations. The options are limited only by your imagination.

Worldizing

The generally preferred approach in sound effects is to record sound elements dry and process them later to match environments

Worldizing a Sound Effect inside a Bathroom

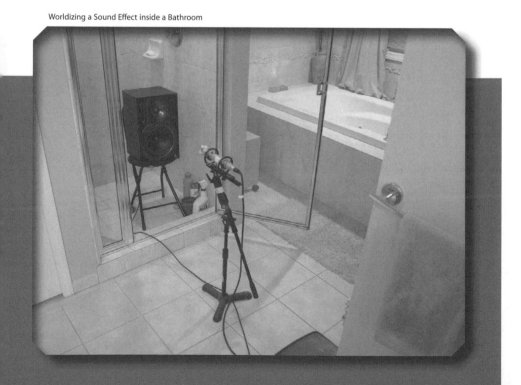

through plug-ins. Worldizing is an extension to this line of thinking. Rather than using digital or analog processors, worldizing involves playing the source recordings back through speakers that are placed in real-world locations and re-recording in the new environment. This gives the sound a whole new character and believability. The practice of worldizing goes back as far as the 1950s, but the term was first used by George Lucas and Walter Murch. Worldizing is primarily used in filmmaking.

Sweetening

Some sounds are dull in real life. Explosions can be one of these types of sounds. When this is the case, you'll need to add something to help sell the effect. This is called sweetening. Sweetening is the process of flavoring the sound with additional elements, equalization, or other effects. In the case of an explosion, the sound could be sweetened by increasing the low frequencies and layering a pitched-down gunshot underneath with some additional debris such as glass or wood.

Film sound designers commonly layer animal growls underneath explosions to make them sound ferocious. For an extreme example of animal growls in explosions, watch — or, rather, listen to — *The Mask Of Zorro*. When sweetening, be sure to preserve the integrity of the original sound. A cake's main ingredient isn't sugar, but it doesn't taste the same without it!

Mixing

Once you have your sounds laid out in your DAW, you'll need to mix them down to a final mono or stereo file. Mixing is just as much an art form as sound designing. It is very subjective and stylistic. In the end, you need to decide what the listener is intended to hear, when it should be heard, and how it should be balanced with the rest of the sounds.

Taste and judgment come into play at this stage. Every chef has access to the same ingredients, but not all chefs get their name on the building. Why? The head chef knows how to mix the ingredients in such a way that they become delicious. In the same way, you should aim to make tasty sound.

When you first start mixing, you'll instinctively want to push everything up in terms of level. Doing this will only create white noise. Everything full-on at once starts to sound like an ocean. Good mixing has dynamics. Instead of starting with your levels all the way up, try building a mix that sits around -18dB and work from there. This gives you lots of headroom to play with. Now your hits and impacts will sound bigger. Your lulls and valleys will create a balance.

Combining multiple sounds together can create overlap in the frequency spectrum. If you boost the low end on several tracks, the overall tone of the mix could sound muddy. Conversely, increasing the high frequencies on several tracks could result in a crisp and brittle sound. Create a balance with frequency as you would with levels. This will help produce ear-pleasing mixes.

Mastering

Mastering is the last step in the chain of creating a sound effect. It is important that the sound is prepared properly and fine-tuned at this stage. L-I-S-T-E-N to the sound. Be very critical. Make sure that file is perfect. Final equalization should be done at this point. The overall level should not exceed digital zero.

Record More Source Material!

Once you get the hang of sound design, your ears will start to hear things in different ways. You'll walk into rooms and hear ballast hums you might not have noticed before. A squeaky refrigerator door will come to life the next time you open it. Fans, motors, and power windows will start to sound like source material for a robot. Always be on the lookout for fresh and new sounds to tinker with when you are recording. Let your ears see your environment. Experiment, experiment, experiment!

CHAPTER EIGHTEEN

The Sound Effects Encyclopedia

How to Create the Sound of...

OVER THE YEARS, MANY SOUND designers have explored new methods, techniques, and philosophies for creating better sound effects. The purpose of this encyclopedia is to provide a starting point for recording and designing different types of sound effects. As clichéd as it may sound, there are no wrong ways of recording sounds, just *better* ways. Experimentation is the key to becoming a successful sound designer. The following pages contain information on how to record, edit, and design commonly used sound effects.

Examples of these sounds can be found at *www.soundeffectsbible. com*.

■ AMBIENCE SOUNDS

Ambience sound effects are extremely useful for creating scenes, filling in room tone, and setting a mood. They can be the main focus of a scene, emphasizing time of day, interior/exteriors, a character's perspective, etc. But they are mainly reserved for subtle cues in a film's soundtrack, like a soft bird chirping through a kitchen window to indicate morning or the drone of traffic through an office window to suggest a city outside. These sounds immediately give the listener a sense of location.

The major challenge with ambience recording is that you will usually have little or no control over your environment. So you'll likely have background noise or other sound events in the recording that will need to be filtered or removed during the editing process. An example of background noise might be the constant hum of traffic in the distance, which can sometimes be removed through equalization.

The best approach for ambience recordings is to record more material than you need. This will give you a surplus for layering or replacing elements of your track that may be polluted by extraneous sounds. For a minute of usable ambience, you should record at least five minutes of material on location. It is also a good idea to use a microphone stand, which guarantees a consistent perspective and lessens the chance of picking up sounds from clothing, arm movement, or vibrations. Your arms will thank you later.

Ambiences can be artificially created, but the best results are recordings gathered on location. Ambiences that are created from scratch in the editing process can produce hyperrealistic environments or can be used to enhance location recordings that yielded mediocre results. Some locations may be impractical to record because of access, budget, or even historical limitations (for example, a World War II battlefield). Once again you're going to need a little elbow grease and imagination.

Recording levels will vary from location to location. Generally, -40dB should be the lowest level for ambience recording. Recording at lower levels might result in unusable audio. If you've raised your levels and the sound is still below -40dB, try moving closer to the sound source. In the edit, you can use filters and noise reduction plug-ins to remove any hiss that's noticeable from raising the volume. If the levels are still too low, try finding a different location to record your ambience. Always record ambiences in stereo.

Here are some techniques and tricks for recording and editing ambiences:

Airport Interior Terminal

Airport security laws make it more and more difficult to gain access to key places to record at an airport. Be aware that with homeland security on full alert, a recordist can look very suspicious. If you are unsuccessful obtaining permission, try recording incognito using a Zoom H4 or other mini-recorder and a pair of earphones. Find a good location near crowds. Higher elevations like a second-floor balcony can give a good room sound and help wash out distinct conversations.

Airport Runway

Find a road near the runway. Most airports have nearby hotels that have parking lots directly underneath the flight paths of planes going to and from the runway. If you can, try to record near the fence line. Again, be aware that security will probably confront you. Wear hearing protection when working close to the planes.

It's difficult to use layering techniques with this type of ambience, as it will be quite noticeable that there are several planes landing or taking off at once. Try cross-fading the silent sections out with more plane activity to make the ambience sound full.

Airport Terminal Announcement

Most airports have announcements over the PA system, but real ones often contain the copyrighted names of airlines and other businesses. Creating your own personalized announcement can be faster and more efficient. Use any microphone to record the voice. Make up a fictitious airline company (for example, North Compass Airlines) and write a script of what to say. Don't read the script. It's better to have a sense of what to say than to read it verbatim.

Once you have a recorded message, you need to process the voice to make it sound like it is coming through a PA system. Use an equalizer to filter out all of the low frequencies. Start by cutting everything below 1KHz and go from there. Some slight distortion will also sell the effect of a PA system. Now take the voice and add some delay and reverb to place the sound in the terminal environment.

Speakerphone, from Audio Ease, is a great plug-in for simulating these kinds of effects. Simply select one of their presets and you're ready to go.

City

When you think of city ambiences, a few specific sounds usually come to mind: car horns, traffic, and sirens. Try to incorporate these elements for a general city background. If you don't happen to get a siren during the recording, you can always add it in later.

Brian Kaurich Recording City Ambience in New York's Times Square

The ambience should sound busy with all of the hustle and bustle of city life. If your location is not as busy as you would like, record more material and layer it during the edit. Street-level placement will bring the listener into the heart of the action. A rooftop or window perspective works well for the overall sound of a city.

Highway Traffic

Traffic is one of the easiest ambiences to record. Roads are everywhere, and car sounds seem to show up in every recording anyway. A roadside placement of the microphone will give a good left-to-right pass-by perspective. Recording over the side of an overpass will provide a constant, even stereo field. Semi trucks are more than willing to honk their horn when they drive by. Just give them the universal honk sign and watch your levels.

Office Cubicle

Cube farms and the hum of modern business equipment can lull the listener (and the employees) to sleep. The key to recording ambiences with people in offices is to record without them knowing. Be invisible. If people are aware they're being recorded, they will overact, ask questions, or won't talk at all. You do have a responsibility to honor people's privacy. If a conversation is noticeable and seems private, be sure to edit it out of your recording.

Restaurants

The main challenge with recording fast-food restaurants is the constant bombardment of the establishment's name. "Welcome to XYZ Burger Stand, can I take your order?" "Would you like to upsize your XYZ Burger Stand Burger?" These phrases can be difficult to edit out and still keep a usable portion of the ambience. Talk to the manager and see if they are willing to say "Hello, can I take your order?" for the few minutes that you do record. It never hurts to ask.

Standard sit-down restaurants are easier to work with. Managers are usually willing to let you come in and record. The only problem is that they are often reluctant to turn off the music playing in the background. Do some schmoozing to see if you can get them to kill the music for a few minutes. And while you're there, see if they'll let you record the kitchen ambience. Don't forget the walk-in coolers and industrial dishwashers.

Subdivisions — Urban Versus Suburban

Think about what a suburb sounds like. Undoubtedly in your head you're hearing a combination of a dog bark, a lawn mower, kids playing, and a sprinkler. Now think about an urban street. Undoubtedly the dog bark got more ferocious, the lawn mower became a distant siren, the kids grew up to become teenagers playing basketball, and the sprinklers became random gunshots. Welcome to sound stereotypes!

Stereotyping an environment is what ambiences are all about. These sound cues help the listener identify with the location. I have yet to watch a single episode of NBC's *Law and Order* without hearing a police siren coming through every open window in the courthouse, squad room, and apartment buildings. For the best results, record in layers and mix the sounds together for a colorful background track.

■ ANIMAL SOUNDS

It has been said by many great film directors that one of the top five things to avoid working with in filmmaking is animals. This is primarily because even trained animals can be unpredictable or stubborn. The problem is greatly amplified, so to speak, for the sound recordist.

In a film, it's easy for the director to decide to enhance an animal's performance in postproduction through the use of sound effects. In addition, a film can be cut so that the trumpeting elephant in the distant jungle is heard but not seen. The audience's cue to the animal is a low-cost sound effect that saves the production from hiring an animal wrangler and bringing an elephant on location. And it still accomplishes the same effect. However, for the recordist, if there is no performance by an animal in the recordings, the animal does not exist for the audience.

Here are some techniques and tricks for recording and editing animals:

General Animal Recording

Despite their noisy behavior in film, most animals are generally not very vocal (at least not until you're recording dialogue on location). You're sometimes going to need to employ certain techniques to help influence an animal's desire to perform. One such technique — albeit, a potentially dangerous one — is to hold a lit cigarette upwind of the animal. The smoke will gently float toward the animal, causing it to react and vocalize.

The time of day will also influence an animal's desire to speak. Feeding time is best for some animals, while morning or evening may be better for others. If you are going to set up a session to record animals at a zoo, it's best to work with a trainer who can coax the animal into making vocalizations.

Recording a Lion's Roar

Use a shotgun microphone to capture the animal's performance and reduce the amount of background noise that is picked up. A boom pole will help get the microphone closer, but be aware that the animal may feel threatened and strike. Ease your way into the session. Slowly approach the animal and don't make any sudden moves; avoid laughing or talking too loudly.

Bats

The high-pitch screech of a bat can be created by vocalizing a screech and raising the pitch. For a group of bats, record additional screeches. Avoid using the same screech over and over as this will sound digital and fake. A pair of leather gloves flapping around works well for the wings. Be sure to equalize excessive low frequencies, which can make the wings sound too large for a bat.

Beetles in a Pyramid

Insect movements can be designed by taking a vegetable and tapping your fingers in rhythm on the surface. A cabbage or melon is a good place to start. Take your recording and raise the pitch. This will cause the sound to become thin and smaller, and the movements will be faster.

You may want to roll off frequencies below 1KHz to help give the sound a small feeling. Create the beetle squeaks the same way as you would the bats, but make them higher in pitch. Lastly, add some reverb to place the sound inside the pyramid.

Crickets

A cricket's chirp correlates directly to the temperature. According to the *Old Farmer's Almanac*, you can count the number of chirps within 14 seconds and add 40 to get the temperature in Fahrenheit; the more chirps, the warmer the temperature. When recording crickets in the field, try recording during spring, winter, and fall to get samples at different temperatures.

Traffic noise is always a challenge when recording nature. The frequency of a cricket's chirp is between 7KHz and 8.5KHz. Most traffic noise shows up between 200Hz and 900Hz. Cutting these frequencies with an equalizer will reduce or eliminate the traffic altogether. If you are only after the sound of the cricket, you can use a spectrum analyzer to find the exact frequency of the chirp and then increase that frequency.

If the background noise is too intense, you can try to find a single chirp and use that as the basis for designing the sound from scratch. Layering dozens and dozens of these sounds can make a great cricket bed. Some people have the unique talent of making a cricket sound with their mouth. Nothing beats the real thing, but in a pinch you can use vocalization like that to design a believable sound. It works particularly well for creating the sound of a single lonely cricket.

Snakes

No matter what kind of snake is in the movie, you will always hear it rattle. It's a Hollywood sound staple. For a rattlesnake sound, you can use a baby rattle. Record the shaking sound and pitch it up. You can edit out some of the silence between rattles to make it sound faster. You can perform the hiss yourself with your mouth, then pitch it up. Try layering multiple hisses for an interesting sound.

Voiced Animals

If you strike out with zoos and other locations, you can try to vocalize the sound effect yourself. With the right techniques and processing, voicing animal sounds can be very convincing. One method is to find recordings of the real thing from television shows or movies and use that as a reference. Take a sample of the recording and listen to the playback through headphones. Now try to emulate the sound with your voice.

This method works best when you pitch the animal's recording up or down to bring it into the human voice range. This will help your performance sound closer to the real thing. Try projecting your voice into cups and empty garbage cans to help make it resonate like an animal with a big chest or body. After you've recorded your track, pitch your voice up or down the same amount as you did to the original animal recording.

■ CARTOON EFFECTS

Cartoon sounds are naturally comical and greatly exaggerate the already-outlandish actions on screen. Cartoon sounds have musical origins. Percussion, wind, brass, and stringed instruments were used for everything from footsteps and talking to crashes and explosions. These cartoon sounds are not literal and can be derived from just about anything that emphasizes or juxtaposes the action. Modern cartoons are far more advanced in technique and style and rely on more sound design-based material that complements the hi-tech computer animation.

When you set out to tackle cartoon recording, research the sounds you want. Watch *The Three Stooges* and old Hannah-Barberra cartoons. These sounds are old and recorded in low fidelity, but the performances are classics. Notice how and when the sounds are used. Take some cues from the masters before setting out to make your own audience laugh.

Here are some techniques and tricks for recording and editing cartoon sound effects:

Cartoon Musical Effects

Keyboards and synthesizers really aren't very useful for cartoon effects. There are some sounds that will work, like xylophones, but nothing can replace the real deal. High school band teachers can be a great source for musical sounds. They usually have tons of instruments and often have the talent to play each one (at least well enough to make them sound funny). The catch is that most school band rooms have flat cinderblock walls that generate loads of reverb. Sound blankets can be brought in to help tame the room, but a better solution might be the school's theater, which probably has been acoustically treated.

Save time by creating a list before you arrive. Remember, whoever you get to help you is probably volunteering their time. Be respectful of this. Work quickly and professionally. You never know when you might need another favor. If you spend hours and hours trying to get the "right" sound, they may be less likely to volunteer their time again.

Many instruments can be played so that they talk and convey emotion. This is what makes a good cartoon effect. Try to get each instrument to do the following emotions and actions:

Anger
Exclamation
Happiness
Laughing
Mocking
Phrases (Tada! What?)
Sadness
Screams
Sighs
Slides (Up and Down)

For microphone selection, try cardioid mics. Dynamic mics will handle the high SPLs of brass instruments. Condenser mics will work better for strings and woodwinds.

Here is a list of good instruments to use:

Brass Instruments
Bugle
French Horn
Saxophone
Trombone
Trumpet
Tuba

Stringed Instruments
Banjo
Cello
Harp
Mouth Harp
Piano
Violins

Woodwind Instruments
Clarinet
Flute
Oboe

Cartoon Percussive Effects

In cartoons, percussive instruments are used for just about everything: crashes, footsteps, even knocks on the head. The performance is more important than the actual instrument itself, although there are many signature cartoons sounds that can only be made from a specific instrument (for example, tympanis).

Miking a Cymbal from above the Bell

Percussion sounds are naturally loud. For the drum instruments, try using dynamic mics instead of condenser mics. In general, sounds with higher timbre should be miked with condenser mics. Avoid damaging condenser mics with loud instruments by placing the mic a few feet away. Cymbals should be miked directly above the bell. Placing the mic near the edge of the cymbal can create a wavering sound as air is moved to and from the mic.

Here is a list of good instruments to use:

Conventional Percussion Instruments
Bass Drum
Bells
Bongos
Congas
Cymbals
Snare
Tambourine
Triangle
Tympani
Vibraphone
Whistles
Wood Block
Xylophone

Unconventional Percussion Instruments
Bottles
Garbage Can Lid
Silverware

Joe Parisi Getting Silly in the Voiceover Booth

Cartoon Voices

Wild laughter, wolf whistles, and whining babies are all the result of good old-fashioned voice work. Think big. Think over the top. Think crazy! Everyone has a friend with a thousand voices. Find that friend and give him a list to work from. The list will let the person focus his creativity on the performance instead of what to say next. Be careful of coming too close to a copyrighted cartoon character. This could put you at risk of a lawsuit. For microphone selection, try a large diaphragm condenser mic.

■ CRASH SOUNDS

These sounds work best when they are larger than life. Although enhancements and other tricks can be added in the editing stage, it is the on-set, on-location performances that are the key to creating realistic *and* over-the-top crashes. The recording process for crashes is messy and physical and best performed with an assistant. However, with patience a solo performance can still generate great material.

Of all types of recording sessions, crashes are certainly the most stress-releasing!

The following is a list of techniques and tricks for recording and editing crashes:

Car Crash

Drivers who know they're about to run into something always jam on the brakes. For a typical car crash, start with a nice tire screech. You can record good tire screeches by doing donuts in an abandoned parking lot with an assistant. Have the car drive in circles making sharp turns. Stand in the center and record all the action from a safe distance with a boom pole. Use a shotgun microphone and focus on the tires.

To record the sound of the car approaching, stand on the side of the road with a boom pole. For head-on approaches, hold the boom pole over the road. You can record the approach in stereo, but be sure to change the position of the microphone inside the zeppelin so that when it is held horizontally, the left-and-right field is parallel to the ground.

Now let's discuss the impact. A junkyard will provide all of the resources you'll need to build a realistic crash. Take a sledgehammer and gather impacts from all parts of the car.

Here is a list of things to record:
Bumpers
Fenders
Grill
Headlights
Hood
Hubcaps
Roof
Side Mirrors
Taillights
Trunk
Windows
Windshield

Once you have your elements, start by building the initial impact. The tire screech could be cut/faded at the point of impact to suggest that the car slid into an object or another car and stopped dead. If the crash is a high-speed accident, you can keep the tire screech beyond the initial impact to give a sense of how fast the cars were going. For a crash into a parked car, you can have the crash first, then a tire screech to imply that the parked car is being pushed.

Hoods and trunks give a good metal collision sound for the impact. This impact could be a single hit or could be multiple hits to suggest other objects hitting the car. The first hit should be the loudest element of the effect. Everything that happens before and after the hit should be considerably lower in level. This will give the sense of a hard impact through dynamics. Layer multiple impact elements and pitch-shift a couple of the tracks to give weight to the crash.

Next, add some plastic from the grill and taillights. Keep in mind it doesn't matter if the impact wasn't in the rear. The taillights have a nice plastic crack to them that will help season the mix. Now add the glass impacts. Lastly, sprinkle in some debris. Although windshields are made from shatterproof glass, car crash sound effects always have typical glass debris. You can use the side mirror and headlights for this debris.

For the final touches, you can add steam to simulate a busted radiator. A can of air that has been processed and filtered can create a good steam effect. A hubcap can also be added. If you don't have access to a real hubcap, you can use a metal trash can lid. Record the sound of the hubcap rolling as well as the moment when it starts to spin and wobble to a stop. Finally, try adding a long car horn blast. Car horns don't loop very easily, so you should try to record a nice long honk to work with.

Crash Material

Crashes come in all shapes, sizes, and types. It's a physical world and everything is subject to destruction. Build up a good library of materials to play with when making crashes.

Here is a list of crash material to gather:
Aluminum
Brick
Cardboard
Ceramic
Cinderblock
Dishes
Glass
Metal
Paper
Pipes
Plastic
Rock
Styrofoam
Tile
Wood

In general, you should use stereo mics for crashes. Debris rarely stays in one place. Having a stereo image allows you to capture the left-and-right nuances of the debris upon impact. If you need to focus your sound effect in your production in one specific place, you can select one of the channels to make the sound mono. Because the debris will fly everywhere, you should count on it

Microphone Stand with a Sound Blanket Protecting the Base

hitting your microphone stand. To prevent this from ruining a take, wrap a sound blanket around the base of your stand. Debris will then land on the blanket instead of the stand.

Here are some tips when working with different crash materials:

Glass

A lot of material falls into the glass category: bottles, drinking glasses, fish bowls, mirrors, panes, etc. Unlike most of the crash materials you'll work with, glass is a one-shot take. Once the glass is broken, you can't recapture the initial break by using the leftover debris. Other materials are more forgiving. So try to record glass breaks with multiple microphones and recorders set at different levels. This will ensure at least one usable recording.

Be sure to wear protective clothing and eye protection when breaking glass.

Bottles

You will find that glass bottles don't always break. That's okay. Save those takes for when you need the sound of a beer bottle falling to the ground without breaking. A way to increase your chances of breaking a bottle is to drop it on its side. Dropping the bottle on its top or bottom will create a louder sound, but it won't always break because that's where the glass is strongest. For bottles, try miking from a foot or two away. Bottle crashes sound different when there's liquid inside. If you have several bottles, try to vary the takes by putting water in some of them.

Drinking Glasses

Kitchen glasses and the like are recorded the same way as bottles. The bottoms of most glasses are much thicker than the rest of the glass. Dropping the glass directly on the bottom will give a flat, thick break. Dropping a glass upside down gives a shatter with a thick impact afterwards. Again, having liquid inside some of the glasses will help vary the takes and give you more to work with in the edit.

Panes

For panes of glass, set up cinderblocks to support the pane. The taller the cinderblocks, the farther the glass will fall to the ground. Position the cinderblocks so that only a few inches of the corners of the glass will rest on them. Use sound dampeners like rags on top of the cinderblocks for the glass to rest on to reduce any sound that the cinderblock might make. If the cinderblocks wobble, try placing rags underneath them to even them out.

Nate Richter Smashing a Pane of Glass

Now place the pane of glass on the cinderblocks. Use a hammer and strike the pane in the center. Be careful of your own movements when making the strike so as not to follow through too much or risk cutting yourself. The glass will shatter and fall to the ground, giving you both an impact and a debris effect.

Plastic

Storage bins and old toys (not *Star Wars* figures) can be great sources for plastic crashes. Soft plastics tend to bend, and hard plastics tend to break. Use gloves when breaking hard plastic because you can create dangerously sharp edges. Pop bottles and jugs can be used for smaller crashes and spills.

On garbage days, keep a lookout for discarded DVD and VHS players. These will give great plastic crashes when dropped or smashed. The interior electronics will also provide plenty of plastic debris.

Wood

As you begin to work on crashes, you'll quickly discover that each material has a unique sound. Wood is a good example. Different

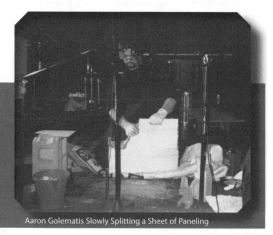

Aaron Golematis Slowly Splitting a Sheet of Paneling

types of wood have signature sounds. Some sound thick and heavy, others thin and light. Wood paneling sheets sound completely different from plywood sheets of the same size and thickness.

Stressing is a great performance technique when working with wood paneling. Stand the sheet on its side longways. Use an ax to start a split in the wood. Once the split is about six inches deep, use your hands to separate the two halves. Do this by pulling one hand toward you and pushing the other hand away. Slow movements will give the best results.

Debris General

Once you've finished smashing and crashing each element, save the debris in separate containers. Keep different types of glass in their own individual containers as well (lightbulb debris, drinking glass debris, windowpane debris, etc.). By keeping the debris separate, you can create additional debris sounds of just one type later.

You should also have a bin of mixed debris for general crash debris effects.

You'll need to mic the elements up close to help increase the level to the recorder. Hold some debris in each hand. Keep your hands a couple of feet apart to create a wider stereo sound. You can move your hands closer together and farther away during the take to help randomize where the debris lands.

Pouring the debris out of your hands can sound fake or planned. Try holding the debris inside your hand

Bins of Various Debris Material

Performing Dust Debris with Rock Salt

while you make a fist. Hold your fist out with the back of your hand up. Gently wiggle your fingers to allow the debris to fall through. Avoid excessive hand and finger sounds.

Dust Debris

Dust debris can be tricky to create. Dust is quiet in real life. As a sound effect, dust needs a little help to be heard. The surface that the debris is dropped on is as important as the actual debris itself. For dust debris, you need hundreds of small objects that can land and bounce on a surface. It's really the surface that is making the sound.

Here is a list of some sources for dust and fine debris:
Popcorn Seeds
Crushed Pretzels
Rice
Rock Salt
Crushed Tortilla Chips

Elevator Crash

One of my favorite sounds I've designed is an elevator crash. Creating complex events can be challenging and equally rewarding. This takes some skill and a fair amount of source material.

The elevator shaft is basically a vertical tunnel. Use reverb to help create this environment for an exterior crash perspective. Start with an ominous metal stress to generate the suspense of something going wrong. Use heavy guitar strings or piano wire to simulate the sound of the cable snap.

Long metal screeches are used for the emergency brakes (that will ultimately fail). One of my favorite sound props is a 12-inch metal candle holder with four feet. Sliding this prop on a glass surface makes the most insane metal screeches I've ever heard. I used this as the basis for the brakes.

Lastly, you'll need the crash at the bottom of the shaft. Wood elements should be used for the wall interiors, but metal and aluminum elements should dominate the sound. Layering and mixing all of these elements together will create a mind-blowing effect.

Lamp Crash

Lamps and other electronic devices don't really shoot out huge electrical bolts when they're smashed. Special effects technicians are the culprits behind these visual effects. For a lamp crash, find an old lamp and drop it or knock it over. More than likely, the bulb won't break. In that case, record a lightbulb smash separately. Add some good electric zaps from an arc welder or a processed cable short and you're all set.

Piano Fall

Since pianos are made of wood, the main impact of the crash will be a hollow wood sound. A nightstand or other wood cabinet can work for the heavy drop. Use a sledgehammer to record some additional impacts and smashes. A wood panel set up on cinderblocks and smashed in the middle can give a nice splinter effect.

Layer the smashes together for a single event that lasts for a few seconds. Remember, pianos are heavy, so make the impact sound heavy. Next, randomly hit and hold some piano keys from a real piano. Don't use a synthesizer because they don't have that smooth, rich tone that a wood body gives. Lastly, add some wood debris along with a couple of short planks or spindles to emulate the legs of the piano.

RV Camper Roll Down Hill

This is not a common sound, by any stretch of the imagination. It made the list because how the sound came about being recorded illustrates the main principle of sound design: improvisation.

While out recording car crash elements in a junkyard one day, a friend and I came across a full-sized motor home/camper. We went inside and smashed everything we could find. It was at that moment that I realized the sounds could be used to create a camper rolling down a hill. With that in mind, we recorded more elements for source material.

We started by throwing debris around inside the vehicle. Then I stayed inside with the microphone while my friend went outside and smashed the windows. The glass debris flew inside the camper and landed on all the other larger debris we'd created. Next, he went to the side of the camper and started rocking it back and forth. Finally, he pounded the sledgehammer on the outside walls.

I raced home and cut up all of the elements and began to layer them. There were hundreds of sounds. I placed markers on the timeline to show where I wanted the sound of the camper rolling on its side to be. I used that as a guide and built the sound around those impact points. The result was magic.

I improvised while I was on location. I wasn't there to record the sound of a camper. But you have to run with inspiration when it strikes. Sometimes it pays off and sometimes it doesn't. But either way you'll gain experience from trying.

Television Implode

I've probably smashed a dozen television sets so far. It never gets old. There are a few ways to record the crash. You can lay the television on its back so that the screen is facing up and drop a bowling ball directly onto the screen. Or you can put the television on the edge of a table and use a sledgehammer to smash the glass; having the set near the edge lets the debris fall over the side. A third method is to pick the television up and drop it on the ground.

There really isn't a huge difference between these crashes. They're all basically a combination of glass and plastic smashes. The sound of the debris might be different, but you can add that in later anyway. If you don't have a television to smash, use your imagination and start with glass and plastic source material. A short processed air blast can simulate the television tube exploding.

Tree Fall on Automobile, Ground, House

Tree falls consist of a wood stress/creak and break along with a foliage impact. Dead trees in the forest will provide some great cracking and stressing with a nice impact. Sound design tree falls can be much cleaner but can lack the echoes that a real forest environment provides. A combination of real-world and design elements will make the sound effect larger than life.

For the foliage impact you can drop heavy items on a pile of leaves. Branches with leaves can help stagger the impact. Because trees are so heavy, a nice thump should be heard at the ground impact. It may be necessary to boost the low-end frequencies on the initial impact.

Other impact surfaces such as cars and houses can be layered on top of the already-designed tree fall. The low-end frequencies should be adjusted to simulate the impact of the surface — a car impact wouldn't produce a heavy bass rumble, for example. A house impact would be a mixture of glass and wood. A car impact would be a mixture of glass and metal.

Window Smash

Windows are expensive and it's unusual to find an unbroken one that someone is throwing away. Abandoned houses can offer a ton of resources, but it is fairly difficult to get permission to smash things up. If you do get permission, call me and I'll come out and record with you!

You'll probably need to recreate a window smash effect in the studio. Windows are firm and solid. Rather than building a frame, record the glass panes separately. Then record some wood splintering and impacts. In the edit, you can layer these elements together for a realistic sound effect.

■ CROWD SOUNDS

Crowd sound effects can be used as ambiences as well as individual sound effects. For example, a walla track can be used to fill a courtroom with a dull drone of voices waiting in anticipation for the trial to begin. But a single gasp of shock from the crowd in response to the verdict would be an individual sound effect. Crowd sounds can be gathered on location or on a stage as a planned event.

Recording Crowds on Location

When recording a crowd on location, it's best to work in anonymity. The moment anyone catches on to the microphone, the candidness of the sound vanishes and it becomes littered with overactors and questions from the crowd like, "Hey, what are you doing?" and "Is that a microphone?" To reduce your chances of being spotted, try planting a mic in an inconspicuous place. Corners work perfectly: They're out of the way and the mic can easily be hidden among lamps, trees, and other decorations.

If possible, place the microphone three feet above the heads of the crowd to allow it to pick up the direct sound. Ideally you should record crowds in stereo because they will almost always be used as a stereo effect in the finished product. The Rode NT-4 stereo microphone is a great selection for crowds but can require stealthier solutions to keep it from being noticed.

Recording Crowds Incognito

A stereo lavaliere microphone can be easily camouflaged on a shirt collar, backpack strap, or other crafty place. However, most stereo lavs are consumer grade and lack the full-bodied sound of a well-designed microphone. An alternative is a pair of TRAM microphones positioned in a stereo pattern. For crowd ambiences, you should position the microphones on the outside of your clothing to get the best recordings. When mounting a lavaliere microphone on your person, be sure to lighten your breathing and reduce body movement so as not to affect the recording. Another solution is the covert Zoom H4 handheld recorder.

Stand perfectly still and do not shift from side to side, which would create a shifting stereo field. Position yourself in various locations around the room to capture different perspectives or to distance yourself from noisy or obnoxious talkers. Signifying sounds, such as a unique or loud voice, can lead to identifiable loop points in the finished, edited sound effect. So be aware of what repeating or signature sounds are being recorded and try to reduce or eliminate them through mic placement — which, in the case of lavs, is your body.

Recording Crowds on a Stage

Crowd recording sessions can be costly or difficult to manage without proper planning. If you've hired an ADR group or voice talent, you'll want to utilize your time wisely to save money. Working with volunteers can be even more stressful. Their schedules are hard to coordinate, they will probably be amateurs, and being cooped up on a stage while being told to be quiet and working for free can only yield so much patience. In either case, preparation is important to keep the session moving swiftly.

Theater groups are often willing to help out. After all, they're actors and you need people who can act. Be sure to offer them a copy of the sound effects to use in their productions. Working with actors can be very efficient. They know their craft and should have the range you need for various sounds. The challenge will be the over-actors in the group.

Over the years, I have yet to work with a single group of people that didn't have that one special person who always wants to be the loudest, the goofiest, and, of course, the last one clapping. When working with these special folks, gently encourage them to blend in with the group. A good crowd should sound like one voice made up of many voices. An anomaly in the crowd will spoil the effect.

Create a list of sounds you would like to record. Use the following as a guide for crowd sounds:
Agony
Ahs
Booing
Chanting
Cheering
Countdowns
Crying
Disagreeing
Gasps
Jeering
Laughing
Moaning
Mumbling
Ohs
Panic
Phrases (Yes, No, Hooray, Happy New Year, Merry Christmas, Surprise, etc.)
Screams
Sighs
Walla

Here is a list of crowd Foley movements:
Applause, Polite
Applause, Various-Size Groups
Applause, Wild
Clapping in Unison
Clothes Movements (Flapping Coats, Rubbing Pants Legs, etc.)

Entering/Exiting a Room
Footsteps (Marching, Running, Walking, etc.)
Jumping
Sitting Down
Standing Up
Stomping

During the session, record at least one safety take per sound. To create larger crowds than what was available, record several takes in order to get enough unique material to use for layering and looping later. Listen carefully to the beginning and ending of each sound for voices that stand out from the rest. The crowd should start and end together as one. Also, have the crowd remove any noisy jewelry or heavy footwear. Use hand signals to communicate with the group.

Some good signals to include are:
Cut
Louder
Softer
Keep Going

Position the crowd in a semicircle. If it's a mixed group of males and females, have them stand alternating male and female. Place the mic six to ten feet in front of the crowd and three feet above head level. Have the group switch positions for the alternate takes; this will make the group sound less distinctive during the layering and looping process.

Recording Crowd Scenes

Battle scenes are very hard to sound design without a crowd track. You can try to record a small group of five or ten people and work with layers, but it won't have the same dynamics that a large group or "army" of people would have. When you assemble a large group of people, take advantage of the situation and gather material you might not have an immediate need for. You'll thank yourself later.

Here is a list of crowd scenes to gather:
Angry Mob
Bar Crowd
Bar Fight
Medieval Battle
Medieval Crowd
Military Battle
Monsters Growling
Pirate Battle
Sports Crowds (Various Sports)
Zombies Moaning

Use primarily men for battle scenes; women can join in by lowering their voices.

Walla Track

Walla can be defined as the unintelligible conversations of a crowd that you hear in the background of a scene. A good walla track is created by having performers speak gibberish that sounds like real conversation. Real sentences should be avoided in a walla track because they can easily be identified and can stand out in the sound. Try having the group repeat the names of vegetables: rhubarb, peas and carrots, avocado, watermelon, etc. They'll feel silly at first, but the effect is very convincing.

■ EMERGENCY EFFECTS

Recording emergency effects poses some unique challenges. Scheduling and permission are the main obstacles. Location and background noise are always problems as well. The emergencies that trained professionals deal with

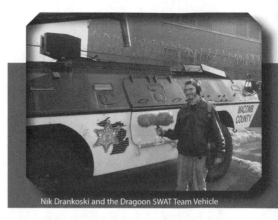
Nik Drankoski and the Dragoon SWAT Team Vehicle

are very real. Their equipment and vehicles are not always easily accessible. When you do get a chance to record them, be respect-

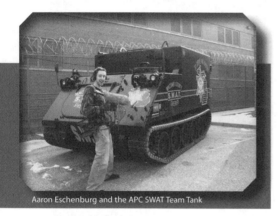
Aaron Eschenburg and the APC SWAT Team Tank

ful, quick, and efficient. Sometimes a call comes in and the session is cut short. Be flexible and ready to move out of the way when this happens.

The following is a list of techniques and tricks for recording and editing emergency sound effects:

Fire Stations

Through six degrees of separation, everyone knows someone whose brother is a firefighter. I myself have three stepbrothers-in-law serving. When they aren't out risking their lives and being heroes, they're at the fire station watching television, working out, and making the world's greatest chili. That said, firefighters usually jump at the chance to do anything but sit around and wait for the bell to ring.

Fire stations are a playground of sounds to record. You could spend hours on the trucks themselves with all of the compartments, levers, and gears. In the equipment room, you'll find coats, masks, oxygen tanks, and other safety gear. There's also usually a recreation room with games, a workout room, locker rooms with showers, and more. Of course there is also the garage itself, with its cargo bay doors and other tools of the trade.

A good contact will often tip you off to the address of a run. They probably won't let you ride along, but you can show up at the scene and record the event from a safe distance. Most stations won't mind running their sirens for you. Because firefighters are often trained by EMS or are EMS personnel themselves, they can give you some good leads to finding an ambulance to record.

Police Radio

The main challenge of creating a police radio sound effect is finding out what to say. You can buy a police scanner and record police calls to use as the basis of your script. You can also listen to police scanners across the country in real time on various Web sites. Be very sure to remove real names, addresses, and license plate numbers from your script. A simple method is to take out one of the numbers from the address or license plate. This will protect the names of the innocent and guilty alike.

To record the script, place a walkie-talkie in front of a microphone and take the other walkie-talkie into another room to perform the police calls. The recorder will hear the filtered sounds coming through the walkie-talkie and not the dry sound of your voice. A police radio can also be simulated by recording a voice dry and filtering the sound to emulate a walkie-talkie.

Police Siren

Police officers are reluctant to turn on their sirens for recording sound effects. It never hurts to ask. You will probably get dozens of rejections, but all it takes is one yes and you've got your sound. Sirens are loud, so stay at least a few feet back from the car. Use a stereo microphone and start with the gain at a low level to prevent overloading the mic preamps. A field or an empty construction site is an ideal recording location. Keep in mind, the location is not too critical because the gains will be turned down so low to compensate for the loud siren.

I've had several experiences where vibrations from the siren actually caused errors on my recorder's micro drive. So I'd suggest using a solid-state medium like a compact flash card. You probably won't get a second chance anytime soon, so you want to make sure you get a good recording the first time.

You don't need to record long amounts of the siren because it will have a natural loop point. Record as much as the officer is willing to give you and work with that. Sirens have a variety of different wails and tones. Try to get a recording of each one. Again, it can't hurt to ask to record an interior car perspective as well. The exterior sound is the most important, though, because you can always use an Altiverb or other reverb unit to simulate the siren from inside the vehicle.

■ ELECTRONIC EFFECTS/IMAGING ELEMENTS

Imaging elements originated as a way of putting sound behind logos and animations commonly seen on sports and news broadcasts. These electronic effects are more abstract than literal, although some imaging elements are derived from real-world sounds such as fireballs and explosions. The most common of these elements is a whoosh. This sound is usually placed behind a flying logo or visual transition element similar to a video wipe.

Electronic keyboards were the main source of the sounds when imaging elements first appeared. The sounds were thus very synthesized and musical. With developments in 3D graphics over the years, the animations have become more sophisticated — and so the sounds portraying their movements have become more complex. Today, one graphic can use a single imaging element that contains dozens of sounds.

The key to creating a good imaging element is finding a source to work with and then heavily processing that source to make it larger than life. A good exercise for creating imaging elements would be to record shows that are graphic-intensive and then replace the show's sounds with your own. With practice, you'll discover ways to make your sounds vocalize and simulate movement.

Here are the definitions of words used to describe imaging elements:

Accent
An element that sounds like punctuation to an event. This is the primary description for all production/imaging elements.

Arpeggio
A musical element with a melody line that ascends or descends a musical scale repetitively.

Ascend
A sound that rises, usually on a consistent incline in pitch.

Bed
A constant sound or group of sounds, usually with a long duration. Unlike a drone, a bed can be musical.

Bumper
An abrupt element that usually contains distortion. Bumpers are used for breaks or short hits.

Burst
An element that gives the impression of separation, such as pixie dust or sparkles.

Chopper
A sound element broken up in a rhythmic stuttering pattern.

Composition
A composite or layering of multiple elements to create a complex single element over time.

Data Element
An element that gives the impression of numbers running in succession, as in a counter or satellite transmission.

Descend
A sound that falls with a consistent decline in pitch.

Distortion
Sounds that are primarily unintelligible, twisted, and overdriven.

Drone
An atonal bed of sound that is constant, with little or no change in pitch or volume. Drones are monotonous sounds that are used to invoke feeling, presence, or emotion. Their tones are usually low pulses but can also include vocal and wispy elements.

Feedback
A sound that feeds back from the original source. Some elements are dry; others may contain reverb.

Glitch
A sound element that appears to malfunction or short-circuit.

Hit/Impact
Generally a single event consisting of an initial, hard-hitting attack. While the duration of the decay and the amount of reverb may vary, these elements are characterized by an impression of instant impact.

Hit to Whoosh
A hit that evolves into a whoosh.

Logo
An element or series of elements that can be used for logos or signature marks.

Musical Element
An element that is musical in nature, but not necessarily in a musical scale.

Power Down
A sound that winds down, simulating a power loss.

Power Up
A sound that winds up, simulating a power start-up or surge.

Ramp
A sound that gradually increases in volume or pitch and that stops suddenly at the peak.

Shimmer/Tinkle
An element that can be used for pixie dust or other magical effects.

Stab
A combination of several elements in one hit, such as a hit and a sweeper combined at the same time.

Station ID
A combination of several elements in succession, similar to a stinger but with an opener and closer, allowing for a voiceover to be added in the middle. This is generally used by radio stations and podcasts.

Stinger
A combination of several elements in succession, such as a hit, a power up, and a sweeper mixed in a series.

Stutter
An element that hesitates or fails to finish.

Sweeper
A musical whoosh.

Swell
A sound that builds to a climax then winds down.

Tape Rewind
An element that suggests a short trip back in time, generally sounding like a real tape player rewinding.

Wash
An element that is usually washed out, or blurred with reverb.

Whoosh to Hit
A whoosh that builds to a hit.

Whoosh
An element that gives the impression of a flyby or transition, generally with an airy, flange, or phaser effect.

■ EXPLOSION EFFECTS

Nothing sells the visual effect of a large fireball overtaking a helicopter and its occupants like the roaring, percussive punch of explosive sound effects. Throughout the 1960s and 1970s, it seemed as if there were only a few explosion sound effects available to Hollywood. These same sounds even seemed to creep their way into television episodes in the early 1980s. Modern television and cinema now deliver far more complicated renditions of pyrotechnic and explosive mayhem through complex layering and compositing of sounds (not to mention much higher fidelity in the recordings).

Given the nature of the real world, it's safe to say that one would be hard pressed to find an original explosion source that did not require the mixing of other elements. In addition to this difficult feat, the contemporary style of picture editing delivers multiple-camera-angle shots of explosions within a few seconds, creating forced perspectives in the sound field. Blasts and explosions now consist of several sound cues, including numerous starts and stops in addition to various debris and impacts.

Source gathering for explosions should be approached with the understanding that there will more than likely be a mixing of sound layers in the editing process. These layers could include glass shattering, metal objects being tossed around, earth elements being littered upon various surfaces, and even fire elements. As with any mixing, the best results are achieved by using the cleanest source material.

The following is a list of techniques and tricks for recording and editing explosion sound effects:

Bomb Timer

Ticking/Beeping
Nothing builds more tension in an action sequence than waiting for the bomb to explode. Whether it's ticking or beeping, the anticipation is still the same. Creating bomb timers is very easy … well, at least easier than disarming the bomb!

Beeping Timer

You should be accurate when timing the beeps or ticks. For beeps, you can use any beep, including those made by microwave buttons or other small electronics. High-pitch beeps tend to sound more high tech. If you are generating the beep using a synthesis plug-in, create a sine wave at 4KHz and start there.

A good length for this beep should be about three frames, or a tenth of a second. Add 27 frames of silence after the beep to create a full second. Then loop the event as many times as necessary. You can increase the sense of pace by timing the beeps every half second. For even more tension, time the beeps every quarter of a second. To create a beeping alarm before detonation, take the beep by itself, add one frame, and loop it.

Ticking Timer

Any short mechanical click will work for the ticks. For the best effect use two ticks (i.e., a tick and a tock). On a clock, the tick sounds higher-pitched than the tock — that's where the onomatopoeic "tick-tock" for the action of a clock comes from. I'm not a horologist, but I suspect this might be due to the tension release of the mechanical gears inside.

The timing of the ticks is similar to the timing described for the beeps. However, keep in mind that the ticks alternate between high tick and low tock. Single ticks can work, but the suspense doesn't seem to build as well. Perhaps this is because the two tones sound musical when played together. Experiment and find out what works best for you.

Depth Charge

These explosive devices were developed during World War I by the British navy to help combat enemy submarines. The weapon was basically a bomb inside a metal barrel that was set to detonate at a certain depth. The explosion occurred underwater, but the aftermath was visible on the surface. So there are two ways of approaching this sound: above water and underwater.

Above Water Explosion

The above water sound is going to be made up of two elements: a low-frequency blast and a huge water splash. You can use any clean explosion (no debris or fire mixed in) to start with. Because the explosion happens below the surface, you wouldn't normally hear the high-end crack of the blast, so roll off the high frequencies by sloping them off from 100Hz to 300Hz. All the frequencies above 300Hz will not be heard.

The splash is basically the debris of the explosion. This can be made up of any large water splash (for example, a cannonball dive into a pool). If your water splash is a little weak, try adding other splashes and pitch-layering them.

For a more involved effect, you can use the sound of a metal drum or garbage can being dropped into a lake or pool for the initial deployment of the depth charge. Add a small splash and some ocean waves and wait for the blast.

Below Water Explosion

This perspective will take a bit of tweaking to dial in the right sound. You can use the same elements that you gathered for the above water perspective, but you will need to process and filter them. The splash will be heard at the front of the effect. There won't be a splash at the end of the effect because you wouldn't hear the surface from this perspective. Pitch-bend the explosion to start normal and then quickly descend in pitch. You should mix in some pitched-down water movement here with the high frequencies rolled off. Finally, a faint water warble and some bubbles can be used for the aftermath debris.

Explosions

Explosions consist of an initial concussion, sometimes followed by debris, then a trail-off possibly with fireballs or flames. It's not uncommon for the debris to continue falling after the trail-off has faded out. Here is the approach:

The Concussion

Explosions are hard to come by in the real world. It's nice to have the phone number of the local historical society or military base that might give you access to the real deal. These sources just might be willing to let you record their tanks, weapons, cannons, etc. Most of the time, though, you'll probably strike out and will need a strong alternative.

Firework mortar shells provide an excellent black powder blast for the initial concussion. This is a good starting point. If possible, use two microphones and split their channels to a two-track field recorder (one mic to the left channel and the other to the right channel). Other alternative blast sources include shotguns, heavy metal impacts, and snare drum hits.

For the first mic, use a small diaphragm condenser such as a Marshall MXL-991. This microphone provides great sound for the price and won't overstretch your budget even if it gets damaged and you have to buy another one. Position the mic two feet away from the mortar and about a foot higher than the edge of the rim. Angle the mic so that it's pointing directly at the hole of the mortar. This perspective will give you a nice in-your-face concussion.

For the second mic, use a short shotgun mic. Place it four feet away and about three to five feet higher than the edge of the mortar's rim. As before, angle the mic so that it's pointing directly at the hole of the mortar. This perspective will give you a full-bodied sound of the blast because the microphone is far enough away to allow some of the lower end of the sound to develop. You will also notice a slap-back or delay from your environment (for example, sound bouncing off houses or trees and reentering the mic). To reduce this echo, try recording the sounds in a more sterile or sparse environment such as a large open field or, for the best results, the desert.

This double miking system allows two perspectives of the same event to be recorded in sync with each other. This also provides a safety take should one of the mics overload or become damaged.

During the editing process you can determine which of the two tracks works best or you may decide to keep both and mix them together. When this source sound is pitch-shifted and treated with some reverb, a rich and powerful blast source will emerge.

Debris

The type of debris to use will depend on the scene. Exterior explosions are usually followed by earth debris. Car explosions may include a hood, car door, or other metal debris. House and building explosions will include glass, brick, wood, and so on. Timing the debris during recording is not necessary; you'll be able to cut and paste your elements together in the edit.

It's best to record the debris in an isolated place or on a Foley stage (the latter being preferred). A stereo microphone works great here. Recording in stereo gets half the work of sound placement done automatically. The stereo field will give the debris a sense of depth and help fill your soundtrack with "tiny tasties" of sonic goodness!

For more intricate results, design a special surface for the debris to fall on. Your surface can be a wood pallet placed on its side to allow the debris to fall through the cracks and bounce off the planks. Or stack a bunch of cinderblocks chaotically so the debris will roll off the sides and fall in between. Piles of junk or miscellaneous debris on a surface also makes a great texture for your falling debris to interact with.

Trail-Off

The trail-off of the explosion is the sound continuing to travel into the distance. This may exist in your source recordings but will probably need to be enhanced or replaced altogether. One technique is to apply reverb to your concussion source before pitch-shifting the sound.

Your reverb should last anywhere from 5 to 15 seconds. This will stretch into a longer duration once you apply the pitch shift. The frequencies affected by the concussion will also be pitch-shifted, resulting in smooth, rich tones. Avoid using crisp, high-frequency heavy reverb settings. Although they'll be pitched down, they'll still maintain a brighter tone that is undesirable for this effect. Find a balance between the dry/wet settings by applying the reverb, pitch-shifting the file, then playing back the results. After a few experimentations, you'll get the feel for how to apply the technique.

Another way to create realistic trail-off sounds is to reverse the concussion file, apply reverb, and then pitch-shift the sound. Save the file under a different name (for example, Concussion Reverse Element), and layer the sound underneath the original concussion sound. Pitch layering also works well for extending trail-offs.

Fireballs and Flames

If your explosion calls for it, you can layer a billowing fireball or even add a layer of fire that creeps up from the flaming debris. Timing is the key for a convincing effect. The fireball should come after the initial attack of the concussion and fade up in such a way as to appear to be a result of the blast. Play with the fade and timing to find the best balance. Try pitch layering for a towering fireball effect.

Fireworks

In Recording Commandment 2 (see Chapter Eight), I mentioned recording my neighborhood fireworks show every year. Although I realized there would be a lot of background noise, such as people cheering, laughing, and even yelling "Mac!", I still recorded the shows because they always give me wonderful amounts of usable material for building explosions. For this setup, I record as described above, but with two additional record decks:

For record deck 2, I use a stereo microphone pointed at the crowd with the fireworks in the foreground. This provides a natural mix to the event. The oohs and ahhs still come across over the thunderous booms and crackles exploding overhead.

For record deck 3 I use a shotgun mic, but pointed away from the fireworks and at the woods nearby. This is sent to one channel of the deck (the left or the right). The sounds from this microphone and its placement give a reflection perspective of the sounds bouncing off the trees in the distance. For the second mic, I use another shotgun on a 20-foot boom pole pointed straight up in the air. This captures great sounds of the exploding fireworks overhead. From this perspective, though, the initial mortar launch from the ground below sounds faint and distant.

Interestingly enough, these sounds from my neighborhood fireworks have ended up in major films, television shows, and even video games like *Medal of Honor* and *Call of Duty*. I remember playing a video game one day and recognizing one of the sounds that I recorded just a few yards outside the window of the very same room I was playing the game in. You never know how or where your sounds will end up. That harmless bottle rocket could be used to design an incoming mortar shell for the next top-shelf video game!

Safe Blown Open

For a conventional safe like those used in the old Westerns, you'll need to start with a good dynamite blast. You can pitch down a gunshot (preferably a shotgun) and use that for the source of the blast. Safes are located indoors, so avoid using explosions with long reverb tails. The blast should be short and abrupt.

Next, you'll need to add a rusty metallic creak for the safe door opening. Once the door is open, add some character to the door by letting it close a little as it settles. Finally, use paper to imitate the money debris created from the explosion. Throwing a loose stack of paper up in the air can work for this. A more controlled approach would be to hold a few sheets of paper in each hand and perform the paper debris.

Wick Burning

A wick is the most down–and–dirty form of an explosion timer. The sizzle and sparking can build the same suspense as an electronic timer. This sound can be created by recording sparklers and layering the sound. The sound will be quiet, so use a shotgun microphone and place it close to the side of the source. The sizzle and crackle are primarily high frequencies. Roll off any excessive low frequencies that intrude on the sound when the levels are raised.

■ FIRE EFFECTS

Fire makes many types of sounds, from a fluttering wind, to crackles and pops, to billowing roars. The materials used for fuel are what produce these sounds.

Here is a list of good sound-making materials to use for fuel:
Cardboard
Dowel Rods
Hay
Kindling
Lighter Fluid
Logs
Newspaper
Tree Bark
Tree Branches

The following is a list of techniques and tricks for recording and editing fire sound effects:

Fire Recording

Fireplaces are a great place to record fires. Because they're indoors, you'll be able to isolate the fire in your recordings with a few sound blankets. If possible, choose a house that's away from traffic because the chimney will allow some sound leakage from the outside. Another option is to use a barbecue grill, although you'll have to watch out for the sounds of birds, traffic, neighbors, etc. On the other hand, a grill allows you to be more liberal with lighter fluid and other larger flame-building techniques.

When miking fire, remember that heat rises and can damage the diaphragm of the mic. Place the mic low and to the side of the fire. Since fires are generally quiet, position the mic as close to the fire as you can without damaging it. Use a hand test in front of the microphone: If your hand can't tolerate the heat, move the microphone back.

A short shotgun microphone will help you achieve a close perspective on the fire by moving the sound of the fire closer without endangering the microphone. A stereo microphone will give a nice stereo image to the fire, but you won't get as close a perspective. You need to determine whether the fire will be used in an active or passive manner. If the fire will be a passive ambience track, a stereo microphone is the best tool for the job. But if it will be an integral part of a scene, a mono microphone might be the better choice.

Remember, once a sound is recorded in mono it cannot truly be made into a stereo sound, but a sound recorded in stereo *can* be turned into mono. The exception to the rule is to create a good solid mono recording and build stereo tracks artificially in the edit by layering the mono sounds and panning them. When layering the sounds you must use different sections of the mono file or the sounds themselves will be out of phase or can reduce the pan effect. When layered properly, the tracks will create an up-close stereo image of the fire. This doesn't apply to all mono recordings but will work here because fire is basically a drone of crackles, rumble, and wind warble.

Many of the fire's cracks and pops will peak your recordings, but that's acceptable because they will be short events that will sound normal during playback. The focus of the recording should be to gather as much usable flame movement as possible. An old-school technique used in radio plays was to handle cellophane to artificially create the crackle of a fire. This might be useful for sweetening a fire sound, but real fires flutter and roar — cellophane merely crackles. If your fire is lacking crispness, try using this method.

Low frequencies can be boosted in the edit to provide a rumble underneath your source recordings that will amplify the size and intensity of the fire. A unique and hard-to-reproduce sound is metal expanding and warping under the pressure of heat. A sheet of ventilation duct or a metal trash can lid left in a fire for 30 minutes will serve as a great source for these sounds.

Fireballs

Torches are great sources for fireballs. Pitch layering can add weight and size to the blast. Boost low frequencies to build a nice rumble. A massive wave of fire can be built by layering dozens of fireballs along with heavy pitch layering. The idea is to create a seamless wall of moving fire. Avoid noticeable peaks and valleys in the sound. Try to layer the fireballs so they move together: When one fireball starts to fade, have another fireball already taking its place.

Fireballs and blast wave sources can also be created by blowing on a microphone. This will generate a warbled low rumble that is consistent with a fireball wave. It's best to use a source like this for sweetening underneath real torch movements. You can also add crackling fire elements. If there is a deliberate shift in sound, such as a pass-by, you should run the fire elements through a Doppler plug-in so that the pitch changes of the fire match those of the torch movement.

Molotov Cocktail

Developed in the early 1900s, this incendiary weapon consists of a bottle filled with gasoline or other flammable liquid and a rag soaked in the liquid that protrudes from neck of the bottle and is held in place by the bottle's stopper. The rag is ignited and the bottle thrown at an object. Upon impact, the glass smashes and the gasoline is thrown in every direction; the lit rag ignites the gasoline and a huge fireball ensues. A Molotov cocktail can be sound designed by combining a torch being ignited, a torch whoosh, a bottle smash, and finally a fireball and flames.

Torch Movement

To make a torch, take a stick or wooden stake and wrap a thick layer of cotton or fabric on the end. Tie off the fabric tightly so that it won't slip or fall once on fire. Dowse the fabric in lighter fluid (hairspray and other flammable liquids can crackle and produce unwanted hiss).

Recording Torch Movement

Be sure to have a bucket of water standing by to extinguish the torch when you're finished. Obviously, this should only be done outdoors or in a very large garage.

Start your recording before igniting the torch. When it's lit, move it back and forth in front of the mic at various speeds. Spinning the torch around in a circle creates an interesting element to use when designing fireballs. After you're done, record the sound of the torch being extinguished in the bucket. Try not to create too much movement in the bucket so that water splashes aren't picked up by the microphone.

■ FOLEY SOUND EFFECTS

Technically, Foley is the practice of performing sound to picture. Many sound effects libraries have Foley collections that consist of the types of sounds that occur during a Foley session, such as footsteps, clothes movements, door knocks, etc. These collections can be very helpful for sound designers who are in a hurry and don't have time or money to schedule a Foley session.

Today, the lines of what a Foley sound is have become blurred. Some Foley sound libraries include what would normally be considered general sound effects. These sounds can be used for picture sync audio as well as multimedia, radio, and other industries employing sound effects. Perhaps a modern definition of a Foley sound effect could be a sound that is either performed to picture or prerecorded using genuine and artificial props to create a specific sound.

Here are some techniques and tricks for recording Foley sound effects:

Body Falls

To make a believable body fall, you'll need a heavy object or a dummy to work with — and by dummy I don't mean a dim-witted intern. At the Chop Shop, we have a body dummy that we've fondly named Vinnie. This body double consists of a leather coat with a pillow and some phone books crammed inside. The coat we use doesn't have a zipper that would rattle. If you are using a coat that makes sounds like this, remove the zipper or gaff-tape it down.

Vinnie, the Chop Shop Body Double

Drop your dummy on various surfaces to create realistic body falls. A real body fall is a combination of two or three sounds. To create this effect, stagger the fall of the dummy so that it yields multiple sounds instead of a single impact. Hold the body horizontal to the surface and let one end drop first, followed by the other. Leather will give a nice fleshy sound to the impact, but the key to a convincing body fall is the weight of the dummy. If your dummy is too light, add weight by stuffing in another phone book or two.

Door Open/Close

Earlier we discussed techniques for recording door creaks. Opening and closing sounds are miked differently. Creaks are generated by the hinges, but the open and close sounds come from the latch. Use a shotgun mic placed close to the handle in order to focus on the sound of the door and reduce the sound of the room.

Brian Kaurich Recording a Door Handle

Even though you're inside, you'll need to use a windscreen because opening and closing the door will create air movement that could be picked up by the microphone. Miking the door from a few feet away will give more sense of the location, which might be the desired effect; however, a close-miked door can be put in a room in the edit with reverb plug-ins.

Flag

A cotton pillowcase can create the sound of a flag flapping in the wind. Hold the pillowcase lengthwise and alternate raising and lowering your hands. Give some of the downward movements a hard snap. Try not to have a rhythm to your movement as this will be noticeable. Instead, randomize your movements to simulate real wind. Slow movements will sound like light gusts of wind. Rapid movements will sound like strong, steady gusts of wind.

Foliage

An old trick for making a grass sound is to use analog tape bunched together. Once you've transferred all of your old cassette tapes to MP3, pull the tape out and create a sizable pile to work with. If you're a purist, you can find fallen branches and leaves in the forest. Leave the live ones alone — first because they're still alive, but also because dead leaves and branches make more interesting sounds. Some imitation plants can sound close enough.

Horse Hooves

I would be remiss if I wrote this book and did not mention the icon of sound effects — coconut shells being used for horse hooves. The technique is very low tech, but it works. Cut a coconut in half — there's a milky fluid inside, so be ready for a mess — and scoop out the fruit. The best surface for hooves walking on the ground is an earth mix of dirt and straw. If the coconuts have a thin, unnatural sound, try padding them with some foam.

Using Coconuts to Perform Horse Hooves

There are two ways to perform hoofbeats. The most common is a three-step sequence. This is an easy task for Foley artists who are not musically inclined (a.k.a. rhythmically challenged). The sound goes like this: buh-duh-dum. It gives an acceptable illusion of a horse gallop, but for those who take their craft seriously and can keep a beat, there is the true four-step cadence, which goes like this: buh-duh-duh-dum. The four-step hoofbeat is most noticeable at slower paces.

Punches

In real life, punches don't sound very exciting (unless you're the one getting punched). They are a quick flesh impact with not really much sonic life to them. In movies like *Raiders of the Lost Ark*, however, they are exciting and full of life. Movie punches are the product of a combination of recording technique and sound design.

There are many props to choose from for the impact. Purists like to stick with flesh sources like steak. Some opt for the less messy newspaper or phone book alternatives. Others choose to hit leather jackets or baseball gloves with wooden baseball bats. Each method gives a unique character to the sound.

Personally, I like to start with a leather impact and sweeten it with some vegetable splats to help emphasize the fleshy tone of the punch. You can also layer bone breaks and other impacts underneath the punch. Some sound designers add a little reverb to create a larger–than-life crack. And speaking of cracks, the crack of a bull whip can also simulate the sound of a punch.

Stone Door

One day, after a long Foley session, I began to clean up and remove the props from the stage. One of the props that I use is a large plastic bin with carpet taped to the inside to make it sound denser and less like plastic. I pushed the bin out of the way and it made an incredible grinding sound as it moved across the floor. I quickly threw on a pair of headphones and pointed the microphone at the ground. I slid the bin close to the mic and discovered an incredible stone movement sound.

I played with the sound some more and discovered that a thin layer of finely crushed rock salt on top of the concrete floor enhanced the stone-grinding quality of the sound. The bin had a great resonance that gave the sound weight. In the edit, I was surprised to discover I didn't really need to pitch the sound down. Instead, I increased the low frequencies to make it sound bigger and voila! I had the sound effect of a large stone door closing.

Using a Plastic Bin on Rock Salt to Create the Sound of a Stone Door

Since then, I've tried using cinderblock and various types of rocks. I would pitch-shift them down and try equalization to enhance the sound, but I could never seem to recreate the girth and presence of the plastic bin. The principle here is that the real thing is not always the best thing. Experiment with alternatives. Create the sound that you're looking for. Don't settle for "Well, I guess that's what it sounds like." Make the sound what you want it to be.

Whip/Whoosh

An airy whoosh made by whipping a wood stick past a microphone can be used for many things. It can give a sense of movement to a kung fu kick. It can be sped up, looped, and layered to make the sound of a boomerang whizzing by. And it can be used as a transition effect like the scene transitions from the television show *Malcolm in the Middle*.

To record a whip sound, you will need to place the microphone about a foot away from the performance area. You will also need a windscreen to reduce the violent air movements that follow the whip. Use a wood dowel rod or stick for the prop. Stand to the side of the microphone and whip the stick up and down perpendicular to the mic. Were you to stand directly in front of the microphone, you'd cause more air to move toward the mic. In the edit, you may need to roll off some of the low end created by air movement.

Different stick sizes and lengths will make different types of sounds. A cheese

Using a Dowel Rod for a Whoosh

grater tied to a rope and swung around can make an interesting airy sound. Multiple sticks at once can also create a unique effect. Try other props like broomsticks and coaxial cable.

■ FOOTSTEP SOUNDS

Footsteps vary by shoe type, surface, weight, and pace. These simple sounds can help save a soundtrack by adding balance to a scene that was more than likely miked from above the actors, resulting in inaudible footsteps. Without footsteps, the scene sounds surreal and too silent. Never underestimate the importance of these sounds in a film.

Most independent films cannot afford to hire a Foley artist or rent a stage to perform Foley. They are at the mercy of the sound designer's personal library of sound effects to fill in the holes that the footsteps leave. A good sampling of shoe and surface recordings can prove to be an invaluable resource for these situations.

Recording Footsteps on a Stage

Close miking works well for footsteps because the shoes them-
selves can be quiet to begin with. A shotgun or hypercardioid mic will help reduce the amount of clothes movements being picked up during the performance.

Recording Footsteps on Gravel

Position the mic about one or two feet in front of the performer on a short stand that elevates the mic six inches above the surface. Angle the mic to point down at the surface between the two shoes.

Stereo miking is generally not preferred as it makes cutting footsteps harder in the postproduction process. Panning and positioning of the footsteps can be done during the final mix phase of the film.

The pace and intensity of the footsteps can convey emotions that the character in the scene might be experiencing. Performance is thus very important during recording. Experiment with different styles of walking, using a heel-to-toe method to emphasize the actually step itself. For running, try landing both the heel and toe at the same time to communicate a sense of pace. With some practice, you'll be able to vary the performance to match what different scenes call for.

Recording Footsteps on Location

When recording footsteps on location, the environment becomes part of the sound. Capturing the full-bodied sound of the footsteps in these settings requires different miking techniques from stage performances. Positioning the microphone at different distances will add depth to the room and allow the location to be a part of the performance. For interior location work, a stereo microphone will provide a nice sampling of the room's acoustics. For exterior location work, use a short shotgun microphone on a boom pole and follow the footsteps.

Recording on location can add character to the sound that a stage cannot duplicate. An old staircase, for example, will likely yield a hundred creaks and moans as you walk up and down — a sonic texture that's nearly impossible to recreate even by building a stair surface on a Foley stage. The old staircase has had years to settle and warp, developing a nice squeaking quality; the newly built surface just hasn't had sufficient aging time to sound right.

If you do have to simulate this effect on a stage, build a set of stairs from 1 x 4 planks; three or four steps should be enough. Starting with the corners, loosen some of the screws on the planks, allowing the wood to stress and move. Spend some time experimenting with the surface to find where the squeaks are. This method can be effective, but it still won't be as convincing as the real thing.

On location, a long boom pole can allow the performer to run past the recordist and give a sense of travel to the sound. When working with boom poles, be sure to limit hand movements. Wear gloves that will let the pole rotate softly and silently in your hands. Cabled boom poles can produce a rattling sound as the coiled cable bounces around inside the pole, so keep your movements fluid to reduce the cable's motion. Use a short shotgun microphone on the end of the pole.

Footwear and Surfaces

Footwear will give character to your sound, but in the end it's all about the performance. I know I've said that before, but it bears repeating. It's all about the performance.

Shoes!

The following is a list of footwear that can help round out your collection:
Bare Feet
Clogs
Combat Boots
Flip-Flops
Hard Sole
High Heels
Sandals
Soft Sole
Tennis Shoes
Work Boots

The following is a list of surfaces to use for footsteps:
Boardwalk
Carpet
Cement
Earth
Grass
Gravel
Hay
Leaves
Marble
Metal
Mud
Rock
Snow
Stairs
Wood, Hollow Surface
Wood, Solid Surface

■ HORROR EFFECTS

From the strange and supernatural to the gory and evil, horror effects call for creative performances, unusual props — and a mop to clean up the mess. The horror you might feel about recording these effects is quickly dispelled when you realize the following: Vegetables and fruits are often the source for the sounds of mangled broken bones and sliced-up bodies in a good slasher film. Supernatural voices are usually well grounded in the voices of very natural humans. And the things that go bump in the night are often the props that go bump on the Foley stage. All of these elements are transformed into shocking, dreadful, and spooky effects during the editing process.

The following is a list of techniques and tricks for recording and editing horror sound effects:

Blood Drips

Blood is thicker than water. This is not just true of relationships: Blood is literally thicker, and the two liquids sound quite different. A blood splat should sound heavier than a water drip. You can thicken up water by adding flour, which will

Performing Blood Drips with a Watermelon

create a nice, bloodlike splat sound. Or try watermelon chunks for even thicker splats.

Flesh Rips

Orange rinds being peeled can produce a tearing sound. You can twist lettuce and cabbage leaves for a ripping effect. Pulling a melon apart will sound like a carcass being ripped opened. Layered together, these

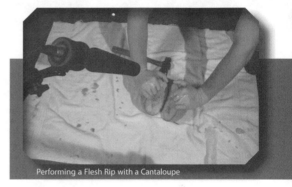
Performing a Flesh Rip with a Cantaloupe

sounds can make the strongest stomach wince.

Guillotine

Some sound effects need to be created by breaking down their elements and starting from scratch. In the case of a guillotine, it's far more economical to layer elements than to try to build a working prop. The sound of a guillotine can be broken down into the following elements:

Blade Drop
Flesh Chop
Head Fall

A real guillotine's blade comes into contact with the wood of the frame as it falls. You can create this effect by layering a sword scrape on metal (i.e., another sword) and a sword scrape on wood. Be sure to match the speed and intensity of the scrapes; they should travel together in one seamless action.

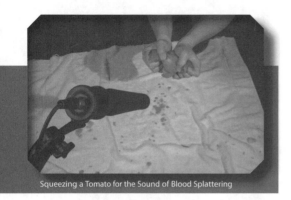
Squeezing a Tomato for the Sound of Blood Splattering

The flesh chop can be built from a quick vegetable rip layered with the sound of a single ax chop into an opened watermelon. For the head fall, drop a head of lettuce. If you want to mimic the sound of a head dropping into a basket, drop the lettuce into a wicker basket like those used for a pet's bed. Dropping the lettuce onto a hollow wood surface will sound like the head falling onto the execution platform. Finally, squeeze a tomato and the let the juice drip for the sound of blood spilling from the neck.

Knife Hacking at Body

A knife plunged into a melon creates a good flesh stab. To avoid too much sound of the rind, open the melon up and hack at it from the inside. A pile of vegetable debris can also offer a good surface. Push the pile together to create more depth for the knife to sink into.

Keep your movements hard and deliberate so the pile doesn't move around too much. Remember, skin is thick and solid, and your sound should emulate that. If you have lettuce, place large leaves facedown on the pile and use that as the flesh surface.

Monsters

Hollywood has been making creature films for decades. The problem is that the creatures are all starting to sound the same. It's very rare to come across a monster growl that hasn't been heard before; there is definitely a clichéd monster sound. This is due in part to the fact that animals are a great source of horrific creature growls and snarls. If you're after that classic monster sound, start with lion growls, jaguar screams, and elephants trumpeting.

The best unique sound effects are those made from scratch. Humans have far more range than almost every other creature in the animal kingdom, so try to produce the sound yourself. Vocalize the sound you're looking for into a microphone and build from there. Avoid using animal sources as the main ingredient, but you might want to try using them to sweeten what you already have.

As described in the animals section, use cups, garbage cans, and other empty objects to give resonance to your voice. If you're planning to pitch-shift the sounds down to make them bigger, perform the growls faster; this will avoid the sound becoming too long when it is lowered in pitch, which can sometimes render it useless. When you're performing, go big. Be animalistic. Let loose. No one is watching — just listening.

Don't limit your creativity to just voices and animals. Organic sources such as a creaky freezer door, a wood chair squeaking across linoleum, and even an engine revving can be processed to create the base for a monster sound. If you are after a unique sound, you'll need to do something that hasn't been done before. Use layering and pitching along with unrelated props and vocalizations to create the bizarre.

Vegetable Abuse

Fruits and vegetables can offer a plethora of sounds to work with: breaks, crunches, dull body sounds, juicy impacts, slimy movements, textures, and more. You can use them to sweeten other sounds, layer them to get juicy hits and impacts, or pitch their movements up to create insects and other creepy sounds. It's really up to your imagination. Remember what your mom told you: "Never underestimate the power of fruits and vegetables."

Use a shotgun microphone up close to record the action. You'll need to use a windscreen or windshield to protect the mic from flying debris. Working with fruits and vegetables is very messy, so it's best to have one person record while another person performs. If you're working solo, have a towel nearby to clean your hands off before touching the microphone or recorder.

Some tools to work with include axes, baseball bats, knives, and spoons. Once you're rolling, you can start the slaughter. Slice, dice, chop, bash, hit, drop, twist, break, snap, and otherwise assault everything in front of you! By the end of the session, you'll have a large pile of culinary debris.

Vegetables Ready to Be Abused

The fun isn't over yet. Now you can work with the debris to create movement and other sound design elements. Once you're finished, double-bag the carnage before taking it out to the trash. After a few days the smell can be unbearable, especially in warm weather.

Below is a list of useful sound-making fruits and vegetables to pick up at the grocery store. They are broken down into sound categories.

Breaks
Carrots
Celery

Crunches
Apples
Bell Peppers
Cabbage
Celery
Lettuce

Dull Body Sounds
Cantaloupe

Eggplant
Potatoes
Watermelons

Juicy Impacts and Movements
Cantaloupe
Oranges
Pineapple
Tomatoes
Watermelons

Textures
Cabbage
Cantaloupe
Lettuce
Oranges
Pineapple

Werewolf Transformation

To create the transformation of a werewolf, you'll need to use a combination of just about everything we've discussed so far. In addition, you can add the sound of a human groaning and writhing in pain. Use chicken bones or celery to create the effect of the body reshaping internally. Hold a couple of stalks of celery together and quickly twist for a gut-wrenching bone break.

You might also want to throw in clothes ripping and tearing. If you want to add hair growth, rub the bristles of a broom against cloth or leather. For a more realistic hair sound, pull a wig tightly through your hand. For the best sound quality, record this effect during a full moon.

■ HOUSEHOLD SOUNDS

Household sounds are the easiest to gather because all of these items are common things found around your home. Recording them will require some cooperation from the rest of the household members, including the cats, dogs, and birds.

The following is a list of techniques and tricks for recording and editing household sound effects:

Appliances

Large appliances will have to be recorded where they are. Use sound blankets to help control the room. Record a minute or so of the appliance operating. Place appropriate props inside the appliance to get a realistic sound. For example, a toaster ejecting sounds different when there's bread inside. Also, record any switches, buttons, doors, drawers, and other components that the appliance has.

Isolate small appliances like blenders and coffee grinders from countertops and kitchen tables to prevent these surfaces from resonating, which would give an undesirable low end to your sound. For complete isolation, hold the appliance in you hand or place it on top of several folded towels.

Doorbell

A doorbell can be recorded up close with a shotgun mic to isolate it from the room. To give the doorbell more character, use a stereo microphone a few feet away to incorporate the sound of the room. For a distant perspective, point a stereo mic away from the doorbell. You can also try recording perspectives from different rooms, to capture, say, what the doorbell would sound like from upstairs. Keep in mind that doing this might introduce other, undesirable background sounds and significantly lower the recording level.

Shower

For the record, don't take recording equipment into a shower when the water is running. That said, you can safely point a stereo microphone over the shower door or curtain, centering the stream of water to the microphone. Record takes of the entire sequence of taking a shower as well as individual takes of the water running. Don't forget that the water will sound different when someone is inside using the shower. Have a friend assist you with this. Remember, microphones only have ears and not eyes, so you can keep your shorts on!

With the water running, go down into the basement and record the sound of the water rushing through the pipes. Have someone repeat the actions mentioned above while you're recording from this perspective. Some pipes make a bang when they're turned on or off. Try to find the location and record the bang.

Toilet

There are several perspectives to think about when recording a toilet. You can record behind the tank, up close, a few feet away, and outside the room with the door closed. Each perspective is unique and offers a different type of sound. Of course, you should do each take with the lid up and with the lid down. While you're working with the toilet, lift up the tank lid and record some sounds of the plumbing inside.

Incidentally, sound designer Ben Burtt used a tank lid being taken off the toilet as the sound for the Ark of the Covenant's lid in *Raiders of the Lost Ark*. This goes to show that in the world of sound effects, lofty and ornate visuals can be voiced by the lowest and humblest of props. Burtt demonstrated a clear case of listening with the ears instead of the eyes when he discovered this effect.

100 Household Sounds

A house has far more to offer than you might think. Before heading off into the field, master your recording skills at home. This will build up your experience and familiarize you with recording all sorts of different objects and machines.

Here's a list of 100 sounds to consider recording at your house:
Air Conditioner
Alarm Clock
Animals/Pets
Attic Door
Barbecue Grills
Bathtub
Bathroom Fans
Bicycles

Blender
Bottles
Breaker Box/Electrical Box
Brooms
Cabinets
Cars
Ceiling Fans
Cleaning Supplies
Clocks
Clothes
Coffee Grinder
Coffeemaker
Computers
Cooking
Dishes
Dishwasher
Doorbell
Doors
Drawers
Dryer
DVD Player
Eating
Electric Razor
Electric Toothbrush
Exercise Equipment
Fireplace
Food
Freezer
Furnace
Furniture
Games
Garage Door Open/Close
Garbage Cans
Garden Hose
Glasses
Hair Dryer
Hair Products

Hand Tools
Ice Maker
Jacuzzi
Jars
Ladder
Lamps
Lawn Care Tools
Lawn Furniture
Lawn Mower
Lawn Sprinklers
Lightbulb Remove/Replace
Linens
Liquids
Luggage
Microwave
Mops
Office Equipment
Pantry Supplies
Pill Bottles
Plumbing
Pool
Pots and Pans
Power Tools
Radio
Refrigerator
Rollerblades
Screen Door
Sewing Machine
Shower
Silverware
Sinks
Skateboard
Sliding Closet Doors
Smoke Detector
Snowblower
Sports Equipment
Stairs

Still Camera
Storage Supplies, Bins
Stove
Swing Set
Teakettle
Television
Toaster
Toiletries
Toilets
Toolbox
Toothbrush
Toys
Utility Room Tub
Video Camera
Washer
Weed Whipper
Weight Scale
Windows

■ HUMAN SOUNDS

Perhaps the easiest sounds to record are human elements. The performer can follow directions and instantly create the sounds you need. On the other hand, working with infants and children is far more difficult and takes time, patience, and multiple sessions.

There are two schools of thought on microphone selection for voice work. The first is to record with a large condenser mic such as the Rode NT-2000 or the Neumann TLM-103. These mics will give the voice a full-bodied sound. Some outboard processing such as a microphone preamp and some compression might be commonplace with these mics, but for sound effects purposes, try recording the voices without using outboard gear. Position the microphone less than a foot away from the mouth; you'll also want to put a pop filter in front of the microphone to reduce the strong plosive sounds that occur during words that begin with the letters "b" or "p." This placement will produce a strong and clean radio-ready voice.

The second microphone choice would be a short shotgun mic. Place the shotgun as you would during an ADR session: a few feet in front of and above the talent and angled toward the mouth. This position helps match the type of dialogue that is typically recorded on film sets and gives a sense of air or room around the voice.

In either case, be sure to have the talent wear headphones that fully cover the ears to stop sound spill from reentering the mic. Avoid recording right after the talent has eaten a meal or consumed soda or other sugary drinks; this can coat the mouth and create wet smacking sounds when the mouth is opened and closed. Your talent should only drink room temperature water during recording sessions.

The following is a list of human sound effects to record:
Blow Nose
Breathe
Burp
Chew
Clear Throat
Cough
Cry
Fart
Gag
Gargle
Giggle
Grimace
Groan
Grunt
Hiccup
Laugh
Moan
Phrases (Hello, Goodbye, I Love You, etc.)
Raspberry
Reactions (Ah, Oh, Aww, etc.)
Scream
Shush

Sigh
Sip
Slurp
Smack Lips
Sneeze
Sniff
Snort
Spit
Swallow
Whimper
Whistle

■ IMPACT EFFECTS

An impact is defined as two objects colliding. Falls, hits, drops, and scrapes are in this category. Recording techniques for impacts are very much the same as for drums. Back in the analog days, small levels of distortion were acceptable and often desired for impacts; they gave the sound a larger-than-life quality. In digital recordings, distortion sounds harsh and brittle, so it should be avoided. There is, however, a trade-off to consider.

Lowering the level of an impact during recording so the sound doesn't clip also lowers the rest of the sound, not just the initial attack. As a result, the decay of the impact is diminished. Compressing the impact in the edit will restore the decay, but at the cost of potentially adding hiss to the sound.

The trade-off is that you might want to let the initial impact deliberately clip in order to preserve the rest of the sound. This is not advised for the beginner; you need to experiment over time to perfect this practice. In a pinch, you can record multiple takes with and without clipping and cut the two together. This will give you a clean attack and a good level of decay.

In general, impacts are a single-source element. Shotgun mics are a good choice for fieldwork. For studio work, you might want to try a larger diaphragm mic to help capture the beefiness of the impact.

The following is a list of techniques and tricks for recording and editing impacts:

Bullet Impacts

A bullet impact is basically a fast surface impact. The hit needs to be hard. Debris and splintering should be added underneath wood hits. Glass impacts don't always need to break. You can record a realistic glass splinter by hitting a pile of glass debris with a hammer. Metal impacts can be created by taking a hammer and hitting a shovel.

Some sound designers go to extreme lengths to record realistic source material for bullet impacts. One such extreme is to use a pig carcass as a target on a gun range; the impacts have a resonance close to that of a human body. But a cantaloupe or watermelon will give much the same effect.

You can sweeten the impact with a bullet ricochet. There are several ways to create the sound of a ricochet. You can record the real thing on a gun range with a microphone near the target. You can also simulate the whizzing sound by using a slingshot to shoot quarters, screws, or large washers over the top of a microphone. A sound design technique is to take race car pass-bys, filter out the engine with equalization, and process from there.

Earth Impacts

Heavy earth impacts are hard to imitate on a Foley stage. They're often enhanced and sweetened with low-frequency boosts that add weight and the effect of ground vibrations. If you're going to create the effect in Foley, start with a thick pile of earth mix to help separate the sound of the floor. To give character to the impact, drop textured objects such as a balled-up leather jacket on the surface. In the edit, you can play with the pitch of the sound and sweeten it by adding an LFE sound underneath.

Metal Impacts

These impacts make great source material for crashes and sound much bigger when pitched down. Large hollow objects like a dumpster can create deep, rich tones. Try to find a dumpster that's completely empty; objects inside will dampen the sound and may rattle. Record the impact from both inside and outside. The inside sound will be huge, so watch your levels.

Sheet metal has a distinct tone: The metal vibrates very easily and has a reverb-like tail. To demonstrate this, take some sheet metal into the studio and stand at the opposite side of the room. Now clap your hands once — you'll hear the sheet metal vibrating. In Foley, it's a good idea to remove any sheet metal from the stage when it's not in use because of its tendency to generate unwanted sounds in response to other vibrations. When you're using sheet metal, pitching the impacts down will create amazing hits that can be used for explosion sources.

Recording Mud Suction in a Bucket

Mud Impacts

Recording mud impacts is messy. If your stage allows for it, bring in dirt and water and play to your heart's content. A cleaner alternative is to use wet towels or wet newspapers for the impacts. The only catch is that you won't get any of the suction sounds associated with mud. Without much mess you can add suction sounds with a deep mud-filled bucket.

■ INDUSTRIAL SOUNDS

Industrial sounds come from tools and machinery that tend to be loud or percussive. Some of the motors in this equipment will cause interference or glitches in digital recordings. And as with loud sirens, some micro drives will malfunction or stop recording altogether. It's best, therefore, to use compact flash cards that are not affected by specific vibrations.

Some larger machines such as stamping machines, conveyor belts, and mill presses can't be moved onto a sound stage, so you'll have to record them on location. Factories and work plants may allow you access to their facilities at night or during a light shift when the building is quiet or less active. Don't forget to turn off any fluorescent lighting that might produce a buzz or hum.

The following is a list of techniques and tricks for recording and editing industrial sound effects:

Arc Welder

Arc welders produce fantastic electric zaps that can work as science fiction source material. Use a boom pole and a shotgun microphone to get close to the machines and help isolate them from the rest of the room. You'll need to wear eye protection. To record someone working with an arc welder as a sound effect instead of source material, use a stereo microphone and stand a few feet away for perspective. The power supply for an arc welder also makes an interesting hum. Be sure to record the sound of it starting up, running, and shutting off.

Assembly Lines

Automaker Henry Ford is credited with introducing the assembly line into the American culture. As a Detroiter, I can attest to the fact that there are far more assembly lines in Michigan than Starbucks! Other industries have adapted the assembly line and applied its principles to making everything from food to toys. Today there are assembly lines everywhere across America.

It's not always easy to gain access to facilities with assembly lines, but if you do, you'll find a myriad of sounds to gather. Bring a shotgun and a stereo mic, along with a boom pole. Use the stereo mic for ambiences and room tones, and the shotgun for up-close sounds of conveyor belts, robotic arms, and other machinery. It should be noted that some factories will only allow you on the factory floor if you're wearing protective footwear. If you have them, wear steel-toed boots.

Pneumatic Tools

You'll find pneumatic tools in auto repair shops as well as the garages of neighbors who own construction businesses. In the latter case, you can ask them to bring their equipment into your studio for isolated recording. A pneumatic tool operates with air produced by an air compressor. Be sure to record the air compressor running as a separate event. For the actual tool sound, place the compressor in another room and run the hose into your Foley stage. Great sounds to consider include removing the tool from the hose and air blasts with an air trigger.

It's very difficult to record tools at an auto shop without the room shaping their sound. This might be desirable if that's the environment in which the sound effect will occur. Because the location plays such a heavy role in the sound, use a stereo microphone and record different perspectives — close and distant. Be sure to keep the pneumatic tool centered to the mic.

Power Tools

You shouldn't have any trouble finding power tools — most likely in your own garage or workroom. It's also easy to bring them onto a Foley stage for good isolation. Remember that you'll want to record them working, not just running. Bring some screws, nail gun packs, wood, and other supplies to use the tools with.

A cardioid or hypercardioid microphone placed 12 to 18 inches away should provide a good recording. Watch your levels — and your ears. Some of these tools — a circular saw, for instance — can be very loud. You might want to take off the headphones (just this once!) and wear earplugs.

Warehouse Door

The wheel track of a cargo bay door can be a great source sound for mechanical movements. You can place a shotgun mic close to the track in a stationary position or follow the movement of the door as it opens and closes. A stereo mic placed in the center of the door a few feet back will give a good, general sound of the door's movements.

■ LFE (LOW-FREQUENCY EFFECTS)

LFE is the .1 in a film's 5.1 surround sound track. These effects are normally used as sweeteners for other effects and rarely as effects in themselves. They can add profound bass character to an otherwise plain sound. This track enhances and extends the full body of a sound effect.

The frequency range for an LFE is 20Hz to 120Hz (these standards differ between formats like Dolby Digital and DTS). The 20Hz-50Hz range has an almost subsonic quality that makes the sound more felt than heard — it's more a vibration than an audible sound. These powerful, teeth-rattling frequencies are the culprits for picture frames falling off your walls when you watch films like *Pirates of the Caribbean* and *Spiderman*. Typically they'll only come across through a subwoofer. In order to develop these effects correctly, you'll need to have a subwoofer in your studio.

Impacts, rumbles, and thumps are the primary types of LFE effects. LFE sounds can be made by taking any normal sound and rolling off all of the frequencies above 100Hz. You may need to apply an EQ filter numerous times to fully remove all of the upper frequencies. Compression should be added to help thicken the sound.

Steady, constant rumbles can be created by taking white noise, rolling off the frequencies as described above, and pitch-shifting down the sound. For rumbles that fluctuate, you can use just about anything. For example, a highway traffic ambience can be filtered and pitched down so that it becomes a sporadic LFE rumble. Experiment with different sources to see what works best for your sound.

■ MULTIMEDIA EFFECTS

Multimedia effects are electronic and organic sounds that correlate with images on cellular phones, DVD menus, CD-ROMs, Web sites, and so on. These sounds can be used in a literal or a metaphorical manner. There are many techniques for creating them. Perhaps the best way is to work with the visual that the sound is intended for. What does it look like? What do you think it would sound like? Start there.

The following is a list of techniques and tricks for recording and editing multimedia sound effects:

Beeps

A beep can be recorded from an "organic" source such as a digital alarm clock or microwave button. Some ENG field mixers have a 1KHz tone generator that could be recorded directly into your field recorder. Beeps can also be created electronically through a synthesis plug-in or tone generator inside your DAW. Once you have a solid tone to work with, it just becomes a matter of pitch shifting and processing.

Multiple beeps can be cut together and pitched up to create a single beep. Layering various pitched beeps together can yield interesting musical tones. Distortion and equalization can give a negative quality to the beeps, which helps if you're after an alert tone. You'll quickly find that high-pitched beeps don't need much level to sound loud. Protect your ears and keep your levels low. High-pitched beeps do not need to be normalized.

Buttons

Button sound effects confirm a digital action. These sound cues indicate that a command was received and is in progress. The type of sound used can help give a sense of style to the button. Sources for these effects can be organic or electronic.

Organic sources include:
Fans
Flashlights
Joysticks
Lamps
Mixers
Mouse Clicks
Power Switches
Staplers
Toys

Keep in mind that you can edit, pitch, and layer any combination of the objects listed above to create slower, faster, and multiple clicks. A button doesn't have to be limited to a single or double click. Gears, ratchets, and springs can be layered to create more complex sounds.

Mouse Overs

A mouse over is the sound associated with a menu item that expands when the cursor is placed over it. The sound usually communicates a sense of movement or expansion. Take any short sound source and process it with a delay, then reverse the sound, then add more delay, then reverse it again, and finally pitch the sound up. This produces a straightforward electronic sound. Repeating the steps above several times will create even more exotic sounds. Experiment with organic sounds as well. Objects sliding can create a sense of movement that can work well with the visual.

■ MUSICAL EFFECTS

Musical effects are sounds made with musical instruments that are not songs. Examples include a guitar tuning, a cymbal crash, and a drumroll. You mic these sounds just as you would when recording a song. The key to recording musical instruments is to find where the sound is coming from. For example, an acoustic guitar's sound comes from the appropriately named sound hole. A piano's sound comes from under the lid.

Be sure that the music you make is original. For example, when played in succession, the three notes that make up the NBC logo are copyrighted. You can parody these notes, but you cannot play them exactly. When working with music boxes, check for the copyright information of the tune being played. Failure to do so could infringe on the copyright holder's legal rights and result in a lawsuit. When in doubt and no information is available, choose another source. An electronic keyboard may have a comparable sample that you can use to perform your own tune or a song in the public domain (such as "Twinkle, Twinkle Little Star").

Here is a list of musical elements that you can record:
Bells
Cymbal Crash
Drumroll
Gong
Guitar Feedback
Guitar Lick
Guitar Tuning
Musical Scales
Orchestra Tuning Up
Piano Chords
Piano Sliding through Keys
Rim Shot
Singing Bowls
Synthesizer Stab
Tambourine Shake
Tribal Drumbeat
Trumpet Blare
Xylophone Sliding through Notes

■ OFFICE SOUNDS

An office building can offer hundreds of sounds to record. You'll find office machinery, office supplies, elevators, and computers galore. Try setting up a time to record at an office after hours. If people will be there, use a stereo mic to gather ambiences. If you're working with objects, bring a shotgun microphone.

Most offices have fluorescent lighting, which can cause a buzz or hum in your recording. If you have to, work with the lights off. You may also need to turn off machines like printers and copiers that might have fans running. Another noise problem is the heating and air conditioning system. Find a thermostat and disable it while you work (get permission to do this). It's a good idea to make a list of what was changed or moved while you were recording. Use the list at the end of the session to put everything back the way it was.

When working in an office or a business establishment, focus on the sounds that are harder to find elsewhere. You can always record scissors and staplers on the Foley stage, but a real office may be the only place to record something big like a copier.

Office and business sounds to look for include:
A/V Carts
Binding Machines
Cash Boxes
Cash Registers
Copy Machines
Elevators
Fax Machines
File Cabinets
Laminators
LCD Projectors
Office Doors
Office Furniture
Office Phones
Overhead Projectors
Paper Cutters
Paper Easel

Paper Shredders
Paper Trimmers
Printers
Printing Calculators
Projection Screens
Time Clocks
Vending Machines

■ SCIENCE FICTION SOUNDS

Science fiction sound effects give carte blanche to the sound designer. This is mainly because the bulk of the sounds are purely fictional and don't have a real-world counterpart to record. Alien creatures, laser blasters, and spaceships do not exist — or at least they're not available for you to record. So imagination is the key to producing realistic fictional sounds (pardon the oxymoron).

A common technique for creating science fiction sound effects is to look for comparable real-world props or vehicles. Start with present-day objects that might evolve into something used in the future. Make this source the base for your sound, and design from there.

Electronic sounds and synthesizers served as the primary source for sound effects in the early years of science fiction movies. This practice greatly diminished in the 1980s largely because of pioneer sound designer and multiple Academy Award winner Ben Burtt (*Star Wars, Raiders of the Lost Ark, Willow*). He singlehandedly redefined the sounds of science fiction and other film lore by utilizing organic material such as film projectors, guy wires, and walruses to engineer authentic-sounding science fiction sounds.

The following is a list of techniques and tricks for recording and editing science fiction sound effects:

Air Bursts

A can of compressed air can be a useful source for air blasts and pneumatic sounds. Aim the blast away from the microphone to avoid damaging the diaphragm. Experiment by blowing the air into cups, jars, PVC pipes, and other objects to create unique sounds. A single air blast with some reverb added can make a very effective processed air release.

Laser Gun

The *Star Wars* laser guns were created by recording a hammer hitting a guy wire. This gave the weapon a blast or hit as the basis of the sound. It served as the laser equivalent of a concussion followed by a trail-off, which in this case was the sound of the aftershock vibrations traveling down the wire. You can get a similar effect by processing an interesting impact sound with delays and pitch bending. Electronic-based laser gunshots can be created by taking a synthesized beep or tone and pitch-bending it.

Planet Atmospheres

These sounds are droning in nature but can also contain signs of life. The standard psychological sound of a desolate planet is desert wind. Don't always stick with the obvious. Try building scary, suspenseful, or even ethereal sound beds without using wind as the main ingredient. Ambiences that have been pitched down and processed could be used as the primary sound. Experiment with forest or jungle ambiences that have been reversed and filtered. You could even use your voice to create interesting elements to process and shape. Experiment. No one has heard the sounds of other planets. So, technically speaking, there's no wrong way to make one.

Robots

Robots usually consist of a series of servo movements. Servomotors can be found in automobile side mirrors, toys, or even DVD player trays. Record these sources and build up a library of servo samples. Bring these samples into a loop-based DAW to layer and pitch together as seamless calculated movements. To add a human element to the robot, try using organic sounds to create vocalizations. This could include processing a human voice.

Spaceship Door

A spaceship door is a movement sound. Electronic sounds don't work nearly as well as real-world sources. Play with objects of various textures to find the sound you're after. A sheet of paper can give a natural flanging sound when pulled from a stack. An automatic sunroof or car window can provide an interesting glass shield effect with some slight processing. You can layer pneumatic air blasts to suggest airlock mechanisms.

For character, try to make the opening sound and the closing sound differ in pitch. An opening sound could start off slightly lower in pitch and rise as the door opens. A closing sound could start off slightly higher in pitch and then drop. Reversing the opening sound to create the closing sound should be done with care. Sounds that are reversed with no additional processing are easy to spot and can spoil the effect.

Spaceship Pass-By

Rocket ships and other spacecraft can be sound designed from real-world vehicles. Planes, jets, cars, and helicopters offer great starting points. It's difficult to build a sound from scratch and create a Doppler effect using only plug-ins. Recording these vehicles in the real world gives a natural Doppler effect and sense of movement. Try to filter the original source so that it isn't easily recognizable. Phasing and flanging effects quickly add an unusual texture to the sound and help separate it from our world.

■ TECHNOLOGY SOUNDS

Technology is constantly evolving and new devices emerge every year. Many of the sounds generated by these devices are in fact sound effects created by sound designers. A few years ago, the sound of a camera shutter was a mechanical sound. Today, digital cameras recreate that sound from an electronic file created by a sound designer and stored in the camera.

Other basic technology effects include PA systems, recording devices, and other electronic equipment. The sounds of modern-day technology can be used as source material to create science fiction sound effects, spy gadgets, and multimedia effects. These effects are getting more and more difficult to record as advanced production of the devices themselves has resulted in noiseless or ultraquiet machines. You should, however, be able to bring such devices to the Foley stage and close-mic them with a shotgun microphone to achieve a usable recording level.

The following is a list of techniques and tricks for recording and editing technology sound effects:

Cell Phone Rings

Most cell phone rings are copyrighted. But don't worry: They're much easier to create than you think. A single sine wave from a tone generator is all it takes to make advanced and elaborate ringtones. Use a loop-based DAW to layer and pitch-shift your sound effect.

Import the sine wave (for example, a five-second 1KHz tone) into your DAW and copy the sample to multiple tracks. Now place the samples on the timeline at various intervals. Use the DAW's timeline grid as a guide for timing the placement of the samples. You can even change the pitch of one, some, or all of the samples to create musical ringtones.

Here is a quick, down-and-dirty tutorial for making a simple ringtone:

1. Start with one frame (1/30 of a second) of a 1KHz tone.
2. Add one frame of silence after the tone.
3. Repeat steps 1 and 2 until there are eight tone samples with seven sections of silence in between.
4. Add eight frames of silence to the end of the file.
5. Repeat steps 1 through 4.
6. Add one second of silence at the end of the file.

What you will now have is a basic cell phone ring that is about two and a half seconds long. Loop this sound over and over until someone answers the phone or it goes to voicemail.

Microphone Feedback

No matter who's at the pulpit in the movie, the microphone will always produce feedback as soon as they start to talk. I guess Hollywood has had some bad experiences with live sound engineers and has decided to make them the subtle butt of the joke for these scenes. The reality is that the PA system probably isn't even turned on during filming — the feedback is added in post.

A quick way to create your own feedback is to hold your headphones up to the microphone while recording. This will save your ears from the painful shriek, at least until you get to the edit. Headphone feedback is usually very high in pitch. You can lower this pitch and add some reverb or delay to give it a PA system sound. For a more true-to-life sound, record a large speaker or guitar amp with a microphone plugged in.

■ VEHICLE SOUNDS

Transportation sound effects cover a broad range of mechanical, electrical, and fuel-powered vehicles, including public transportation, aircraft, and watercraft. Recording techniques can vary drastically from one vehicle to another. One of the most popular techniques used in recording vehicles for film is onboard recording.

This technique records from a vehicle perspective while in motion. Many recordists will place several microphones in various positions inside and outside the vehicle; these perspectives are recorded to one or more recorders, to be used in sync or as isolated tracks. In a film, these synchronous recordings give the sound designer more options to choose from.

There are four major groups within the transportation category:
Aircraft
Automobiles
Boats
Trains

The following is a list of techniques and tricks for recording and editing transportation sound effects:

Aircraft

As discussed in the ambience section, standing near the end of a runway on the outside of the perimeter fence will yield some pretty good results. It's always nice to get closer to the action, but today's security concerns make that nearly impossible, especially if you're not attached to a major film or video game project.

Smaller aircraft are far more accessible. Through six degrees of separation, everyone's firefighting brother knows someone who owns a plane or has a pilot's license. Riding along inside a plane with a stereo microphone will give you the sound of being in the cockpit. On the ground with the engine off, be sure to have the pilot flip as many switches and gears as possible, and record these sounds with a shotgun microphone.

Here is a quick reference of things to record on an airplane:

Interior and Exterior Perspectives
Start
Idle
Shut Down
Taxiing
Takeoff
Climbs
Dives
Landing

Automobile Drive-Bys

Cars, motorcycles, trucks, and just about everything else roadworthy with an engine and wheels can fit into this category. When producing sound effects for picture sync, be sure the driving surfaces match the images. A rough concrete surface sound won't work for a smooth highway surface image. And dirt roads recorded after a rainfall will produce a bumpy texture that may not match what is seen on screen. Make the textures of the sound and image match.

Standing on the side of a road that has intermittent traffic will give you isolated pass-bys of all sorts of vehicles. Look for a location

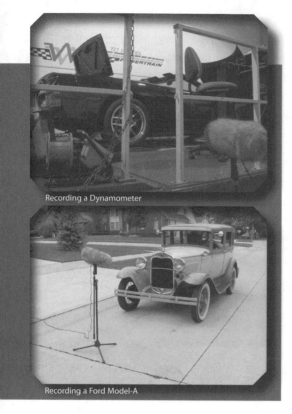

Recording a Dynamometer

Recording a Ford Model-A

without any birds or insects that could spoil the recordings. Slate the make and model of the vehicles that pass by so that you can name them correctly in the edit. If you don't have time to slate with your voice for fear of spoiling the sound of another approaching vehicle, take notes on a pad of paper and reference the take number or counter location of the field recorder.

Have friends or family drive to the location and perform some drive-bys for you. This will give you performance control over a variety of vehicles. As discussed in the Ten Recording Commandments (see Chapter Eight), record the vehicles at different speeds to give yourself more sounds to work with in the edit and to build up your library.

Automobiles, Onboard Recording

The following are the main positions for onboard mic placement for cars:

1. Engine Perspective/Under the Hood
2. Tailpipe Perspective
3. Interior Cabin Perspective

Engine Perspective

This perspective is perfect for car chase sequences because it gives you the purring and roaring of the engine as it idles, takes off, and rips through the gears. It produces the in-your-face voice of an engine. Place a lavaliere microphone under the hood above the engine block. Be careful with your placement; exposing the microphone to the heat of the engine can result in permanent damage. Some recordists use less-expensive dynamic microphones. Run the microphone cable out of the hood, along the side of the car, and through the window to the recorder. Never mount or leave the recorder inside the engine compartment.

Tailpipe Perspective
The tailpipe is responsible for the guttural and throaty rumble of a car. Place a microphone close to the end of the tailpipe, using a cloth or other material to buffer the vibrations of the metallic surface; this will also isolate the microphone from the heat of the tailpipe. A heavy-duty windscreen can be fashioned from fabric and materials such as windjammers or a Hi-Wind cover. It's also wise to surround the microphone to shield it from strong airflow by placing it inside a PVC tube or small coffee can lined with carpet or foam.

Interior Cabin Perspective
This perspective gives the general ambience of riding inside the vehicle. The effect is useful by itself, but a nice mix of this perspective and the engine mic perspective will provide a seemingly more realistic effect. In reality, modern vehicles tend to isolate the cabin interior from engine noise. Nonetheless, the sound feels right when mixed properly.

Here is a list of general sounds to record on an automobile:

Interior Vehicle
A/C on Low, Medium, High for 60 Seconds (No Engine)
Door Ajar Alarm
Door Locks Up/Down
Door Open Light/Hard
Engine Drive Up/Shut Off
Engine Revs
Engine Start/Drive Off
Engine Start/Idle for 60 Seconds/Turn Off

Gear Shifter
Glove Box Open/Close
Hazard Lights
Hood Open/Close
Horn Blast Short, Long, Multiple
Key Insert/Remove
Mirrors Adjust
Seat Automatic Adjust
Seat Belts Fasten/Unfasten
Seat Recline Back/Forward
Sunroof Open/Close
Trunk Open/Close (Interior Perspective)
Turn Signal
Windows Up/Down
Windshield Wipers on Low, Medium, High for 60 Seconds (No Engine)
Windshield Wipers Wash Window/Mist (No Engine)

Exterior Vehicle
Door Locks Up/Down
Door Open Light/Hard
Engine Drive Up/Shut Off (Close Perspective)
Engine Drive Up/Shut Off (Distant Perspective)
Engine Revs (Distant Perspective)
Engine Revs (Grill Perspective)
Engine Revs (Tailpipe Perspective)
Engine Revs (Under Hood Perspective)
Engine Start/Drive Off (Close Perspective)
Engine Start/Drive Off (Distant Perspective)
Engine Start/Idle for 60 Seconds/Turn Off (Distant Perspective)
Engine Start/Idle for 60 Seconds/Turn Off (Grill Perspective)
Engine Start/Idle for 60 Seconds/Turn Off (Tailpipe Perspective)
Engine Start/Idle for 60 Seconds/Turn Off (Under Hood Perspective)
Gas Cap Remove/Replace
Gas Door Open/Close
Hood Open/Close

Horn Blast Short, Long, Multiple
Mirrors Adjust
Sunroof Open/Close
Trunk Open/Close
Windows Up/Down
Windshield Wipers on Low, Medium, High for 60 Seconds (No Engine)
Windshield Wipers Wash Window/Mist (No Engine)

Note: Treat different speeds on fans, wipers, etc. as different sounds. Turn the device on, let it run, then turn it off. Repeat these steps for each speed. Record the engine revs as complete events. Rev the engine and then allow it to return to the normal idle before revving again. This will give you a natural edit point later.

Boats

Boats offer nearly as many elements to record as automotive vehicles. Out on the water, turn the motor off to record waves against the hull and other objects on the boat. It's a good idea to secure your recording equipment in the center of the boat. Strap the equipment to a chair or other object mounted to the boat to prevent it from moving around and getting wet. Cover the gear with towels; plastic covers are noisy and may interfere with recording.

Use a stereo mic for sounds that incorporate the water, such as motoring and waves splashing. The wind will be an issue, especially at high speeds. Be sure to bring a Hi-Wind cover to combat this. Try recording different perspectives while the boat is moving. Record some of the takes with the microphone facing forward and away from the motor and some takes with the microphone facing toward the motor.

Here is a list of general sounds to record on a boat:
Anchor Up/Down
Cabin Interiors
Docking Sequence
Horn Blast Short, Long, Multiple
Inboard Motor Drive Up/Shut Off

Inboard Motor Driving Onboard
Inboard Motor Pass-Bys
Inboard Motor Revs
Inboard Motor Start/Drive Off
Inboard Motor Start/Idle for 60 Seconds/Turn Off
Life Preserver over Side
Outboard Motor Drive Up/Shut Off
Outboard Motor Driving Onboard
Outboard Motor Pass-Bys
Outboard Motor Revs
Outboard Motor Start/Drive Off
Outboard Motor Start/Idle for 60 Seconds/Turn Off
Paddles
Sails Up/Down
Throttle Movements
Waves against Hull

Wave Runners

Recording a Swamp Buggy from the Shore

Wave runners offer an interesting challenge for recording onboard perspectives. A surefire way of recording the constant movement is to follow alongside in a boat. Use a long boom pole and a shotgun microphone to help separate the sound of the boat you are recording from and the wave runner. This should produce a solid onboard sound without putting your equipment at risk of getting damaged. Pass-bys for a wave runner could be recorded from a boat or a dock.

Trains

For train pass-bys, find a quiet location with very little automotive traffic. An intersection with no crossing bell will give you a clean pass-by. If you can't find an intersection without a crossing bell, head down the track on foot about a quarter of a mile so that you won't pick up the crossing bell after the train passes. Stay a safe distance from the track. Trains are loud, so you don't need to be up close — and you'll also want to turn down your gains.

Recording a Train Crossing Bell

Use a stereo microphone pointed at the track perpendicularly; this will give you a stereo perspective as the train moves past you. A shotgun microphone could be used to record the perspective of the wheels. The difference between the two perspectives might not be that noticeable because of the high volumes of the sound. You might be better off recording in stereo and mixing down to mono during the edit.

Get a train schedule for the track you're recording, either online or by calling the train station. You don't want to waste time sitting by the tracks all day — unless, of course, it's a nice day. As a train approaches, motion for the engineer to blow the horn or whistle. They're usually up for it.

Subway Train

If you're looking for a good subway train sound, you can take a section from a train pass-by and loop it. Remember, the train's engine is moving toward you or away, so its sound will be constantly changing in pitch, making it difficult to loop. Use a clean section in the middle of the sound where the engine is far enough down the tracks not to be heard. Find a piece of the sound that is just the clicks and clacks of the wheels. Metal screeches can be added for brakes. Place the sound in a tunnel with a reverb plug-in. For a pass-by, use a Doppler effect plug-in.

■ WARFARE SOUNDS

The sounds of war include nearly infinite layers of bullet fire, shell casings, explosions, yells, screams, bullet impacts, tanks, airplane flybys, and much more. This is the chaos of combat. In films, though, it's a very controlled chaos. Special effects engineers plan every stage of every scene. Sets are designed right down to all the pyrotechnics. Stunt actors rehearse their actions until they're perfect.

The recorded aspects of these scenes are just as controlled. Tanks are recorded separately from the tank fire, gunshots are recorded separately from the gun handling, and the actors' screams are recorded separately from the bullet impacts. Although the real-world sounds might not be as bedazzling as their sound designed equivalents, it's best to start with real source material before manufacturing the sounds from scratch.

The following is a list of techniques and tricks for recording and editing warfare sound effects:

Gunshots

The sonic characteristics of gunshots are directly related to the environment in which they're recorded. A gunshot is merely a quick pop. If recorded near a mountain range, the pop transforms into a thick report as it rips across the flat plains, bounces off the mountains, and returns with an echo, giving the sound a nice trail-off feature. If recorded at an indoor gun range, the pop will quickly grow into a monstrous and murky boom as it reverberates around the room with dozens, if not hundreds, of echoes. If recorded in a forest, the pop will become a thin, weak crack as the sound bounces off thousands of leaves and dozens of tree trunks.

Be selective in choosing a location. Remember to listen with your ears and not your eyes (is that concept sinking in yet?). A great-looking location may not be a great-sounding location. Do some tests before inviting your gun handler out to the location.

Because guns are difficult to record and firing locations difficult to find, it's a good idea to record with multiple recorders and multiple mic placements. You'll need to use pads or attenuators because the initial attack of the gunfire will undoubtedly overload your mic preamps. When you're recording, have the shooter pause between shots so you can capture the trail-off without the interruption of the gun being reloaded or cocked. Set up visual signals between you and the shooter to communicate when to reload and fire the next shot.

In setups with close mic placements, bullet casings hitting the ground might get recorded unintentionally. Use a sound blanket to provide a silent landing surface for the shells. This also makes it very easy to clean up the shells after the session. After a while, the shells may start landing on each other, so do a quick cleanup between takes. Save the spent shells to use as props in Foley.

Just about every gun differs in the volume it produces. Always play back a test recording of each gun before continuing with the session. Failure to do so may result in a set of wasted recordings that can be costly and time-consuming to re-record. In addition, always record safety takes of each weapon. You can never record enough source material.

It will be difficult to slate each take with your voice because of microphone levels and placement, so plan on keeping a written log. If you have one, you could use a bullhorn to slate the takes.

Exercise extreme caution when monitoring the sounds produced by the guns. Do not use headphones during the actual gunshots. Instead, wear earplugs and monitor the levels on the recorder's meters. Use headphones for playback and listen at low levels during the initial gunshot, then at higher levels after the shot to check for background sounds and trail-off. If you do not take these precautions, you could permanently damage your ears.

Gun Recording — Exterior

The following setup employs four recorders that will allow up to eight individual tracks. These tracks will provide safety recordings in the event of distortion or undesired results from one of the

microphones. You'll also get different distances and sound qualities that can be mixed together in the edit process.

Position 1
Send to Recorder 1 — Channel 1 (Left) and Channel 2 (Right)
A stereo mic placed behind the shooter and facing the firing range
gives an overall general perspective of the event. The microphone
will capture more of a crack than a concussion.

Position 2
Send to Recorder 2 — Channel 1
A dynamic cardioid microphone placed beside the barrel of the
gun captures more the mechanics of the weapon than the actual
shot itself. This recording will rarely be used alone, but it is an
excellent sweetener for the other perspectives. The sound is dry
and isolated.

Position 3
Send to Recorder 2 — Channel 2
A larger diaphragm condenser microphone placed directly in front
of the gun captures the bravado of the event. This distance provides the space that the sound needs in order to develop the large,
low-frequency waves. This will be your typical gunshot sound
effect.

Position 4
Send to Recorder 3 — Channel 1
A short shotgun microphone pointed toward the gun captures
the crack and flyby of the bullet. This unique placement captures
a good balance of attack and decay that can give a larger-than-life
sound to the weapon.

Position 5
Send to Recorder 3 — Channel 2
A second short shotgun microphone pointed downrange and away
from the gun focuses more on the pass-by of the bullet and less on
the crack of the shot.

MXL 991
60' From Gun /
2' From Ground
Angled Away From Gun

MXL 991
60' From Gun /
2' From Ground
Angled Toward Gun

Sennheiser 416
25' From Gun /
2' From Ground
Angled Away From Gun

Sennheiser 416
25' From Gun /
2' From Ground
Angled Toward Gun

Advanced Gun
Recording Set Up
Outdoor Range

Rode NT-3
10' From Gun /
2' From Ground
Angled At Gun

Shure SM57
5' From Gun /
Level With Gun
Angled At Gun

Shooter

Rode NT-4
10' From Gun /
10' From Ground
Angled Parallel To Barrel

Gun Exterior Microphone Placement

Recording a
Pistol Shot
from Various
Perspectives

Position 6
Send to Recorder 4 — Channel 1
A small diaphragm condenser microphone placed farther down-range and pointed toward the gun captures a good distant perspective of the event that's difficult to simulate in the edit process.

Position 7
Send to Recorder 4 — Channel 2
A second small diaphragm condenser microphone placed down-range but pointed away from the gun captures more of the pass-by and trail-off reflections.

Combinations of these recordings will provide a vast array of options in the edit process and can be used to match nearly every scenario your production might require.

Gun Recording — Interior

This setup uses three recorders that will allow up to six individual tracks. As before, these tracks provide safety recordings in the event of distortion or undesired results.

Position 1
Send to Recorder 1 — Channel 1 (Left) and Channel 2 (Right)
A stereo mic placed behind the shooter and facing down the firing range gives an overall general perspective of the event. The microphone will capture more of a crack than a concussion.

Position 2
Send to Recorder 2 — Channel 1
A dynamic cardioid microphone placed beside the barrel of the gun captures more the mechanics of the weapon than the actual shot itself. Again, this recording will rarely be used alone but works as an excellent sweetener for other perspectives. The sound is dry and isolated, with very little reverb.

Position 3
Send to Recorder 2 — Channel 2
A larger diaphragm condenser microphone placed directly in front

MXL 991
5' From Target Or Wall /
2' From Floor
Angled At Target

MXL 991
5' From Target Or Wall /
2' From Floor
Angled Toward Gun

Advanced Gun
Recording Set Up
Indoor Range

Rode NT-3
10' From Gun /
2' From Floor
Angled At Gun

Shure SM57
5' From Gun /
Level With Gun
Angled At Gun

Shooter

Rode NT-4
10' From Gun /
10' From Floor
Angled Parallel To Barrel

Gun Interior Microphone Placement

Using a
Sound
Blanket to
Catch the
Shells at an
Indoor Gun
Range

of the gun provides your typical gunshot sound effect. There will be a heavy amount of reverb from this position.

Position 4
Send to Recorder 3 — Channel 1
A small diaphragm condenser microphone placed farther down-range and pointed toward the gun captures an equal amount of reverb and attack from the shot.

Position 5
Send to Recorder 3 — Channel 2
A second small diaphragm condenser microphone pointed away from the gun and toward the target or range wall captures ricochets and bullet hits. This also gives a mix of the event that contains more reverb than attack.

Combinations of these recordings will provide fewer options in the edit process than exterior recordings and are highly subjective in their perspective. An exterior gunshot can be processed to simulate an indoor gunshot, but the reverb signature of an interior gunshot is too prominent for the reverse to work. However, this reverb makes interior gunshots great sources for explosions. Pitching down the sound will create a powerful blast and the room's reverb tail will turn into a rich, even trail-off.

A Sheriff's Deputy and the Author at the Macomb County Sheriff's Department

Automatic Machine Guns

Access to fully automatic machine guns and heavy artillery may be as simple as a phone call to your local National Guard base or sheriff's department. You might be surprised at how eager they might be to help. You'll need to scout the location before the sessions to ensure that the background noise is acceptable and that the surroundings will produce minimal echo.

If you're unable to secure a location or weapons to record, you can produce the sound artificially with a non-automatic weapon. Start by determining the bullet caliber of the automatic machine gun you wish to simulate. Next, find a non-automatic weapon with the same caliber. Record sam-

Having Fun between Takes with an M-16 Machine Gun

ples of the weapon, bring them into a multitrack editor, and layer single shots together to create an automatic sound.

Avoid using the same single shot for layering; it will sound digital and fake. Also, let each sound play out. Don't cut the shots back to back because some of them will sound cut off. Layering allows each bullet to travel off while the next round is fired, which will make the sound closer to the real thing. To be accurate, you should do some research to determine what the firing rate of the automatic weapon is and match your designed shots to that speed.

Gun Foley

Every type of weapon has unique movement sounds. Be sure to record everything that each weapon has to offer. Most gun owners are reluctant to let you drop their expensive weapons on the ground, but you can simulate the effect with staple guns and other tools. The action of most weapons isn't very loud. Use a shotgun mic up close to help create an in-your-face sound of the weapon.

Gun movement sounds don't really exist in the real world. In film, though, any time the hero raises his weapon to take aim there's an associated sound. Holding several props together can create this effect. Try using a leather

The Gun Vault at the Macomb County Sheriff's Department

belt with a loose buckle wrapped around the staple gun you just dropped on the floor.

Here is a list of Foley sounds to record with guns:
Barrel Open/Close
Bolt Close
Bolt Open
Bolt Open and Close (Single Event)
Bullet Loaded/Unloaded into Chamber
Chamber Spin
Dry Fire
Hammer Pull/Release
Magazine Insert Empty/Full
Magazine Load/Unload Bullets
Magazine Remove Empty/Full
Pistol Remove from/Replace in Holster
Racking
Safety On/Off

Missile Pass-Bys
Producing a missile pass-by involves a very simple trick: Take a commercial jet pass-by and pitch it up. You can pan the sound to help sell the movement. An explosion can be added at the end of the sound for the impact. Match perspectives between the missile and the explosion. At the end of the pass-by, the missile will sound distant. The explosion should then follow suit and sound distant as well. If you want the explosion to be up close and powerful, cut the missile in the middle of the pass-by, before the Doppler shift, and insert the explosion there.

Ninja Star Throw
The sounds of martial arts weapons such as nunchakus, ninja stars, and throwing knives are based on movement. For a ninja star throw, you'll need multiple stick whips layered together for the length of time the weapon travels. Next you'll need a small metal ring for the impact. You can up-pitch a knife or sword strike for this. Add the impact of the object the star hits. For a human target,

use a combination of a punch for the impact and a squish for a blood element.

Sword Impacts

A sword impact or scrape can be created by using two long pieces of metal. Home improvement stores have steel straps and rods that work perfectly. Of course, you can purchase the real thing at a store or online at a site like *www.bestbuyswords.com*. You don't have to swing the props hard to get a convincing sound. In fact, you can keep one prop stationary and strike it with the other. Hold the props lightly, using only your fingers, so as not to dampen the ring of the metal. To get a muted metal impact, hold both props firmly. For scrapes, put both props on a slight inward angle and slide one across the other.

Performing a Sword Scrape with Real Swords

Performing a Sword Hit with Metal Straps

You don't need to strike the sword into a surface to get an impact. For example, impacts into surfaces like metal, stone, or wood can be layered against a solid sword hit to sell the effect of the surface. You can add a swoosh sound at the front of the effect by using a stick whip to mimic the sound of a sword traveling through the air.

■ WATER SOUNDS

Water offers unique recording challenges primarily because water and electronics do not make good bedfellows. Equipment can suffer

from prolonged exposure to humidity and direct contact with water. Special care must be taken to ensure that your microphone stays nice and dry — while the recordings sound sopping wet.

The following is a list of techniques and tricks for recording and editing water sound effects:

Aaron Eschenburg Recording Splashes Up Close

General Water Sounds

Pools and lakes are great sources for big splashes and water movements, but background noise can be a problem. A bathtub works for small sounds like drips, but their splashes tend to be very tub-sounding. If your Foley stage allows for it, bring a children's pool inside for isolated recordings. A large blow-up pool works better than the hard plastic ones. Use an electric water pump to remove the water when you're finished recording. Simply run the hose from the pool to an indoor drain or to the outside.

Splashes and violent movements will of course send the water in every direction, making microphone placement difficult. Water effects should be miked high and to the side. Use a zeppelin to stop water from damaging the microphone, but keep in mind that water can seep into the fibers of the fabric surrounding the zeppelin's shell. A few drops here and there should be fine, but avoid dousing the zeppelin.

Unless a specific effect calls for a low-frequency texture (such as an ocean roar, a waterfall, or deep underwater gurgles), the frequency range for liquids is 200Hz and higher. Therefore, the majority of the material recorded can be edited with low-cut filters to keep only the frequencies affected by the liquid. This will help to remove unwanted background noise and other extraneous sounds and produce a clean, natural result.

Bubbles

Water bubbles can be created by blowing into a glass of water with a straw. For deeper and bigger bubbles, use large bowls or pots. The diameter and length of the straw will also affect the girth of the bubbles. Use a section of garden hose or a snorkel in a children's pool to produce enormous bubbles. If you're going to record water boiling, you'll need to mic the pot from a few inches back and to the side. Keep in mind that the heat from the stove will rise along the side of the pot and can damage your microphone if it's too close.

Drip

A water drip is much quieter than you might think. The levels it will produce on the recorder will be relatively low. Use a shotgun mic with a zeppelin to get closer to the water. A bathtub or sink is a perfect place to record, but don't use a running faucet because the sound of the faucet itself will interfere with the take. Dip your finger into a glass of water and let the drips fall into a sink or tub full of water. For louder drips hold your finger higher above the water.

For multiple drips, hold a wet sponge over the water. Don't squeeze the sponge, which could be heard in the recording. Instead, let the water naturally find its way out of the sponge. Record several takes of this and cut them together to produce longer sounds.

Sewers and Caves

A sewer can be recorded on location, but there's an easier way than dealing with all the stench and rats. Take water drips from a sponge source and cut them into long sections. Use layers to create more drips. Offset the layers so that the same drips don't occur at the same time on different tracks.

If you have a 30-second loop, break it up into three tracks. On the

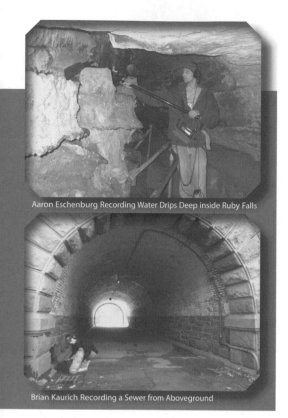

Aaron Eschenburg Recording Water Drips Deep inside Ruby Falls

Brian Kaurich Recording a Sewer from Aboveground

first track, start the loop at the beginning. For the second track, start the sound ten seconds into the loop. For the third track, start the sound 20 seconds into the loop. This will give you a full sound without noticeable loop points. If the loop is in mono, pan track 1 to the left, keep track 2 in the center, and pan track 3 to the right. Avoid hard-panning these tracks. Instead, find a compromise — for example, 50% left and 50% right. This will create a natural-sounding stereo field.

Once you have a steady bed of drips, you can apply reverb plug-ins to create environments like caves and sewers. Pitch-layering the loops can help build depth into the drips. For example, water dripping farther down the cave would sound lower in pitch than drips that are closer.

Waves on a Beach

Nothing is more relaxing than the sound of waves crashing against the beach. And what better way to spend the day than recording on the beach? You've been looking for an excuse to play in the sun and here it is. The catch is that shoreline locations can be difficult to record because of the patrons on the beach. Look for a stretch of isolated beach, perhaps on private property (be sure to get permission).

If you strike out on a location, try a different time of day. Recording at night — when the populated surf transforms into a marine desert — can be a great solution. Select a location that's free of traffic noises and other superfluous sounds. If you're lucky, you won't get mobbed by seagulls.

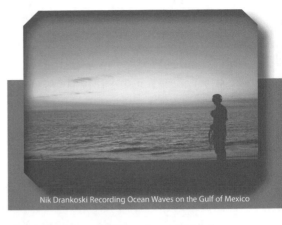

Nik Drankoski Recording Ocean Waves on the Gulf of Mexico

Windy days are perfect for recording waves. Bring a Hi-Wind cover just in case. Set up a stereo mic centered to the horizon; this will balance the sound of the waves. If you miss spending time with the winged rats, try early morning sessions when the beach bums are still sleeping underneath the pier.

Underwater Recording

Now that we've discussed how dangerous it can be to record near water, let's discuss putting your microphone into the water. A hydrophone is a unique submergible microphone that records the vibrations and sounds heard underwater. DPA Microphones' DPA8011 Hydrophone is a high-end solution for true aquatic recordings, but its cost exceeds $2,000. There's a cheaper and dirtier solution. It's called the condom trick.

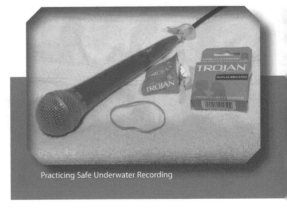

Practicing Safe Underwater Recording

Place a microphone inside a condom. If you use a lubricated condom, it's your own fault. An omnidirectional microphone works best, but a cardioid pattern will suffice. Use an inexpensive microphone in case of a leak. Seal the condom off by wrapping rubber bands tightly around the cable. Submerge the microphone and start recording. You might be surprised at how well the recordings turn out. Be sure to dispose of the condom when you're finished so your significant other doesn't get suspicious.

Note: Do not try this with microphones that you are not willing to throw away. If any liquid enters the microphone, it can become permanently damaged.

Another approach to creating underwater sound effects is to record water material from above the surface and design the sounds in the edit. Remember that high frequencies are subdued or nonexistent underwater. Use equalization and pitch shifting to achieve the right sound. For example, ocean waves pitched down low enough will produce an underwater ambience.

■ WEATHER AND NATURAL DISASTER SOUNDS

Weather sounds can be produced artificially, but the best results come from real sources. Natural disasters need to be designed from scratch. Because of their scope and size, you'll need to have an arsenal of elements to create disasters like twisters, avalanches, landslides, and earthquakes. Weather can be recorded whenever it happens. Sometimes that's the problem.

Rain

I've spent many days waiting to record rain. The irony is that I've also spent many days waiting for the rain to stop so that I could continue recording something else. Over the years, I've gotten into the habit of recording rain and thunderstorms whenever they happen — even if I don't need the material at the time.

Whenever I hear thunder or rain, I grab a recording package and set up in the garage — it's one of the reasons I always keep a package ready to go at a moment's notice. I use a stereo microphone on a stand with a zeppelin and windscreen and place the assembly a couple of feet inside the garage. This shields the gear from the rain and doesn't interfere with the sound. I press record and go back to work (or sleep), letting the recording roll for an hour or two.

I keep the recordings on a hard drive until I need the material for a sound I'm working on. Sometimes I don't use the material for months or even years. But when I need it, I've got it. Besides, you never know when the perfect lightning bolt will strike. The more you record, the better chances you'll have of recording it when it happens.

If the rain hasn't fallen in your neck of the woods for some time, don't start beating the drums and dancing on the lawn. There's a trick to artificially producing rain. Rain is essentially thousands of drops of water landing on a surface. So grab a garden hose and press the red button on your recorder. Keep the stream steady and constant. Once you have a good sample, you can loop it in the edit and build monsoons from it.

Try spraying the water on different surfaces, such as a window on the side of a house, concrete, brick, shingles, grass, etc. For the sound of rain on a lake or ocean, spray the water into a pool and layer the drops over waves. Using a hose also works great for recording the interior of a car with rain hitting the windshield. Use your imagination.

Earthquake

An earthquake sound effect can be as simple as a low-frequency rumble (see the LFE section) or more complex, with the ground splitting open along with other chaos and debris. Texture is important for the ground movements. Pitching the sound of a balloon being rubbed, dragging heavy objects across earth surfaces, and processed wood cracks all make good sources for this.

Be careful not to muddy up your track by boosting the low frequencies on all of the elements. Be selective with what you enhance. Most of the time, you're better off using the low-frequency rumble for your low end and keeping the other elements crisp and bright. This will create a sound that has good frequency balance.

CHAPTER NINETEEN

The Future of Sound Design

Breaking the Sound Barrier...Again

F I COULD SUMMARIZE THIS book in one statement, it would be this: *There is more than one way to make a sound effect. Make it any way you can — just make it better than what you've heard before.*

Inspiration and Influence

Inspiration and influence are polar opposites. One can give you a boost of creative energy and send you hurtling off in a new direction. The other can lock you into thinking in a specific direction and can give you tunnel vision. Everyone works differently.

Some musicians listen to other songs in their particular genre to inspire them to create their own original songs. Other musicians refuse to listen to other songs or influences while writing music so as to avoid tainting or altering their natural songwriting direction. Sound design is musical in nature. It is an orchestration of various sound elements blended together to create a symphony of what would otherwise be considered everyday noises.

For each person there is a balance between being inspired and being influenced. Inspiration can lead to artistic breakthroughs, while influence can stifle the creative process. To date, millions of sound effects have been created, and hundreds of thousands of them are for sale in stock libraries. The world doesn't need the same sounds regurgitated over and over. Audiences want to hear fresh, new material. Make something new and different. Move past the preconceptions of what an explosion sounds like. Design something cooler.

Listen to Films, Don't Just Watch Them

There are movies that you watch and then there are movies that you listen to. Great sound films don't have to have incredibly deep storylines or award-winning acting to be entertaining ... although it definitely helps. They do, however, need great sound designers and talented Foley artists. When you combine a deep storyline with great acting and superb sound design, you end up with an Academy Award-winning film like *Lord of the Rings*. Below is a list of some great movies to listen to and the sound designers involved. Study the sounds and the way they're layered and focused upon. For some scenes, turn the screen off and just listen.

The Sound of the Rolling Boulder in *Raiders* Is a Honda Civic Coasting on Gravel. *Raiders of the Lost Ark*, ©1981 Luscasfilm Ltd., All Rights Reserved.

Great Sound Movies

Aliens ... Don Sharpe
Apocalypse Now ... Walter Murch
Backdraft ... Gary Rydstrom
Contact ... Randy Thom
Fight Club ... Ren Klyce
The Haunting ... Gary Rydstrom
The Incredibles ... Randy Thom
Jurassic Park ... Gary Rydstrom
The Long Kiss Goodnight ... Paul Berolzheimer, Steve Flick, Charles Maynes
The Lord of the Rings ... David Farmer
The Matrix ... Dane Davis
Monsters, Inc. ... Gary Rydstrom
Raiders of the Lost Ark ... Ben Burtt
Saving Private Ryan ... Gary Rydstrom
Snatch ... Matt Collinge
Star Wars ... Ben Burtt
Toy Story ... Gary Rydstrom
True Lies ... Wylie Stateman
Twister ... Greg Hedgepath, Charles Maynes, John Pospisil
Underworld ... Scott Gershin

Analyze these films for sound content, timing, mixing techniques, and impact. Having great sound effects and using them in a way that builds emotion, tension, and action are two different things. While listening to these and other films, ask yourself these questions:

Is that sound effect realistic or does it seem forced?
How does that sound relate to the rest of the mix?
What did they use to make that sound?
How could I make that sound effect?

Giving Credit Where Credit Is Due

Although sound is half the experience of a movie, the sound design credits are often buried deep at the end of the film — after all of the production assistants, craft service people, and producers' girlfriends. It's a shame. A good filmmaker knows the value of great sound design. These filmmakers often see to it that the sound designer's credit is listed where it belongs — on the front credits, with the rest of the designers and artistic leads in the film.

Here are some sound designers who have had a big impact and influence on my work:
Gary Rydstrom
Ben Burtt
Randy Thom
Scott Gershin
Dane Davis
Charles Maynes
Ren Klyce
Alan Howarth

Sound design is often a thankless job. One of the best compliments is when no one notices what you've done. Sure, all of your hard work and passion goes undetected. But what it really means is that you did your job right.

The Future of Sound Effects

There's a greater need for sound effects today than ever before. From the crude thunder sheets of centuries ago to the birth of radio and on to the Internet, sound effects continue to play a major role in storytelling. With cinema, television, radio, video games, multimedia, cell phones, and now the popularity of *YouTube*, sound effects production is increasing. These resources are becoming available to everyone, not just the pros. The technology is becoming more affordable, and with digital filmmaking on the rise, a new breed of sound designers is beginning to crest the horizon. I hope this book helps you in your journey.

Sean Viers, Future Sound Designer

Resources

Keeping Up with Technology and Techniques

BELOW IS A LIST OF books, magazines, manufacturers, trade organizations and unions, and online resources.

Caveat emptor: Although I fully endorse some of these companies and organizations, inclusion in this section does not necessarily mean endorsement.

Books

Acoustic Design for the Home Studio
Mitch Gallagher
Thomson Course Technology

Audio Pro Home Recording Course
Bill Gibson
Mix Books

Complete Guide to Game Audio
Aaron Marks
CMP Books

Modern Recording Techniques
David Miles Huber, Robert E. Runstein
Focal Press

Recording and Producing in the Home Studio
David Franz
Berklee Press

Sound Design
David Sonnenschein
Michael Wiese Productions

Understanding Audio
Daniel M. Thompson
Berklee Press

Trade Magazines
Audio Media
www.audiomedia.com

Electronic Musician
www.emusician.com

EQ
www.eqmag.com

Keyboard
www.keyboardmag.com

Mix Magazine
www.mixonline.com

Post Magazine
www.postmagazine.com

Pro Audio Review
www.proaudioreview.com

ProSound News
www.prosoundnews.com

Recording
www.recordingmag.com

Sound on Sound
www.soundonsound.com

Online Resources

www.filmsound.org
This Web site offers a wealth of information about professional sound design.

Sound Effects Bible
www.soundeffectsbible.com

Yahoo Sound Design Group
sound_design@yahoogroups.com
This group consists of Academy Award-winning sound designers as well as amateur recordists. This is a great place to ask questions, research information, and network.

World Wide Pro Audio Directory
www.audiodirectory.nl

Organizations and Unions

AES — Audio Engineering Society
www.aes.org

AMPAS — Academy of Motion Picture Arts & Sciences
www.oscars.org

ATAS — Academy of Television Arts & Sciences
www.emmys.org

CAS — Cinema Audio Society
www.cinemaaudiosociety.org

Dolby
www.dolby.com

European Broadcasting Union
www.ebu.ch

GANG — Game Audio Network Guild
www.audiogang.org

Library of Congress
www.loc.gov

MPSE — Motion Picture Sound Editors
www.mpse.org

NARAS — National Academy of Recording Arts and Sciences
www.grammy.com

PACE Anti Piracy
www.paceap.com

SMPTE — Society of Motion Picture and Television Engineers
www.smpte.org

THX
www.thx.com

Sound Effects Companies

Blastwave FX
www.blastwavefx.com

Hollywood Edge
www.hollywoodedge.com

Noise Fuel
www.noisefuel.com

Pro Sound Effects
www.prosoundeffects.com

Sound Dogs
www.sounddogs.com

Sound Ideas
www.sound-ideas.com

Soundsnap
www.soundsnap.com

Stock Music.net
www.stockmusic.net

Equipment Retailers

B&H Photo Video
www.bhphotovideo.com

Broadcast Shop
www.thebroadcastshop.com

Custom Supply
www.mediasupplystore.com

Full Compass
www.fullcompass.com

Guitar Center
www.guitarcenter.com

Markertek
www.markertek.com

Musician's Friend
www.musiciansfriend.com

PSC (Professional Sound Corporation)
www.professionalsound.com

Sweetwater
www.sweetwater.com

TAI Audio
www.taiaudio.com

Trew Audio
www.trewaudio.com

Microphone Manufacturers

AKG
www.akg.com

Audio Technica
www.audio-technica.com

Audix
www.audixusa.com

DPA
www.dpamicrophones.com

Holophone
www.holophone.com

MXL
www.mxlmics.com

Neumann
www.neumann.com

Oktava
www.oktava-online.com

Rode
www.rodemic.com

Rycote
www.rycote.com

Sanken
www.sanken-mic.com

Schoeps
www.schoeps.de

Sennheiser
www.sennheiser.com

Shure
www.shure.com

TRAM
www.trammicrophones.com

VDB
www.vdbboompolesuk.com

Plug-In Developers

Altiverb
www.altiverb.com

PSP
www.pspaudioware.com

TC Electronic
www.tcelectronic.com

Universal Audio
www.uaudio.com

Waves
www.waves.com

Recording Equipment

Edirol
www.edirol.com

Fostex
www.fostex.com

On-Stage Stands
www.onstagestands.com

Pelican
www.pelican.com

PortaBrace
www.portabrace.com

Roland
www.roland.com

SilicaGelPackets.Com
www.silicagelpackets.com

Sony
www.sony.com

Sound Devices
www.sounddevices.com

Zoom
www.zoom.co.jp

Software Developers

Ableton
www.abelton.com

Adobe
www.adobe.com

Apple
www.apple.com

Cakewalk
www.cakewalk.com

Digidesign
www.digidesign.com

Lexicon
www.lexicon.com

Reason
www.propellerheads.se

Sony Media Software
www.sonymediasoftware.com

Steinberg
www.steinberg.net

Studio Equipment

Alesis
www.alesis.com

Argosy
www.argosyconsole.com

Auralex
www.auralex.com

Dorrough Electronics
www.dorrough.com

Ebtech
www.ebtechaudio.com

Foam Factory
www.usafoam.com

Furman
www.furmansound.com

iLok
www.ilok.com

Mackie
www.mackie.com

M-Audio
www.m-audio.com

MOTU
www.motu.com

Noren Products
www.norenproducts.com

Omnirax
www.omnirax.com

Presonus
www.presonus.com

Raxxess
www.raxxess.com

Studio RTA
www.studiorta.com

Tannoy
www.tannoy.com

Tascam
www.tascam.com

Yamaha
www.yamaha.com

FILMOGRAPHY

OTHER REFERENCES

ABOUT THE AUTHOR

Ric Viers has worked in the film and television industry for more than ten years. His location sound credits include nearly every major television network, Universal Studios, *Dateline*, *Good Morning America*, Disney, and many others. His sound design work has been used in major motion pictures, television shows, radio programs, and video games. In 2007, Viers launched his own label, Blastwave FX, to celebrate the release of his 100th sound effects library. To date, he is considered to be the world's largest independent pro-vider of sound effects, with more than 150,000 sounds and more than 150 sound effects libraries to his credit. He has produced sound libraries for numerous pub-lishers, including Apple, Blastwave FX, Sony, Sound Ideas, and The Hollywood Edge.

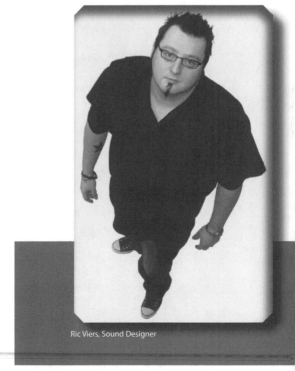

For more information visit *www.ricviers.com*.

Ric Viers, Sound Designer

SOUND DESIGN
THE EXPRESSIVE POWER OF MUSIC, VOICE, AND SOUND EFFECTS IN CINEMA

DAVID SONNENSCHEIN

The clash of light sabers in the electrifying duels of *Star Wars*. The chilling bass line signifying the lurking menace of the shark in *Jaws*. The otherworldly yet familiar pleas to "phone home" in the enchanting *E.T.*

These are examples of the many different ways in which sound can contribute to the overall dramatic impact of a film. When it comes to crafting a distinctive atmosphere for your film, sound design is as important as art direction and cinematography, and it can also be an effective tool in expressing the personalities of your characters. In addition to introducing basic theory and analyzing specific examples of sound design in well-known films, this groundbreaking book shows you how to use music, dialogue, and sound effects to provoke an emotional reaction from your audience. Interactive, simple exercises nurture your creative ability to hear and compose the most effective sounds to express the story and then seamlessly integrate them with all the other cinematic elements.

"I'm very impressed with the broad range of well-researched information and David's fascinating reflections about the emotional power of sound and music. His 'Try This' sidebars are clever, stimulating exercises. The need for such a book is great indeed, fulfilled in this obviously heartfelt project."
> — Gary Rydstrom, Academy® Award-winning Sound Designer,
> *Terminator 2, Titanic, Jurassic Park, Saving Private Ryan*

"The scope, seriousness, and depth of this book give it a unique value. Sonnenschein has articulately assembled a great deal of thought and information about the deeper aspects of the sound design craft."
> — Dane Davis, Academy® Award-winning Sound Designer,
> *The Matrix, Boogie Nights, The Hand that Rocks the Cradle*

"A comprehensive guide that any sound professional can't live without. David's research is penetrating and thorough, with detailed analysis and straightforward commentary on one of the least understood areas in filmmaking."
> — George Watters II, Supervising Sound Editor, *Pearl Harbor,*
> *The Hunt for Red October, The Rock, Naked Gun 2*

DAVID SONNENSCHEIN is an award-winning Sound Designer who directs feature films and teaches vibrational healing and sound design.

$19.95 · 245 PAGES · ORDER NUMBER 11RLS · ISBN: 9780941188265

FILM DIRECTING: SHOT BY SHOT

VISUALIZING FROM CONCEPT TO SCREEN

STEVEN D. KATZ

BEST SELLER
OVER 190,000 COPIES SOLD!

Film Directing: Shot by Shot — with its famous blue cover — is the best-known book on directing and a favorite of professional directors as an on-set quick reference guide.

This international bestseller is a complete catalog of visual techniques and their stylistic implications, enabling working filmmakers to expand their knowledge.

Contains in-depth information on shot composition, staging sequences, visualization tools, framing and composition techniques, camera movement, blocking tracking shots, script analysis, and much more.

Includes over 750 storyboards and illustrations, with never-before-published storyboards from Steven Spielberg's *Empire of the Sun*, Orson Welles' *Citizen Kane*, and Alfred Hitchcock's *The Birds*.

"(To become a director) you have to teach yourself what makes movies good and what makes them bad. John Singleton has been my mentor... he's the one who told me what movies to watch and to read Shot by Shot.*"*
> – Ice Cube, *New York Times*

"A generous number of photos and superb illustrations accompany each concept, many of the graphics being from Katz' own pen... Film Directing: Shot by Shot *is a feast for the eyes."*
> – *Videomaker* Magazine

"... demonstrates the visual techniques of filmmaking by defining the process whereby the director converts storyboards into photographed scenes."
> – *Back Stage Shoot*

"Contains an encyclopedic wealth of information."
> – *Millimeter* Magazine

STEVEN D. KATZ is also the author of *Film Directing: Cinematic Motion*.

$27.95 · 366 PAGES · ORDER NUMBER 7RLS · ISBN: 0-941188-10-8

SETTING UP YOUR SHOTS, SECOND EDITION

GREAT CAMERA MOVES EVERY FILMMAKER SHOULD KNOW

JEREMY VINEYARD

This is the 2nd edition of one of the most successful filmmaking books in history, with sales of over 50,000 copies. Using examples from over 300 popular films, Vineyard provides detailed examples of more than 150 camera setups, angles, and moves which every filmmaker must know — presented in an easy-to-use "wide screen format." This book is the "Swiss Army Knife" that belongs in every filmmakers tool kit.

This new and revised 2nd edition of *Setting Up Your Shots* references over 200 new films and 25 additional filmmaking techniques.

This book gives the filmmaker a quick and easy "shot list" that he or she can use on the set to communicate with their crew.

The Shot List includes: Whip Pan, Reverse, Tilt, Helicopter Shot, Rack Focus, and much more.

"This is a film school in its own right and a valuable and worthy contribution to every filmmaker's shelf. Well done, Vineyard and Cruz!"
— Darrelyn Gunzburg, "For The Love Of It" Panel, *www.ForTheLoveOfIt.com*

"Perfect for any film enthusiast looking for the secrets behind creating film... It is a great addition to any collection for students and film pros alike....." Because of its simplicity of design and straight forward storyboards, this book is destined to be mandatory reading at films schools throughout the world."
— Ross Otterman, *Directed By* Magazine

"Setting Up Your Shots is a great book for defining the shots of today. The storyboard examples on every page make it an valuable reference book for directors and DP's alike! Great learning tool. Should be a boon for writers who want to choose the most effective shot and clearly show it in their boards for the maximum impact."
— Paul Clatworthy, Creator, StoryBoard Artist and StoryBoard Quick Software

JEREMY VINEYARD is currently developing an independent feature entitled "Concrete Road" with Keith David (*The Thing, Platoon*) and is working on his first novel, a modern epic.

$22.95 · 160 PAGES · ORDER NUMBER 84RLS · ISBN: 9781932907421

THE WRITER'S JOURNEY
3RD EDITION

MYTHIC STRUCTURE FOR WRITERS

CHRISTOPHER VOGLER

BEST SELLER
OVER 170,000 COPIES SOLD!

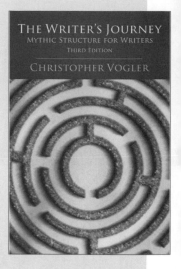

See why this book has become an international best seller and a true classic. *The Writer's Journey* explores the powerful relationship between mythology and storytelling in a clear, concise style that's made it required reading for movie executives, screenwriters, playwrights, scholars, and fans of pop culture all over the world.

Both fiction and nonfiction writers will discover a set of useful myth-inspired storytelling paradigms (i.e., "The Hero's Journey") and step-by-step guidelines to plot and character development. Based on the work of Joseph Campbell, *The Writer's Journey* is a must for all writers interested in further developing their craft.

The updated and revised third edition provides new insights and observations from Vogler's ongoing work on mythology's influence on stories, movies, and man himself.

"This book is like having the smartest person in the story meeting come home with you and whisper what to do in your ear as you write a screenplay. Insight for insight, step for step, Chris Vogler takes us through the process of connecting theme to story and making a script come alive."
> – Lynda Obst, Producer, *Sleepless in Seattle, How to Lose a Guy in 10 Days;*
> Author, *Hello, He Lied*

"This is a book about the stories we write, and perhaps more importantly, the stories we live. It is the most influential work I have yet encountered on the art, nature, and the very purpose of storytelling."
> – Bruce Joel Rubin, Screenwriter, *Stuart Little 2, Deep Impact,*
> *Ghost, Jacob's Ladder*

CHRISTOPHER VOGLER is a veteran story consultant for major Hollywood film companies and a respected teacher of filmmakers and writers around the globe. He has influenced the stories of movies from *The Lion King* to *Fight Club* to *The Thin Red Line* and most recently wrote the first installment of *Ravenskull*, a Japanese-style manga or graphic novel. He is the executive producer of the feature film *P.S. Your Cat is Dead* and writer of the animated feature *Jester Till*.

$26.95 · 300 PAGES · ORDER NUMBER 76RLS · ISBN: 193290736x

THE MYTH OF MWP

In a dark time, a light bringer came along, leading the curious and the frustrated to clarity and empowerment. It took the well-guarded secrets out of the hands of the few and made them available to all. It spread a spirit of openness and creative freedom, and built a storehouse of knowledge dedicated to the betterment of the arts.

The essence of the Michael Wiese Productions (MWP) is empowering people who have the burning desire to express themselves creatively. We help them realize their dreams by putting the tools in their hands. We demystify the sometimes secretive worlds of screenwriting, directing, acting, producing, film financing, and other media crafts.

By doing so, we hope to bring forth a realization of 'conscious media' which we define as being positively charged, emphasizing hope and affirming positive values like trust, cooperation, self-empowerment, freedom, and love. Grounded in the deep roots of myth, it aims to be healing both for those who make the art and those who encounter it. It hopes to be transformative for people, opening doors to new possibilities and pulling back veils to reveal hidden worlds.

MWP has built a storehouse of knowledge unequaled in the world, for no other publisher has so many titles on the media arts. Please visit www.mwp.com where you will find many free resources and a 25% discount on our books. Sign up and become part of the wider creative community!

Onward and upward,

Michael Wiese
Publisher/Filmmaker